7/19

CONTEMPLATING
ADULTERY

Contemplating Adultery

THE SECRET LIFE OF A VICTORIAN WOMAN

LOTTE HAMBURGER

and

JOSEPH HAMBURGER

FAWCETT COLUMBINE
New York

A Fawcett Columbine Book
Published by Ballantine Books

Copyright © 1991 by Lotte Hamburger and Joseph Hamburger

Library of Congress Cataloging-in-Publication Data

Hamburger, Lotte, 1924–
Contemplating adultery : the secret life of a
Victorian woman / Lotte and Joseph Hamburger.
—1st ed. p. cm.
ISBN 0-449-90307-9
1. Austin, Sarah, 1793–1867—Correspondence.
2. Pückler-Muskau, Hermann, Fürst von, 1785–1871—
Correspondence. 3. Wives—Great Britain—Correspondence.
4. Marriage—Great Britain—History—19th century.
5. Authors, English—Correspondence. I. Hamburger, Joseph,
1922–   . II. Title.
HQ1593.A97H36 1991
306.73′6′092—dc20   89-42838
CIP

Text design by Debby Jay

Manufactured in the United States of America

First Edition: August 1991

10 9 8 7 6 5 4 3 2 1

To KATE LEVY,
mother and mother-in-law

CONTENTS

ILLUSTRATIONS

ILLUSTRATIONS APPEAR FOLLOWING PAGE 176.

ACKNOWLEDGMENTS

A PROJECT of this sort cannot be undertaken without generous help from many persons and institutions. We are grateful to all of them.

Our thanks, first, to our daughter, Annette, for suggesting the title. She and her brothers Jeffrey and Philip also provided a wonderful sounding board, often by long-distance telephone, for their parents' preoccupation with adultery—happily not their own. Our children's amusement and skepticism helped to keep us on an even keel.

We are grateful to Rosemary Ashton, of University College, London, who drew our attention to the location of Sarah Austin's letters to Pückler.

We also wish to thank Mrs. Carinthia Beevor for her generous hospitality and for permission to publish passages from Sarah Austin and Duff Gordon letters.

Many other persons and institutions have generously allowed us to publish passages from manuscript letters and other papers: Mrs. Georgiana Blakiston; The Trustees of the Bowood Manuscript collection; British Library; British Library of Political and Economic Science; Bodleian Library, Oxford; The Reverend Michael R. Buckley, Weybridge; the Syndics of Cambridge University Library; Durham University Library; Historical Society of Pennsylvania, Philadelphia; Huntington Library, San Marino, California; Manchester College Library, Oxford; John Murray, publisher; National Library of Scotland; National Forschungs und Gedenkstätten der Klassischen Deutschen Literatur, Weimar; St. Bride Printing Library, London; Mme. Gruner Schumberger, Val Richer (Guizot Papers); Staats- und Universitätsbibliothek, Hamburg; the Master and Fellows of Trinity College, Cambridge; University College, London; Department of Special Collections, University Research Library, University of California at Los Angeles; University of Michigan Library; University of South Carolina Library; Victoria and Albert Museum, London; the late Mr. Gordon Waterfield; Dr. Williams's Trust, London; and Yale University Library, including the Osborn Collection. We also record our gratitude to the always helpful staff of the extraordinary Yale University Library.

Dr. Marian Zwiercan welcomed us to the Jagiellonian University Library in Cracow, Poland, and, on behalf of the Library, granted us permission to publish the Pückler, Sarah Austin, and other letters. We are grateful to him and to the library. Dr. Elzbieta Burda, head of the Manuscript Department at the Jagiellonian Library, facilitated our examination of the letters and other papers during our visit to the library and provided us with microfilm. Professor T. H. Pickett, early in our research and in response to Dr. Zwiercan's request, kindly loaned us microfilm copies of Sarah Austin's letters to Pückler.

We had invaluable help deciphering Pückler's letters, most of which were written in the antique German script, from Kate Levy (London), Hana Demetz-Rosskam, Ruth Muessig, Professor Dieter Pilling (Dresden and Cracow), Thomas Sauer (Würzburg), and Dr. Liselotte Davis.

Ruth Muessig's dedication and assistance have been helpful to an extraordinary degree.

Several persons have allowed us to intrude on their busy lives with requests for help with translations: John C. McLucas, L. Jepson, Cora Monroe, Professor Vasily Rudich, and, above all, Marlene Demarque and Professor Victor Gourevitch, who have been unstinting with their time and knowledge of colloquial French.

Our meeting with Katherine Frank enabled us to have a stimulating conversation about Sarah Austin's daughter Lucie Duff Gordon.

We are grateful to Professor Zbigniew Pelczynski for facilitating our visit to Cracow. Dr. Alfred Essa allowed us to exploit his ingenuity with mainframes to solve our simple word-processing problems. William Ludwig generously provided help with photography. A long-standing friend, Professor Beatrice Bartlett, read part of the manuscript and gave it the meticulous care she gives to her own work. The editor-in-chief at Ballantine Trade Books, Joëlle Delbourgo, and our editor, Mary Sagripanti, were encouraging and helpful at every stage; we appreciate all they did to improve the book, including their tireless if not always successful efforts to persuade us to use the active voice.

PREFACE

THIS is a work of joint authorship. Both of us have researched all the chapters and deliberated and argued about them, but each of us has written different parts. Lotte Hamburger is mainly responsible for chapters 1, 3, and 4, and Joseph Hamburger for chapters 2, 5, and 6.

Our earlier work about the Austins, a general and intellectual biography titled *Troubled Lives*, included one chapter ('Escaping Marriage') on the main theme of this book. That chapter was written before the Sarah Austin–Hermann Pückler-Muskau correspondence became available to us, for after years of searching for it we felt bound to accept the reports from German libraries that the papers had become war losses. Fortunately, when the letters re-emerged we found that they confirmed our earlier account but also gave us rich details of the unhappy marriage and love episode that occupy the four central chapters of this work. We draw on the earlier book, however, for general background information and for many of the details of Sarah's youth in the first chapter and of her later years in the final chapter.

Sarah Austin's letters to Pückler, the main source of evidence used in this account, were written in English (except for a few of her later letters and paragraphs of others that are entirely in French), but she peppered all her letters with foreign phrases, usually in German and French. Pückler's letters to her, on the other hand, are generally in

German. We have translated the quoted passages from these letters except where their meaning is obvious or where translation would sacrifice flavor. Since quite a few of the letters are not dated or have an incomplete date, we have, where necessary, used internal evidence to attribute dates. We have also added punctuation to some quoted passages, if the meaning might have been obscure without it.

A portion of the argument and evidence used in this book was included in the article 'Contemplating Adultery,' *London Review of Books*, January 22, 1987, 17–18.

L.H.
J.H.

CONTEMPLATING
ADULTERY

Introduction

❧ ❧

EVERYTHING about the relationship described here is unlikely—nearly too bizarre to be credible—but as a collection of manuscripts bears witness, it all took place during a few years in the early 1830s. An unhappily married Englishwoman, thirty-nine years old, falls in love with a man she has never met—a German prince, author of a bestseller that she is translating into English. As they begin to exchange letters, he encourages total candor; she eagerly complies and confides her inner and outer life to him. Using the German embassy couriers to carry their letters to and fro, they correspond ever more audaciously, right under the nose of her melancholy and preoccupied husband. Swept up by a storm of passion, she writes in the most unveiled way about her disappointment in marriage, her hunger for affection, intimacy, and love. Her self-revelation at times becomes akin to a disrobing of her personality as she describes her sexual longing, voluptuousness, and physical attractions. Yet in spite of her abandoned writing, she is anything but an unprincipled woman, and her wish to protect her vulnerable husband and much loved eleven-year-old daughter runs in tandem with yearning as her thoughts turn increasingly to adultery.

The three main characters in this drama were all persons of substance. Sarah Austin (1793–1867), the writer of these letters, was a learned, vivacious beauty, the wife of the austere legal scholar John Austin. Known in her day as a leading translator of German and French works on history and literature, and as author of one of the first books in English about Goethe, she attracted the admiration and friendship of notable intellectual figures, including Jeremy Bentham, Thomas Carlyle, and John Stuart Mill. She was the youngest daughter of the highly respected Unitarian Taylor family of Norwich; her outlook and ambitions were deeply etched by her upbringing, and to all appearances, and in spite of professional success, she appeared to be the incarnation of the early Victorian middle-class woman.

Sarah Austin's husband, John Austin (1790–1859), today widely acknowledged for his contribution to the philosophy of law, was from a not-too-dissimilar provincial, East Anglian religious background. His family was more obscure than the Taylors, but as his father, a Suffolk miller, grew rich, he encouraged his bookish sons to aspire to professional accomplishments. John and Sarah ultimately abandoned the Unitarianism of their youth, but they were steeped in its moral outlook. They had values and interests in common, but were ill-matched nonetheless, and very early in their marriage Sarah became deeply disenchanted.

The man to whom Sarah bared her soul, a minor Prussian nobleman, Prince Hermann von Pückler-Muskau (1785–1871), is nowadays remembered more for the magnificent parks he designed than for the twenty-nine volumes of travel romances he wrote. He was a meteor on the literary and social scene, a spectacular figure—colorful, amusing, eccentric, outrageous—a Byronesque charmer whom few

women could resist. Ambition and flamboyance were domi-
nant traits in his contradictory and restless personality: often
he himself seemed uncertain whether he would play dandy,
traveler, writer, or park designer. He was as from another
planet compared to the world of the Taylors and Austins.
His roots were in the free outlook of the eighteenth-century
aristocracy, and he moved in an extravagant, unbridled
circle in which sexual intrigue, infidelity, and divorce were
the rule. Marriage for him was a property arrangement, and
the usual setting for love was an illicit relationship. Unburdened by Puritanism, Pückler disdained bourgeois morality
and advocated erotic indulgence—a belief exemplified in
his wild youth, countless love affairs, and Don Juan attitudes. As he declared, 'The entire sum of the social and
moral rules . . . that govern our lives from morning till
nightfall are the most boring tasteless lies.' Pückler's ideas
and life-style were shaped by an emancipating romanticism
that celebrated spontaneity, expressiveness, sensualism, and
erotic fulfillment. It was no accident that Goethe and Byron
were two of his favorite authors, that he was at home in one
of the most free-thinking literary salons of Berlin, and that
he ultimately escaped the constraints of Europe and traveled
for years in the Near East, adopting Turkish clothing and
habits. While Sarah's upbringing emphasized self-discipline
and control, Pückler mocked middle-class social, and especially sexual, conventions and urged the release of Eros and
a return to a more natural state for man and woman.

From the moment we glanced at the Austin-Pückler
correspondence we had little doubt that it was out of the
ordinary. Sarah Austin's well-formed, flowing handwriting
with hardly an inked-out word or any sign of second
thoughts; the long flying crosses on her *t*s; the English,

French, and Maltese addresses from which she wrote; the multitude of dashes that conveyed the rapid, ever-changing flow of her thoughts, were all familiar to us from the numerous other letters of hers that we had read. These letters to Pückler, however, stood apart. They had some of the confiding characteristics of a diary, but in contrast to most nineteenth-century Englishwomen's diaries, in which sexual thoughts generally remained a taboo subject, Sarah was willing to reveal herself to Pückler with entire openness. There cannot be many instances of a woman so articulate and passionate writing such self-revealing letters that have survived.

It is now more than a century and a half since Sarah poured out her heart to Pückler. How did her letters remain hidden for so long? Not surprisingly, the wish to protect reputations played a part in blanketing them from view. The prince was discreet about his correspondent and so was Ludmilla Assing (a writer and niece of his literary mentor, Karl Varnhagen von Ense), to whom Pückler's papers eventually passed. In her biography of the prince, Assing only mentioned an English friend in one inconsequential sentence, and in her massive nine-volume edition of his correspondence, which included many letters to and from women, the name Austin appears but once. It would seem that Assing, who idolized Pückler, was protecting her hero's reputation as much as Sarah Austin's in withholding the correspondence. After Assing's death in 1880, Pückler's papers were placed in the German State Library in Berlin, and Sarah's explosive letters became available to scholars. They were, in a sense, even advertised, for in 1911 Ludwig Stern drew up a massive catalog of the Varnhagen collection which by now included the Pückler papers. Yet well into the twentieth century they lay virtually unexamined in their handsomely decorated boxes.

There was not much interest in Sarah's life to draw researchers to the Berlin archives. Sarah, aware that she had something to hide, had led the way in shaping an image of herself as the most devoted of wives, and before her death she weeded out letters that friends, according to the custom of the day, returned to her. Her immediate survivors outdid her. They destroyed letters that even Sarah had preserved, perhaps to blur the intense unhappiness of the first decades of her marriage. Immediately following Sarah's death, her 'foolish son-in-law,' as a close friend of Sarah's called him, burnt many letters 'in order, as *he* said, "to save trouble"!' and Sarah's sister-in-law, Charlotte Austin, 'burnt everything she could lay her hands on, among them all of Mrs. Austin's letters to her husband and her daughter.'

It would seem that a polite cover-up of a sad marriage was also uppermost in the mind of Sarah's granddaughter, Janet Ross. When in 1888 she published *Three Generations of English Women*, a collection of family letters interspersed with minimal narrative, she initially assembled 2,878 letters from and to her grandmother, but she published only six letters from Sarah's early married years, that is, before she reached her forties. Equally unfortunate, she cut and deftly altered letters, and though she did not disguise John Austin's poor health and professional failure, the anguish of the early decades of her grandmother's marriage was not readily visible. Janet Ross was all too aware that there were still more than fifty close relatives—Taylors, Martineaus, and Austins—anxious to read the book, and the mighty Henry Reeve, Sarah's influential, family-conscious nephew, was hovering protectively in the background. As one can tell from those letters she used where the originals have survived, she systematically removed or altered what was personal—a practice not uncommon in her time. Thus 'I am sad enough' became 'I am overworked,' and when Sarah wrote, 'I have a sort of superstitious hope that I have born the malice of fate for her [i.e., her daughter Lucie],' the letter was excluded. Janet Ross put the finishing touches on the facade of the ever dutiful, self-sacrificing wife who knew so many important people. This image was also in keeping with the one recorded in that Victorian shrine to English worthies, the *Dictionary of National Biography*, where Sarah's marriage to John Austin is described as one to which 'she brought an unusual share of devotion.' The young, restless Sarah was replaced by the conventional dulled older woman. She had become something of a museum piece—the ultimate incarnation of marital devotedness and certainly not a figure likely to draw researchers to the Berlin archives.

Interest in Pückler, on the other hand, led Eliza Butler, a professor of German at Oxford University, to examine the Pückler papers. In her book, *The Tempestuous Prince* (1929), she quoted passages from Sarah's letters in the collection and did not mince words about her flirtatiousness but surprisingly made little reference to the considerable psychological and sexual interest of the letters. A good part of the relationship remained veiled. Not much more was revealed by Sarah's great-great-grandson, Gordon Waterfield, in his book about Sarah's remarkable daughter, Lucie Duff Gordon. He, like Butler, quoted passages from the correspondence but played down the relationship as a sentimental 'indiscretion' that lightened Sarah's burdened life and that could not have led to a sexual encounter.

World War II saw to it that the letters disappeared from view for almost half a century, for the war played havoc with the Varnhagen collection. To protect major manuscripts from allied bombing, officials of the German State Library in Berlin moved their invaluable music manuscripts, including original scores of works by Bach, Mozart, and Beethoven, to a Benedictine monastery in Silesia. The Varnhagen papers were included in the shipment. The safety of the collection was thus enhanced but its recovery greatly delayed. The monastery that sheltered the papers happened to be in an area ceded to Poland in the postwar settlement, and the 505 crates of manuscripts fell into Polish hands. Eager to keep important manuscripts as war reparations, the Polish authorities held onto the collection but concealed it, fearing that the Soviets might seize it for one of their libraries. Even in the late 1970s the papers were still being described by German libraries as a war loss. Finally, in 1980 librarians and archivists became aware that the collection was in the Jagiellonian University Library at Cracow, and it emerged from obscurity only more recently. We feel considerable gratitude to Rosemary Ashton of the University of London for drawing our attention to its new location.

After years of searching and speculating about Sarah's correspondence with Pückler, at last we could satisfy our curiosity. Initially we read most of it on microfilm and then visited the library in Cracow to examine the actual letters, to attempt to decipher illegible portions, and to browse for additional material. As we read Sarah's letters, written on different sized and colored paper (white, ivory, blue, pink), we were acutely aware that they were meant for Pückler's eyes alone and then for the flames. The intense emotions that had gone into these letters was palpable, and here we were holding them up to the gray, cold, December Cracow light to examine some faint sentences. We could read most of Sarah's letters with relative ease. The parts that were most difficult were those where she indulged her habit of cross-writing—squeezing more onto a page by writing vertically over the already completed horizontally written lines—in order to save paper and, when not using the courier, postage costs.

Quite a few of Pückler's letters, however, were a struggle to decipher. Sarah eventually burned those she received, and it is only because he wrote drafts and kept copies of some of his letters to her that any record of his side of the correspondence remains. His handwriting in the old German script was legible, but the penmanship of the copyists he sometimes employed was highly idiosyncratic and difficult. Then we found additional Pückler letters in special copy books that he used later in their correspondence. These were small notebooks in which he wrote not with ink but with a hard, pointed metal stylus on fragile, transparent tissue-like paper. The books originally were interleaved with double-sided carbon sheets, allowing the paper beneath the carbon to receive a dark emphatic imprint; these pages were posted to Sarah. We were left, as he was, with the scratchings on the tissue paper. Since Pückler took care to write neatly in these copy books, a good deal was surprisingly legible, but for some ambiguous parts we resorted to the back of the tissue where the exposure to the carbon paper had left darker markings. Here, however, the writing was 'backward,' and only a small make-up mirror put that right. Fortunately, the library was open for very long hours.

As anyone who has tried to tell a story knows, one crucial

and perplexing question is how best to present it. We pondered whether to publish Sarah's letters as they were written but found arguments against this. The letters did not tell the full story and seemed to raise more questions than even long footnotes and an introductory statement could adequately answer. Sarah Austin wrote boldly, with gusto—what she called 'my wild way of writing'—and unerringly found the telling word, but in these letters she leapt from subject to subject, as in an urgent, fragmented conversation (for examples, see Appendix). She darted from politics to her husband's health, from literature to London gossip—all of this interspersed with self-disclosure and declarations of love. 'I scrawl as quickly as I think,' she explained. This spontaneous, pressured writing established intimacy and mood, but did not make for systematic presentation or for an overview of the story. We also wished to include Pückler's part in the dialogue, as it could be deduced from remnants of his letters to Sarah, letters to other women, and his attitudes generally. In addition, much was missing about the circumstances that led to this relationship which could only be found in hundreds of other letters written by Austin and her friends. Consequently we decided to highlight the events and personalities involved, keeping Sarah's voice in the forefront as much as possible by using short and long quotations from her letters to Pückler and to others. This approach required an abundance of quotation marks, but it allowed us to present Sarah's pungent words while explaining this strange relationship in the context of her marriage and the circumstances of her life.

Sarah's audacious letters are fascinating for their biographical detail, but they also raise some broader issues. How are they to be reconciled with the image of middle-class Victorian women? To find a woman of her class so able and ready to recall erotic passages in literary works and so willing to assert the force of her passion and yearning for sexual fulfillment challenges the still widely held assumption that Victorian women were prudish, inhibited, and often fearful of sexual experience. Sarah obviously does not fit this portrait and her letters lend support to revisionist historians who have told us that the stereotype of the sexually passive Victorian woman is a caricature that does not do justice to the variety of sexual attitudes and behavior in Victorian times.* What convention demanded was not necessarily what prevailed in private. Nor can one side-step the issue by declaring that, since her letters to Pückler were written a few years before Victoria ascended the throne in 1837, Sarah should be seen as belonging to an earlier, more outspoken era. In fact, 'Victorian' attitudes did not burst suddenly upon the scene at the beginning of Victoria's reign; they were well in place early in the century, and there is no escaping the label 'Victorian' for Sarah. But while she belonged to the Victorian era, this account of her secret act of rebellion shows that she was driven to question some of the fundamental attitudes of her day, especially those relating to sex and marriage.

Sarah's relationship with Pückler occurred two decades before an organized women's movement emerged in England, but in her letters to Pückler, and especially in letters to other women, there is smouldering resentment against

---

*See Peter Gay, *The Bourgeois Experience, Victoria to Freud*. vol. 1, *Education of the Senses* (New York, 1984); vol. 2, *The Tender Passion* (New York, 1986); and John Maynard, *Charlotte Brontë and Sexuality* (Cambridge, 1984).

societal assumptions about women and against the obstacles to speaking out on this subject. The younger Sarah was in many ways a likely candidate to be an advocate for her sex: her social conscience, education, and, above all, her experience in marriage all pointed in this direction—as did her close friendship with John Stuart Mill and others with progressive views. Someone who could toss phrases into her letters such as '*you* are an independent woman, what a miracle,' or echo another rebel by saying, 'society crams us with fictions,' and who was incensed at the treatment of women in Germany with its 'slavish, base prejudice as to all that regards our sex,' clearly harbored resentments about the condition of women in her day. Often her sense of grievance would be vented in a sudden outburst, as when she complained about having 'no separate or independent existence—the vowed helper, servant, nurse, friend of another, with all the disabilities of sex—poverty—everything.' Yet given Sarah's opinions, she was intensely guarded about expressing them in public. A conversation that took place in the privacy of her living room explains some of this reticence. One of her radical friends complained that there were certain subjects, such as religion, about which a man was bound to lie if he could not stand martyrdom, whereupon Sarah retorted, 'and 300 on which a woman must lie who cannot stand infamy.' With this in mind, she sought 'quiet and peace with society and its opinions,' and on another occasion she explained, 'I have resolved *not* to publish anything on a matter on which I cannot say what I think, i.e., all I think.' The social pressures on women and her own vulnerable position silenced her most effectively.

The passage of time has been kind to Sarah. All her life she feared the discovery of her 'wild, mad correspondence' and the subsequent disgrace and ignominy that would be heaped upon her and her family. When late in life she came across a book describing another woman's indiscretions, she once more recalled her own. Maintaining privacy was essential, she told a friend, and added, 'I am not a bad woman in the main, and why should my faults and follies be printed?' She could hardly have foreseen that by the time her letters finally emerged a century and a half later, attitudes would have changed so drastically that her situation may now elicit more understanding than condemnation.

CHAPTER ONE

Her Choice

After all, she was a woman, and could not make
her own lot. . . . Her lot is made for her by the
love she accepts.

GEORGE ELIOT, *Felix Holt*

THE chains of matrimony bound fast in the early nineteenth century when divorce was virtually impossible for
most middle-class women and men. Sarah Taylor made her
momentous choice of a lifelong partner in 1814 when, at
twenty-one, she became engaged to John Austin and then
spent 'five years feeding on love and severe study to be
worthy of being a wife.' When the marriage finally took
place in the summer of 1819 in Norwich, the young couple
chose to forego a honeymoon. As Sarah's mother explained,
'They wish to do nothing but go quietly home to their own
lodgings, and after settling themselves for a while come
down here for a short time to see us and pack up what is
left behind.' The decision not to bow to the conventions of
romantic love fits well with what we know of John Austin's
personality. This was a rational saving, a sign of his determi-

nation to practice the most stringent economy and lead a purposeful life. With married life in London in sight, Sarah was not likely to have wasted any regrets on the relinquished honeymoon. After all, what was this small sacrifice compared to the expectation of enduring happiness?

The wedding, on Tuesday, August 24, 1819, was a quiet, nearly somber affair, accepted by all her family with a sense of inevitability. By contrast, the announcement of the engagement half a decade earlier had caused quite a stir. Then it had seemed incongruous that this lively, attractive girl who sparkled in society should prefer the austere, serious John Austin to all her other admirers. Was this perhaps just another of 'Sally's' triumphs to be chalked up to flirtatiousness and irresponsibility? Her incautious entanglements had stirred gossip before, but this was an official engagement acknowledged by her family. To outsiders the alliance between the ebullient youngest daughter of the Taylors and an untried, not-so-young law student was bewildering.

Sarah had in fact known John Austin for almost two years before the engagement announcement. They met in 1812 in Norwich, probably introduced by John's sister Anne, a close friend of Sarah's. They might well have come to know each other without this introduction, for both were from well-to-do East Anglian middle-class Unitarian families, had common acquaintances, and nineteen-year-old Sarah was striking and not easily overlooked. When she met John he had just left the army where he had served for five years since enlisting shortly before his seventeenth birthday. The unpredictability of army postings had taken him to Sicily, where he spent three years with his regiment defending the island against an invasion by Napoleonic forces that never came, and then to Malta for more waiting and stagna-

tion. Well before he finally turned his back on the army he
had become utterly disgusted with himself for succumbing
to what he regarded as the indolent, aimless existence of an
officer in the enclosed atmosphere of an army camp. When
he wrote in his diary, 'I am . . . convinced that my own
happiness is commensurate with and inseparable from the
progress I make in the acquisition of knowledge,' he can
have had little doubt that he was not well-suited to military
life.

He was still pondering whether to resign from the army
when a family tragedy helped him reach a decision: a distraught letter arrived from his father informing him that a
younger brother had died from yellow fever while serving
in the navy. His father pleaded with him to return home
and offered financial help to enable him to rechart his
course. John Austin thus returned to Ipswich, about forty
miles from Norwich. It is not known what he was doing
in those first two years back home, except perhaps reading
and brooding over the decisions that lay ahead. At a time
when he should have plunged single-mindedly into a new
profession, he apparently allowed his mind and heart to
speculate about Sally Taylor. Evidently he fell in love
regardless of his unsettled prospects. Finally, in October
1814, he moved to London and began three years of law
studies at the Inner Temple, and a month later proposed to
Sarah by letter.

John Austin was a young man who did not fit the common mold. His upright character was evident, but his blend
of intellectual arrogance and nervous diffidence could be
unsettling. Characteristically, John Austin never sat for a
portrait, but it appears he was slim, on the tall side, with
large deep-set hazel eyes, and the erect bearing of his early

military training. Born in 1790, he was three years older than Sarah, and surprisingly, when he proposed he had already turned gray, adding a distinctive quality to his appearance. What also marked him was his strong mind and the earnest, emphatic manner with which he stated his opinions. As a friend put it, 'One could not see him at all without knowing something of the intellect which lay hidden in him.' The impression he made varied greatly with his mood. When in good form, he was 'glorious in talk' and drew listeners by his vehement eloquence, but at other times he seemed extinguished, a banked-down fire, until stirred into flame. When approached in such a burnt-out mood, his fierce pride often led him to find cover in a cold, self-protective aloofness that intimidated hapless well-wishers. One unexpected visitor described how, on delivering some message, he was greeted by an 'icy response,' and a woman friend of Sarah's, for whom he had little regard, spoke of always being afraid of him, 'I don't know why.' As he himself was aware, he utterly lacked the common touch or any easygoing geniality with which to glide over the rough patches of everyday life. John Austin could not disguise his mental power or his unusual personality, and he did not make friends easily. The reverse was true of Sarah. They seemed born under different stars.

While John kept people at arm's length, Sarah drew them to her. If beauty, as she once said, was a scepter bestowed by nature, she reigned with its aid. Yet it was not her good looks, her striking coloring, her 'well-filled' figure, or those unusually large, 'deep grand,' and 'lustrous' gray eyes, so arresting under emphatic dark brows, that her friends dwelt on. What engaged them was her animation and warmth. This is what Sydney Smith referred to when he congratulated her for not being among the cold blooded—'a tribe to which you have no relation.' These qualities also attracted Thomas Carlyle when he first met her. He described her to his wife as an 'exceedingly vivid person not without insight' and as having 'a pair of clearest, warm blue eyes (almost hectically intense).'* So many others were to feel this same overflow of zest and warmth. It was Sarah's hallmark, and it thawed the reserved, proud John Austin.

At times, however, Sarah's ready feelings spilled over and led her into what her mother gently called 'scrapes' and what a friend spoke of as 'extremes of display and flirtatiousness.' She did not always conform to the demure behavior expected of a young woman in an era when Jane Austen was still alive and the reins of decorum bridled the behavior of a middle-class woman. Stimulated by vanity and love of admiration, Sarah could be tempted into wild feats of horsemanship and physical daring or allow herself the more dangerous pleasures of a romantic chase, all of which drew a barrage of censoriousness from the city matrons and others. There was little 'becoming' reserve in her clear enjoyment and ease in male company; there was no mistaking that she was attracted to men and they to her. As the youngest in a family of five brothers and two sisters, she had enjoyed the social traffic of her convivial family and since childhood had mixed with clever persons of all sorts, developing a formidable poise and confidence. Now she relished displaying her charm and ready wit to the aspiring ministers, young merchants, and radicals who gathered at the Octagon Chapel, the center of the influential Unitarian congregation, where her parents were among the leading

---

*Carlyle was mistaken; their owner declared them gray.

members. Sarah's social manner was not the vapid, fan-fluttering kind; she liked to spar and hold her own in the fray of conversation, and there may well have been an audacious edge to her clever talk. Of course, most of the young men of her circle were not among her critics; one of them noted admiringly how she was 'all that was dazzling, attractive, and imposing.' Evidently, however, she also was imprudent and played havoc with the hearts of numerous men, and the gossip she aroused was proportionate to her success.

Yet merely to bask in the sunshine of social success was unacceptable to a Taylor, and Sarah used her formidable energy and lively mind to engage with life. It cannot have taken John Austin long to discover that she was remarkably well educated for a woman of her time, with an intense interest in the world outside Norwich. Beneath the sociable, gay surface, there was ambition and a determination not to be one of 'the common herd of little Misses,' as Jane Welsh Carlyle called them. Certainly she was vain and all too conscious of her powers, but there was no mistaking her capacity and drive, and there were those in Norwich who felt that in spite of occasional 'giddy' behavior, she was a young woman of great promise. If she would settle down, this youngest daughter of the Taylors might well add luster to this middle-class family's dynasty of talent.

Sarah's sterner qualities had been carefully nurtured. She might be high-spirited but her parents had ensured that she applied herself to study, and they had also inculcated moral values highly compatible with John Austin's. Without in any way intending that Sarah marry an earnest, intellectual suitor, they laid the foundations for this match. Sarah had been raised with a burden of expectation, for the Taylors of Norwich, without being arrogant, thought of themselves as superior people. John Taylor, Sarah's father, was a powerful man in the city, known for behind-the-scenes efforts on behalf of humane causes, and, above all, for business enterprise that had made him a well-to-do, though not rich, local wool aristocrat. The Taylors and their influential friends were part of the nonconformist elite in East Anglia. They were productive, public spirited, well read, and had helped to make Norwich into one of the most prosperous and cultivated provincial cities at the turn of the century. Sarah's network of relatives, past and present, on both sides of her family, including the Meadows, the Rigbys, and the Martineaus, were merchants, physicians, solicitors, writers, and scholars known to most citizens of Norwich. In keeping with the social conscience of their religion and the belief that virtue should be active, they could be found as members of the common council, the board of guardians, and the library and music committees; Sarah's father, brothers, and cousins were at the forefront of the struggle for civil and religious liberties, not only for Unitarians but for all religious dissenters. Twice in the eighteenth century, even though as religious nonconformists they were officially barred from office, Sarah's maternal ancestors had been mayors.

In Sarah's youth the flame of family pride burned high and was much fanned. She was taught to venerate her great-grandfather—a famous eighteenth-century Hebrew scholar and theologian who had played a vital part in the history of dissent, and who became the first minister of the Octagon Chapel.* His numerous descendants, including the Martineau branch of the clan, congregated every five or six

---

*This beautiful eighteenth-century building still stands and continues to be used as a Unitarian meeting house.

years 'to celebrate a feast of family love' and to exult in the
memory 'of those admirable characters to whom we owe
our existence.' The songs and verses on these occasions were
naive and explicit:

> Here at this kindred altar bow we down
> Here breathe the wish for virtue, for renown

There were affirmations of 'our first desire, a spotless name
to raise,' and self-congratulation on the 'vigorous scions,' on
'the rank we possess in public estimate,' and on the relatives
'who now stand distinguished in society by their professional talents, their virtues, and their usefulness.' The seven
Taylor children had little doubt about their heritage and
what was expected of them. Sarah inherited an ample portion of this family pride. Late in life she was to take a French
friend back to her old city, proudly to show him the cultivation that had prevailed in homes such as her own: 'the
books, the pictures, the fine engravings, the scientific culture.' Her ancestors, she said, 'possessed neither riches, rank,
nor titles . . . it was by their virtues alone that they left the
name they have done.'

Her parents cemented family feeling with unstinting affection. John Taylor was the most conscientious of fathers,
ever thoughtful about the 'weight of care' of his fatherly
role, which he tried to carry out as his grandfather, the
minister, had explained it: The duty of parents was 'to
lighten the understanding of their children, to excite them
to proper action, to moderate and direct their passions, and
to do all [they] can to set them upon the right way of life.'
In keeping with these principles, Sarah's father wrote verses
about his pleasing fatherly toil, sweet solicitude, watchings,
and broken sleep, comparing himself to a gardener tending

his young plants according to their varying natures. Some of his children, like Sarah, it would seem, needed

> More firm resolve to check the wild desire,
> More skill to guide it to its proper end.

Others, who lacked self-confidence, needed 'more prudent warmth to flatter and commend.' All, however, were steered to

> Meekly bend to my indulgent reign
> Which asks no tyrant's rod, no mind subduing chain.

John Taylor was convinced that 'Unitarian breeding' was best, but his rule was skillful and mild.

By and large, the seven children lived up to the hopes of their fond parents. Sarah's brothers created a hubbub of intellectual curiosity and activity that swirled around her from childhood, and their striving and prodigious energy were always before her. At times it seemed like a chain reaction with each of the seven inspiring the next in line. All the brothers eventually became influential in their various fields. There were to be an outstanding mining engineer, a professional musician, an inventor and entrepreneur, and two Taylor publishers and printers—one of them a learned and outstanding publisher of scientific works. Sarah's sister, Susan Reeve, married early and was a widow by the time she was twenty-six. She applied herself to raising her only surviving child, a son who became an influential publicist and editor. Just after her husband's death, Susan expressed her sorrow in terms of Taylor values: 'I have lost a companion from whom I confess everything did derive its interest. I must now seek to love Reading, Music, Conversation, for themselves alone, and from a feeling that the more I can do for my own mind, the more I shall be enabled to do for my children; for *his* children.'

A glimpse of Sarah showing off her progress in self-improving studies can be found in a letter written to a brother. She was reading Julius Caesar in Latin and had begun *Gil Blas*, which she expected to be a great treat. 'The style is rich in idiom and those odd and droll expressions which make the French so good a colloquial language. In English I am reading one of those books which foreigners esteem an ornament to our language. I mean Clarissa. I must say I think it rather a laborious task.' She also attended a lecture on mnemonics which succeeded in 'converting the driest parts of learning, dates, numbers, etc., into a play.' An air of enjoyment in mastery blew through the Taylor household. No wonder that one of their contemporaries reported 'feeling an ignoramus amongst those clever girls, and remembering to this day Sally Taylor presiding over the historical commerce.'

Susanna Taylor, Sarah's mother, had great force of character, and she channelled her children's surging energy, setting an example that was not lost on Sarah. 'She was one of the most agreeable women I ever knew,' said a friend, 'full of information, the mind cultivated in a considerable degree, of very cheerful disposition, and promoting cheerfulness all around her.' As manager of a large household with a constant flow of visitors, Mrs. Taylor could by no means forget economy, and she worked alongside her servants. Yet somehow she found time for an interest in literature and politics and was something of a learned woman, joining friends in discussion groups and relishing 'feats of reason' with friends, visiting ministers, scholars, and barristers on circuit. She also kept in touch with some of the

literary women of her day, and had a deep interest in
education, especially in the education of girls, a subject on
which Unitarians, with their commitment to rational enquiry, were far ahead of public opinion and practice.

Mrs. Taylor was unrelenting in her insistence that her
daughters' minds should be steered away from the common-
place, and she and her friends agreed that women should not
be tied only to 'nursing children and mending stockings.'
Improvement of the mind was a pleasure and a noble occupation, she told her daughters, and since mankind—and that
meant women as well as men—was distinguished by its
rationality, it was also most emphatically a duty. Active
endeavor and well-directed energy were the keys to satisfaction. The notion of being born to be simply a lady, destined
for frivolous occupations, was as much a travesty of God's
purpose and a stumbling block to everything worthwhile
in existence as the assumption that women should be confined to domestic drudgery. A well-furnished mind was a
lifelong protection against tedium and a resource against
adversity. 'A well-educated young woman may always provide for herself, while girls that are but half instructed have
too much cultivation for one sort of life and too little for
another.' What became of women who failed to marry or
those who lost their husbands and were left with small
children? she asked. And there were quite a few of these to
point to in their circle.

Sarah and her sister were given plenty of vigorous mental
exercise. They were instructed in the usual subjects as well
as in Latin, mathematics, philosophy, and political economy, and were submitted to mental drill similar to that
given to their brothers. Though Sarah went to school, she
also received much additional instruction from her mother

and from tutors who taught her along with several friends. With a relish that was infectious, Mrs. Taylor threw herself into her daughters' lessons. When reading Latin with Sarah's sister she exclaimed, 'Nothing at present suits my taste so well. . . . When we get to Cicero's discussion of the nature of the soul, or Virgil's fine descriptions, my mind is filled up. Life is either a dull round of eating, drinking, and sleeping, or a spark of ethereal fire just kindled.'

The instruction was not all theoretical. Along with study went training in the numerous chores of a nineteenth-century household. Sarah later spoke of being expected to 'go to market, to direct the management of food, to judge of quantity and quality of the various articles of domestic consumption; to know how every thing in the house is cleaned, repaired, kept in order; to cut and make clothes; to direct the washing, to wash and iron fine linen, lace etc.' It was an established belief in their circle of friends that 'literary characters must now and then descend from their altitude.' Thus Sarah, like her younger cousin Harriet Martineau, was 'saved from being a literary lady who could not sew,' and in later years she was to wallpaper rooms and housekeep meticulously on very narrow means.

Looking beyond the horizons of Norwich, Mrs. Taylor also encouraged Sarah to learn the fundamentals not only of the conventional languages such as Latin, French, and Italian, but also of German, at that time an unusual language in a girl's curriculum. For her daughters' improvement and pleasure, she also arranged visits to friends and relatives with wide interests. Susan, for example, was sent to visit the parents of Florence Nightingale, and Sarah repeatedly stayed in London with Mrs. Letitia Barbauld, a highly educated Unitarian writer. Here she tasted metropolitan life—went to parties, attended the theater and opera, practiced the art of conversation, and discussed the English classics with her hostess. It is hardly surprising that none of the seven Taylor children remained in the city of their birth.

Sarah's youth was free and full of enjoyments that included swimming, riding, singing, dancing, picnics, and trips on Norfolk's broads and rivers. Yet despite all this, she was bombarded with relentless didacticism, not only about the need for mental effort but about maintaining the highest moral standards. Her moral education was closely tied to the religious sentiments that suffused the Taylor household. The affairs of this life were seen in reference to the next, and charity, kindness, selflessness, duty, remembering God and one's fellow men were not mere Sunday maxims. Mrs. Taylor, like her husband, was unsparing in her efforts to guide her children's characters to enable them to negotiate 'the mazes of life.' Sarah was still in her early teens when her mother wrote, 'Even at your early age, the great points of moral conduct must be understood, and I think I may safely trust that they will in no instance be deviated from by you either in thought, word, or deed.' At the end of one of these tutorials, her mother checked herself and sighed: 'And now, my dear, if all my moralising can but give you right views and feelings.'

Her youngest daughter's headstrong ways presented something of a challenge to Mrs. Taylor. Repeatedly she warned Sarah not to be careless in her behavior and to avoid 'foolish ebullitions of vanity and selfishness.' At fourteen she was reminded that 'there is a kind of intoxication produced by being an object of attention which is apt to lead us into little follies.' When she was almost eighteen and sexual consciousness was heightened, Mrs. Taylor became more insistent in her warnings:

> What I am most anxious to know is, whether you steer clear of scrapes and difficulties: whether upon an impartial review of yourself there is a tolerable degree of satisfaction in what you have said and done? I am not afraid for you in those cool moments when nothing occurs to drive reason from her throne, but in periods of excitation, which are so frequent in youth (*that* being the peculiar season of excitation), then, if possible, consider!

The numerous reminders Sarah received about holding herself in check indicate that she easily ran afoul of the proprieties of her day. Looking back on her youth, Sarah said, 'I was admired, courted, loved, and loving,' but this was not the whole story. Her specific transgressions are unknown; only a few tantalizing hints remain, such as John Austin's allusion to stains on her reputation and his comment that she '*may* have erred.' Mrs. Taylor, writing to a son, implied that his sister's misdeeds had been a matter of misunderstanding brought about by liveliness and a gift for being entertaining, and her comment to Sarah expressed regret rather than distress. 'The experience you have had,' she told her, 'is considerable for your age, by a more rigid plan with you I might have spared both you and myself some pain, but you would have known much less of the human heart.' Sarah evidently relished flirtation and was vain, bold, and often incautious in testing her sexual attractiveness or giving play to what she spoke of as her 'loving character.' Later, in another context, she was to ask herself, 'Why and why am I always so impetuous, why do I always write, speak, act without reflection and so accumulate stores of repentence.' The misunderstandings she caused are likely to have been intensified by her verbal agility. She could voice her mixed feelings in fine shades that her admirers may not have bothered to decipher. Clearly she had many suitors and there were some embroilments that caused concern. Her confused feelings may have led her to encourage and then drop a suitor, toy with more than one at a time, or break an understanding or even an engagement.

Whatever Sarah's transgressions, even a slight disregard of the social code, especially if it involved relations between the sexes, drew strong censure in the Taylor milieu. Apparently some fairly heavy moral artillery was directed toward Sarah's behavior, which various members of the family knew about and deplored. There may have been conversations, appeals to conscience, even possibly from the minister, and perhaps finger-wagging from one of her brothers. Sarah was acquiring a reputation as a flirt and a tease, attracting the sort of talk that was threatening to a family so proud of their respectability. Harriet Martineau later described 'the censorious gossip which was the bane of our youth' and sarcastically referred to 'what exceedingly proper people we were, and how sharp a look-out we kept on the morals of our neighbours.' Gossip, it would seem, was a powerful weapon in their circle and one not to be underestimated, and Sarah came under intense social pressure.

The young woman who occupied John Austin's thoughts displayed a mixture of failings and strengths. There was 'Sally'—ebullient, challenging, given to display, who attracted men's attention and could show the sort of vanity and foolishness that the proud, fastidious John Austin despised. Yet the Sarah he knew also had a generous spirit,

idealism, sympathetic insight, and a well-stocked mind and
political interests well attuned to his own. Her affectionate,
enthusiastic manner was the breath of life to his cerebral,
self-doubting nature, and her Taylor background was entirely congenial to his own. So John Austin found himself
in a predicament. While still dependent on his father for an
allowance, he had fallen in love with a young woman who
was far from perfect but who promised so much. If he was
to apply himself to his years of study, his peace of mind
demanded that he settle whether she would stand by him.
The dilemma seems to have gnawed at him until mid-
November 1814, when he finally wrote his letter of proposal.

It was one of the unlikeliest of such letters. Love, in fact,
is barely mentioned and at most is only intimated. Instead
of an expression of feeling, Sarah received an involved
legalistic statement resembling a draft for a contract or a
negotiation for a business transaction. This document
throws a beam of light on John Austin's enigmatic personality and on the mystery of what helped draw this gifted,
ill-matched couple together.

As John's letter made clear from the outset, he was determined to reduce the terrible risks of love by applying his
strong powers of analysis and reason to a situation usually
clouded by emotion and gallantry. Plain speaking, he felt,
was essential to his purpose and he therefore disdained 'all
those paltry tricks and devices and obliquities, with which
it is sometimes, I believe, thought necessary, or graceful, to
introduce an avowal of love.' In this spirit he began cautiously: 'Assuming then that we feel a mutual inclination to
each other, our great object should be to enquire as calmly
as we can whether it is or is not likely that we should

promote our well-being by *yielding* to that inclination.' He then developed his strange transactional proposal. The agreement to marry was, he implied, an exchange to promote not happiness so much as greater well-being, and this required that they both look at their own weaknesses and identify those needing improvement. It was crucial to avoid misunderstanding of what he expected from her and what she could expect from him, and absolute candor about this was imperative. As prelude to a possible engagement, he suggested what amounted to a calculation of costs and benefits. 'I shall sincerely endeavour to lay before *you* those harsh but useful truths relating to myself, without a due consideration of which you would be mad to decide in my favour.' Sarah on her side was to do the same; she should 'with equal sincerity intimate to *me*, whatever might render it expedient for me to withdraw these merely conditional proposals.'

He then led the way in self-criticism by laying out the least encouraging facts about his situation. In ever more pessimistic estimates he carefully enumerated 'those evils which you must or might undergo from an attachment to me.' '*Primo*,' he wrote, it would take at least three years, until November 1817, before he could complete his legal training. By then he would be twenty-seven and would still have to establish himself in practice, which would require another two years or so. 'It is therefore morally impossible that my professional exertions should enable us to marry before I am thirty, and very improbable that they will enable us to marry before I am four or five or six and thirty.' Altogether, it might be twelve years before he would be financially independent. Worse was to come, for he was anything but hopeful about his ability to break into the legal profession. '*Secundo* . . . it is also very probable that my profession may never bring me into one shilling,' and Sarah in waiting might find she had sacrificed her youth for nothing, her distress 'enhanced and aggravated by the unworthy spectacle of my protracted dependence [on his father].' He also questioned his capacity to stay the long course, for '*Tertio*,' he wondered whether caprice, impatience of poverty, or other unruly motives might waylay him. 'It is, too, not impossible that I *may* play the fool and the scoundrel, and prove false both to myself and you. . . . that at the moment you are expecting from fortune the completion of your long deferred hopes, I may forget your love and your faith in the wane of your beauty; or that basely yielding to despair, I may damn myself to wealth and contempt in the arms of age and ugliness and folly.' Mercifully, however, he added as an afterthought that he was 'vain enough to think that of all our adverse chances, *this* . . . is to be dreaded the least.' The scenario that put him in the arms of a rich but ugly woman was perhaps too fanciful to give Sarah much anxiety, but his three-tiered account of his risky future left little doubt that he feared the steep road ahead and doubted whether he had the stamina to ascend it.

This is where Sarah's contribution to his well-being came in. She was to lend her efforts 'to prop and secure my constancy,' and her ministering efforts were to include a 'fortitude of affection which could wipe the damps of anguish from my forehead, or playfully teaze my sinking spirits into alacrity.' His ornate language could have been mistaken for mere rhetoric, but his army diary (presumably unknown to Sarah) could have given an ominous reality to his words. The diary was haunted with a sense of guilt and worthlessness for not living up to his own exacting standards. In it he accused himself of an inability 'to establish habits of regulated industry'; for 'lethargy of the faculties'; for a tendency to consume days in listlessness and ennui; and for 'indolence—always the most prominent vice in my character.' Only by conquering 'this corroding disease' could he hope to fulfill his ambitions and overcome his 'fears of never emerging from obscurity.' Now Sarah was to save him from these demon. Could she, he asked 'have really *nerve* enough for the deep-toned, steady, and consistent enthusiasm upon which both my pride and my tenderness might securely rely; which would strengthen and sustain the weakness of a spirit that must cling to sympathy for support and would urge me on to heroic industry.' With her at his side, he would have 'that strongest of all motives' to apply himself to work.

If these truths did not 'appal' her, if she could brave all this for him, he still had another condition. 'I shall require you to submit to a self-examination which may perhaps severely wound your vanity, but which you must triumphantly encounter before I can dare to hang the fate of my feelings upon the chance of your consistency.' She was to face her own weaknesses as unsparingly as he had his own, but meanwhile, just in case she would be too easy on herself, he undertook the examination. A near-sermon about the evils of trifling with the affections of men followed. He demanded that she determine whether she was 'in truth that volatile, vain and flirting thing, hackneyed in the ways of coquetry, and submitting its light and worthless affection to the tampering of every specious cox-comb.' Could she, he asked, 'restrain the wanderings of your coquetry and your vanity . . . by cultivating that quick and subtile perception of propriety, that anxious and vigilant prudence which would surround you with an atmosphere of purity and safety?' Obviously he was all too aware that Sarah was reputed to fan flames of passion that consumed others while she remained unscorched herself, and he was not going to submit himself to that sort of pain and indignity.

Caution and desire were locked in struggle. In spite of the language of analysis, calculation, and negotiation, John was 'tortured by an interest too vehement and too painful for doubt.' He wished to make certain that she would not 'inmesh [his] affection by artifice' and was not going to commit himself by offering a proposal without a most earnest pledge on her part. 'Proceed to examine your past conduct, and then determine whether you can either in honour or safety accept my proffered love.' If she could reassure him, he would risk a commitment instead of these exploratory negotiations.

What he offered Sarah in his stilted prose was a bargain of sorts. She would help him conquer his deficiencies and, in exchange, he offered to help her overcome hers. If she would exercise self-control, he would cleanse her reputation by the simple solution of bestowing on her the respectability of marriage. 'A more guarded deportment,' he told her, 'combined with my respectful and (may I presume to say?) *protecting* attachment,' would gradually wear away 'those slight stains on your reputation.' An alliance with him would provide 'an asylum to your innocence from every calumny and every indiscretion,' and, in an echo of the Bible, he assured her that his virtue and propriety would shield her: 'in *me* alone is your hope and your stay.'

Strange as it may seem today, Sarah on reading this did not see reason to pause. She was not dismayed by the self-absorbed tone of the letter and the demand for an infinity of support for his weaknesses while he stormed about hers; nor was she appalled by his condescension in offering marriage as a means of acquiring a respectability that he assumed was in jeopardy. Nor did it strike her that he made demands on her for self-improvement without offering the equivalent assurance that he could mend his own ways. It was only much later, after his death, that she recognized the imbalance of the letter, reflecting that her 'destiny [was] distinctly put before her,' and noting, 'All his love-letters, during our five years' engagement, speak, not of the happiness he hopes to enjoy or to give, but of his reliance on me as his prop and comforter. And this tempted me.' At the time, however, she was far from thinking his letter excessive or bizarre, but, on the contrary, was eagerly and joyfully ready to submit to his conditions.

Sarah's parents cast a cooler look at her prospects and initially were strongly opposed to the match. They appreciated Austin's fine character and mind but they seem to have worried about his unworldliness and wondered whether his will and energy came up to his forceful manner. The Taylors put great store on decisiveness and application in a young man, and John's path until then had hardly displayed these qualities. His first choice of a career in the army was not to their taste. Young men should be 'chemists and mechanics, or carpenters and masons, anything but destroyers of mankind,' was Mrs. Taylor's view. Military life was a hindrance to that early mental self-discipline which was the foundation for future achievement. John had become deeply disillusioned with the army, but why had it taken him so long to extricate himself? His two years of dilatoriness before beginning law study cannot have allayed their fears.

If the Taylors sensed some defects in John's temperament,

there were other concerns they could raise with greater ease. John Taylor was always forbearing and sensitive in offering counsel to his children, but he was bound to question an engagement to a man with three years of study ahead of him, to be followed by the hazards of establishing a practice—and this without any private means to cushion possible pitfalls. It was hardly the time for John Austin to take on more commitments, and Mr. Taylor appears to have had the painful duty to point out, as he later told one of Sarah's brothers, that it was 'a matter of prime consideration, when the ways and means for supporting a family come to be reflected upon,' to be coldly realistic in calculating income. 'It was as well to consider before marriage what will follow after': What would fill the larder during their first years together? For Sarah to consider marriage while John groped for some foothold on the ladder to independence was most imprudent.

The vulnerability of a young woman before and after marriage was much on her parents' mind in 1814, for this was the year that Sarah's sister, Susan, lost her young physician husband, leaving her with a child to raise. Susan, desolate, was once more living at home alongside Sarah, who tried to contain her new-found happiness. The contrasting emotions under her roof tore at Mrs. Taylor's heart, and anxiety and sorrow eroded her habitual cheerfulness. Trying to find consolation in the girls' support of each other, she wrote to a friend who echoed her thoughts about 'the two dear sisters, whose situation is so different, whose hearts are so much in unison.' Susan stoically attempted to put aside her own feelings: 'How I long to talk about Sally's affair,' she wrote. 'Does it not seem as if it was to be a comfort in time of need to us. I mean by furnishing a matter of deep interest.' Yet Mrs. Taylor brooded about the past, reproaching herself for having consented, against her better judgment, to Susan's engagement when she was merely sixteen. Now she felt that had she resisted Susan's wishes, the young man's precarious health might well have been revealed before marriage. Having agreed to one ill-starred marriage, she was more anxious than ever about sanctioning another about which she had reservations. As Mrs. Taylor reflected, 'The marriage of children has been one of my greatest trials.' She wanted Sarah to remain free for a while longer, and her letters reveal her brooding about the risks of a young woman's situation. Married life, she felt, brought 'too many cares and responsibilities to be entered upon without trembling anxiety.'

Not that everything spoke against this engagement. She and her husband were getting on in years—he was sixty-four and she would soon be sixty. If they died, Sarah would have the comfort that 'the attachment to a man of honour and feeling will afford her.' She had no doubt that Sarah was self-reliant and entirely capable of managing on her own, but there were also subtle pressures that made life uncomfortable for an unattached woman:

Women have many difficulties to encounter if they are left to themselves—independence of mind and such a degree of confidence in their own powers as prevents their being a burthen to others is unwillingly allowed them. People like feeble helpless beings, till they find how troublesome they may become. Seeing therefore that girls are despised if they are insipid, and if they are entertaining, in constant danger of being misrepresented, it may be [that] the wisest way to escape from these evils, if it can be done without encountering greater . . . [is] to accept a proposal which settles the mind as to its future destination.

Susan made a comment in line with this somewhat grudging endorsement by her mother. At least 'this connexion [with John Austin] will crush all the indiscretions we have lamented, for ever.' A brother's comment was equally tempered: 'I hope and trust it may end in her comfort and happiness and I have no doubt that if she becomes a wife she will be indeed an excellent one.' The family's arguments for the engagement were hardly enthusiastic.

Only when John Austin's father stepped in did the Taylors give their consent. Jonathan Austin was a strong-willed Suffolk miller and corn merchant of humble origins, who had become rich on government contracts during the war and now had ample means to subsidize his son's studies and marriage. The subject of money, however, darkened father-son relations, for Jonathan Austin appears to have kept his son on a short financial rein in the hope of steering him toward a greater interest in money-making. An alliance with the energetic Sarah may have appealed to him as the perfect spur for his studious son, and, in addition, he may not have been indifferent to the Taylor family's distinction and connections. He certainly made the match possible by offering to contribute £300 annually once John and Sarah married. John Taylor then responded to this offer by promising another £100 annually. An informal marriage agreement had been reached. Mrs. Taylor summed up: 'Opposition from his parents would have occasioned great difficulties, but their generous affectionate conduct entitled them to liberality and decision on our part.'

Sarah now triumphantly announced her engagement to a friend: 'After some weeks of suspense and anxiety which have been sufficiently trying to me and which have prevented me writing to you on this most interesting subject sooner, I am enabled, thank God, to tell you that my doom is most happily sealed.' Breathless in her happiness, she wrote about 'the overflowing of a full heart.' She could hardly believe her good fortune: 'I assure you that my heart and my judgment are equally satisfied with the man of my choice, that he is all and more than I ever *imagined*, that he loves me dearly, and finally that I am the happiest girl in the world.' Her fiancé had 'superb talents and will I know study hard for my sake, but it must be some time before he can maintain a wife.' The long wait would be no terrible deprivation: 'I have no idea of *impatience* to be married and can imagine no greater happiness than to possess his affection, to write to him and occasionally to see him.'

The Taylor family was reconciled to the engagement, but not much more. Sarah's oldest brother announced in cautious tones that all was settled: 'Our sister Sally has engaged the affection of a young man who from what is said of him seems worthy of her. . . . I must say I am anxious to become a little better acquainted with one whom we may call our brother.' Sarah's father appears to have acquiesced in the spirit in which he had philosophically consented to the marriage of one of his sons. 'Every human Soul wants a very close union with another Being, to whom it can without the least reserve unbosom itself.' Meanwhile, Mrs. Taylor comforted herself that this was destined to be a very long engagement, with marriage as the most distant prospect, for John had promised not to marry until he was established.

Sarah's heart undoubtedly made the choice, and her conscience, sharpened by her family's insistent moral earnestness, confirmed it. It is most unlikely that she practiced her cousin Harriet Martineau's habit of 'nightly examination of hourly conduct,' but John's exhortation that she scrutinize her motives and aim for self-improvement was entirely consonant with family values. Far from resenting his demands, she was uplifted by the idea of living up to his standards. To a doubting brother she wrote of her commitment to self-reform:

> You will imagine that I should not have dared to accept the sacred and weighty deposit of the tranquility and dignity of such a man as he is, if I had not felt myself incapable of trifling with it, and resolute in my determination to exert the most vigilant selfcommand and the most severe self examination to prevent my ever unintentionally or for a moment wounding feelings it is equally my duty and my interest (to say nothing of my inclination) to consult.

Dazzled by love, her mind aflame with visions of redemption, Sarah now set out to change her ways. Her vitality, beauty, and talent did not preclude a hankering for moral improvement. It was a marvel that she who had created such a false image of herself should have attracted a man of his caliber, but from now on she would do justice to 'the dignity and solidity of his character.' She would be transformed by her love—'a love which I firmly believe will do more for the elevation and improvement of my character than anything in the world could.'

While Sarah was joyous about her choice, she realized that others were less so. The impression John made was often so astringent that she feared it might turn even her friends against him. As she wrote to one of them: 'I have great doubts, dear Mary, whether he will entirely please you, as he is certainly stern. . . . At any rate if you don't like him never tell me so. . . . So, dear, let him be all perfection with you. If you tell me he is not I shall doubt your word or your penetration for the first time in my life.' Did John's severity offer a reinforcement to her conscience? This thought may have occurred to her sister, who observed Sarah during her engagement enjoying the 'happiness arising from a quiet conscience.' John's demanding proposal led Susan to comment with astonished amusement, 'You have no idea how strict the hero's notions are. I want to see the man, and yet I dread it, he must be terrific. But I *do think* he's the man for Sally.'

It was not merely the glow of virtue and the calm of an appeased conscience that appealed to Sarah. John also offered her a part in marriage well beyond that available to women in conventional unions of the time. She had no lack of suitors—but here was one who did not appeal to her most superficial vanity, did not tempt her with the dross of riches, or seek to confine her to domesticity. A union with John would allow her to play an emotionally supportive role, but, above all, it held the promise of an intellectual companionship. In his letter of proposal, John, in his convoluted way, had asked her 'sedulously to form yourself to that enlarged yet feminine reason, which could at once enter into my most comprehensive views'—that is, to understand and share the advanced ideas that he was developing in new areas of thought such as political economy, Malthusian doctrine, and Benthamite legal ideas. This offer of a significant part as an intellectual equal and helpmate spoke to her talent, ambition, idealism and was irresistible. Mrs. Taylor had always stressed the crucial importance of intellectual compatibility in marriage:

> I think it impossible to be happy, without each party can say of the other, I have found a companion—for to sit down every day with a person who only interrupts the enjoyment which may always be derived from reading and thinking is a great aggravation instead of an abatement of the evils of life. It was a vigorous mind that Sally always seemed to lay the greatest stress upon in her calculation of qualities—and I expected if such a mind was found with an unblemished character it would determine her choice.

For Sarah, the vision of herself as a partner to a high-thinking man was more seductive than simple flattery.

The emphasis on common interests was a progressive notion at that time. In part it reflected the current of ideas most clearly expressed in the writing of the early feminist Mary Wollstonecraft, whose *Vindication of the Rights of Woman*, published in 1792, a year before Sarah was born, had aroused much interest among Norwich Unitarians. Personal ties also linked the Taylors and Wollstonecraft: Mary Wollstonecraft's husband, William Godwin, had been a schoolfellow of Mr. Taylor's and occasionally borrowed money from him. Yet Mrs. Taylor and her friends, while enthusiasts for wider mental horizons for women, were not inclined to talk the language of women's rights. Their outlook was reflected by a close family friend, Lucy Aikin. In her *Epistles on Women* (1810), Aikin protested against the degraded position of women and demanded that they cast off the 'barbarous shackles' of ignorance to assume their place as intellectual equals and friends rather than as humble dependents of their husbands. In her verses the husband calls

upon 'my life's associate [to] now partake with me . . . my
deepest thoughts' and 'smoothe all my cares, in all my
virtues blend' and exhorted her to 'be my sister, be at length
my friend.' John Austin's engagement letter echoed the
spirit of this appeal, and significantly, some of his few
surviving letters to Sarah from their early years of marriage
were signed, 'your husband and friend.'

With the engagement settled, Sarah continued to live
with her parents in Norwich, pouring all her enthusiasm
into study, while John, in London, took over from her
mother and became her postal tutor for the five years of
their engagement. 'I shall desire to talk with you on all
subjects which engage my attention,' he wrote to her, as he
encouraged her to read the formidable books that occupied
him, including works by Adam Smith, William Blackstone,
Cicero, Hume, Machiavelli, Thomas Malthus, and Dugald
Stewart. She was the most apt of pupils, studied with great
intensity, and waited for his letters 'full of love and of
reason, of wise and high-minded advice.' The engagement
became something of an intellectual apprenticeship for her,
and a list she kept of her reading between leaving school and
entering marriage would have done credit to the most
dedicated and advanced student of politics or philosophy of
law. This sort of intense sharing of reading and ideas as a
prelude to a marriage of companionship was not unique
among striving intellectual couples, and when Sarah eventually came to London she was to meet other exceptionally
clever young women who had also been coached by their
fiancés 'to ascend the steep of learning.' She relished the
mental challenge, which, in its intermingling of the erotic
and the tutorial relationship, offered an acceptable intimacy
between the sexes.

Those who had known Sarah previously were amazed at

the change in her, and the young men in the Octagon congregation took sides as to whether this was the demise of the 'Sally' they had known. William Johnson Fox, who later became an eminent Unitarian clergyman and radical polemicist, gossiped with his fiancée about the transformation:

> I have seen Sally T[aylor], but 'oh, how changed!'—from the extreme of display and flirtation—from all that was dazzling, attractive, and imposing, she has become the most demure, reserved, and decorous creature in existence. Mr. A[ustin] has wrought miracles, for which he is blessed by the ladies and cursed by the gentlemen, and wondered at by all. The majority say, 'tis unnatural, and cannot last. Some abuse the *weakness* which makes her, they say, the complete slave of her lover; others praise the *strength of mind* by which she has so totally transformed her manners and habits.

After four years, in 1818, John Austin completed his law studies and took a position as conveyancer. A year later, after this trial of patience and dedication, Sarah's father felt obliged to relent on the promise that they would delay marriage until John was firmly settled. He had to admit that Sarah had 'wisely taken ample time to prove the sincerity of [Austin's] affection, his temper, and all those qualities of the Mind and Heart, which the married state demands to make it what it should be.' There was also Mrs. Barbauld's advice: 'Two or three years indeed to mature their affections and prove their constancy, I will allow them, but I hope it will not be longer. I own I am a friend to young people venturing a little.' So the wedding was set for August 1819. Sarah's parents' mood was melancholy that summer. A reunion of sixty-five family members scheduled for September reminded Mrs. Taylor of the previous one, in 1814, which had been so painful for her because of the death of Susan's husband. Once more she was not in the mood for merrymaking but had to put on a brave face. She also grieved at having to part from what a friend described as 'so dear a daughter, so sweet a companion and friend.' Mr. Taylor also mourned the departure of his youngest child: 'I believe *my loss* does not excite so much commiseration as it deserves,' he wrote to his son. Without Sarah he would be 'most frequently alone, tho' in Company,' for he would be left with only his book, since 'almost constant somnolency . . . irresistibly comes over your Mother in the Evenings.' His expectations for Sarah's marriage were cautious in the extreme: he wrote to his son Richard in London to prepare him for the arrival of 'Sister Austin—a name which it will require some little time to familiarize your tongue with', and he added, 'She quits tomorrow the paternal Roofs, and from this time becomes the partner in other pursuits, Pleasures and Pains than were found here. I pray Heaven her change may not be for the worse, but for the better!'

The marriage took place in the parish church of St. George's, Colegate, as marriage services were not permitted in nonconformist chapels. As Sarah walked by the family vaults, tablets, and mayoral sword rests of some of her ancestors, her sister stood behind a door weeping. Then, as Sarah and John sat in the London coach waving good-bye to her family, a disappointed suitor threw a magnificent ornate gold watch into Sarah's lap—a watch Sarah treasured—a reminder perhaps that the choice had been hers.

CHAPTER TWO

Second Thoughts

> If ever one is to pray, if ever one is to feel grave
> and anxious, if ever one is to shrink from vain
> show and vain babble—surely it is just on the
> occasion of two human beings binding them-
> selves to one another for better and for worse till
> death part them.
>
> JANE WELSH CARLYLE

> It is too painful to think that she is a woman,
> with a woman's destiny before her—a woman
> spinning in young ignorance a light web of
> folly and vain hopes which may one day close
> round her and press upon her, a rancorous poi-
> soned garment, changing all at once . . . into a
> life of deep human anguish.
>
> GEORGE ELIOT, *Adam Bede*

W HEN Sarah entered marriage, as she said, with 'passionate love and religious devotion,' her devotion was not only
to John Austin but to a vision of him—of them both—in
their new life together. She so wholeheartedly shared his
aspiration to live in the world of ideas, books, and good

causes that she was untroubled by his gloomy forecast and was quite willing to give up the financial rewards and recognition a conventional legal career might have offered. Naturally John would have to earn money to supplement their parents' subsidy by doing routine legal work, but his greatest efforts were to be directed to developing ideas and principles that ultimately would shape what happened in the halls of power. Her husband would be a man of letters—not to pursue abstruse scholarship, but to contribute to human betterment. If a modest income seemed sufficient, it was not that they were undemanding but that their aspirations were so highly pitched.

In their conception of marriage the husband would have the support of a wife who was a companion and helpmate well beyond the domestic realm, and after her arduous study of philosophy and political economy, Sarah was well prepared to understand her husband's work and to collaborate in a life dedicated to public causes. She thought of herself as 'a worthy associate of the best efforts of the best of men,' and adopting the fashionable language of friendship for this kind of wife, spoke of offering the 'generous and courageous devotion of a friend who is also a wife.' Such women, in her mind, became 'the nurses of great thoughts and noble actions in men.' This rhetoric of marriage assumed a close interdependence with a superior husband—a high-minded man, which John surely was, and also one who accomplished significant, useful work, exactly what Sarah thought him destined to do. Her hopes and expectations were focused on him while she saw herself as partner, inspirer, and friend in a marriage in which love was intertwined with high purpose.

John seemed ideally suited to play the part Sarah envisaged. He set out on his legal career determined to contribute his striking intellectual power and considerable learning to the movement for improving the legal and political system. Already during his law studies he had proclaimed his philosophical rather than practical interest by announcing to surprised fellow law students that his goal in life was nothing less than to 'elucidate the principles of law.' A letter he wrote to the famous legal philosopher Jeremy Bentham shortly before his marriage shows where his heart lay politically and how eager he was to serve the cause of reform:

> I have long revered you, and though my deep conviction of the importance of your doctrines has long inflamed me with an earnest desire to see them widely diffused and generally embraced; still, these feelings (as you will easily conceive) have been not a little enhanced by the regard which you have shewn for *myself*. If these feelings remain unimpaired (and, for my own sake, I earnestly wish they may) I shall not be the least zealous amongst those preachers of the gospel who (as I hope) are daily encreasing in numbers and in faith. I regret that my dependent situation will oblige me, for many years to come, to give most of my time to *grimgribber* [legal jargon]; but I am certain that if I can once get money enough to support myself and my wife in independence and comfort, I shall feel no violent desire for any other object than that of disseminating your doctrines. My feelings in this respect I am obliged for the present to conceal from all but my intimate friends. If my father imagined that I entertained any other views than those of getting money and power (but particularly the former) I am convinced he would not leave me a shilling

at his death and there would be no great chance of my making money in my profession if I began, at a very early period of my professional life, to hold up the absurdity of the system to public view. . . . I hope, Sir, you will have patience with all this talk about myself. Nothing but my desire to convince you that I am your disciple, and, as such, earnest for the improvement of human happiness, could have induced me to take up your time with a subject so insignificant when compared with those which you are engaged in.

His wife to be, he explained, shared his willingness to make sacrifices to achieve high public goals: she 'will never try or even wish to turn me aside from the intentions in favour of the public which I now entertain, and . . . a very inconsiderable income (or what most women would think very inconsiderable) will satisfy her as much as myself.' If Sarah saw this letter, she might have noticed that in it he seemed to pour out more devotion and spontaneous feeling than in his letter of proposal.

Bentham needed little convincing that Sarah was prepared to join her husband in his cause, for he was familiar with her father's and brothers' leadership of the reform movement in Norwich. Support of liberal reform was part of the Taylor heritage, for as Unitarians, like other religious dissenters, they were excluded by law from many public offices, and the sting of discrimination was a constant prod to political consciousness. It was not surprising, therefore, that on coming to London in 1819 Sarah and John supported the growing democratic movement against aristocratic monopoly of power. These were tense times—there were demonstrations in the streets and rioting against the king and his government. Within a week of Sarah's marriage the political temperature of the country rose to fever point. In what became known as the Peterloo massacre, mounted soldiers inflicted injury and death by riding through a Manchester crowd that had gathered to protest the corrupt system of government that left so many unrepresented and oppressed. This unprovoked violence aroused indignation that reverberated throughout the country. Married life for Sarah and John began amid unprecedented political agitation, and they felt that they were witnessing historic changes.

During their early years of marriage, Sarah was exhilarated to find that she and John were welcomed into London's radical intelligentsia. Jeremy Bentham, in his seventies and eager for disciples, introduced them to his small circle of intimates, which included politically active writers and lawyers as eager as they were to rid the country of the privileged aristocratic oligarchy. Among those in Bentham's retinue were James Mill, the noted historian and economist and father of John Stuart Mill, the banker George Grote, and a number of gifted younger men, many of them destined to become prominent as writers and politicians. Sarah and John even lived in the epicenter of the reform movement, for they rented part of a house next to Bentham's and near the Mills'. In Bentham's coach house John Austin and young John Stuart Mill practiced the calisthenics that were fashionable at the time; one could observe 'the stern vigor of John Austin balancing on the bars' while young Mill swung from the beam. The precocious Mill, then fourteen, not comfortable with his own family, became like an adopted son in the Austin household. John acted as his intellectual guide and tutored him in law, while Sarah, whom he addressed affectionately as 'Mütterlein,' taught him French and German. Meanwhile Sarah had a playful, even flirtatious, relationship with old Bentham, a man she revered for having lived 'in the service of mankind and the destruction of their pernicious prejudices.' Bentham was so taken with her that on his death he left her a ring with a lock of his hair, she being the only woman, Sarah claimed, he thought worthy of this distinction. During these early years in London John set to work and produced what would be his first published article for the *Westminster Review*, a journal subsidized by Bentham to promote utilitarian philosophy and political radicalism. Intellectually and socially both Sarah and John felt they were making a good beginning.

There was, however, the need to earn money, especially as a daughter—Lucie*—was born in June 1821. Initially John took low-paying, humdrum jobs as a conveyancer and then as an equity draftsman, perhaps to avoid the uncertainties of trying to establish himself as a barrister. After a few years, however, he set himself up in chambers and waited for clients. It was a long wait and a doleful experience. He regarded most barristers as money-grubbers and resented pressure from his father to become one of them—something he left to his brother Charles, who became one of the highest-paid members of the bar. Also, since legal philosophy was his 'belle passion,' he was not inclined to put his best effort into practice.

---

*She was born June 21, 1821. 'Lucy' was the spelling most often used by her mother and her immediate family, but at age 11 she was signing herself with the German spelling 'Lucie,' probably the result of her schooling in Bonn. We are adopting her own spelling and that used by her descendents. On her death certificate her name was spelled 'Lucy.'

Quite apart from his aversion to practice, he lacked the requisite temperament for it. For all his intellectual brilliance, John was overcome by nervousness when he had to speak before an audience—a debilitating trait for a barrister who had to perform in court. His edgy pride and lack of self-assurance were all too evident in the way he dealt with the only brief he ever was given. A friend witnessed the sorry ordeal:

> It was in the City Court. He was the 4th barrister in the Hall and therefore according to a rule recently laid down by the bar that two counsel must be employed in every appeal—he was entitled to a brief. I called to him 'Here Austin is a brief for you.' If a thunder bolt had fallen he could not have stood more aghast. I put the brief into his hand & pointed out the very common question he had to ask. But he could not utter a word. I put the question for him. A very easy one. Now this has happened to many an able, even eminent man before. And I should have thought nothing of it. But when the Attorney offered him his fee, he rejected it with indignation as if he had been insulted. And then I said to [my]self—there is no help for him.

Sarah soon arrived at the same conclusion:

> It became in no long time evident to one who watched him with the keenest anxiety, that he would not succeed at the Bar. . . . Nothing could be worse for him than the hurry of practice, or the close air and continuous excitement of a court of law. . . . Nervous and sensitive in the highest degree, he was totally deficient in readiness, in audacity, in self-complacency. . . . He gradually grew more and more self-exacting and self-distrusting. He

could do nothing rapidly or imperfectly; he could not prevail upon himself to regard any portion of his work as insignificant; he employed a degree of thought and care out of all proportion to the nature and importance of the occasion. These habits of mind were fatal to his success in business.

After six years trying to establish himself in one form of practice or another, Austin finally abandoned his attempts in 1825.

It became clear very early that he had deeper problems than those of finding an appropriate career. The decision to give up legal practice, like many of the major and even routine events in his life, was preceded by terrible indecision, heart searching, self-doubt, and dejection, accompanied by bouts of physical illness. He suffered from attacks of fever, migraine, indigestion, loss of appetite and general lassitude and often had to take to his bed. To Carlyle he was 'a lean gray headed painful looking man, with large earnest timid eyes.' His fevers could have been caused by infectious disease, but friends such as Mill, who knew him well, recognized the psychosomatic dimension of his condition. Mill concluded 'that anxiety was the chief cause of his frequent illnesses.' Any stress, such as a deadline, a lecture, or his mother's last illness, tended to disable him. Yet Austin was reasonably cheerful and well when able to withdraw from challenging situations—for example, when on holiday in Cornwall or France or after leaving employment to live abroad. Sarah soon realized that more than physical causes were at work and she spoke of him as a 'hypochondriacal man.'

There had been early warnings of John Austin's precarious mental state. Reclusive behavior ran through his family—in his melancholic mother and in his brother George and sister Charlotte, who were said to be excessively shy. In the army John had succumbed to fits of melancholy and dejection, and even during their engagement Sarah received what in retrospect seems a self-reflecting gift from him—a copy of Byron's *Lara*, in which the brooding, lonely hero 'stood a stranger in this breathing world, / An erring spirit from another hurl'd; / A thing of dark imaginings.' It also ominously noted that Lara's 'troubled manhood follow'd baffled youth.' Sarah, aware of the unfortunate impression her fiancé could give, began to make excuses for his moodiness even before they were married. She smoothed his way as he accepted an invitation to dine with her brother in London. 'I hope you will find him tolerably *agreeable*, for if he fails in anything I *believe* it is in that. . . . I know he can be so if he tries.' She went on to say that 'he is better and a little recovered from the oppression and stupidity of which he complains.' Yet such episodes recurred, and there were periods when he shut himself up in his study, refusing to leave it even for meals. He spoke of 'my old disease' and often turned down invitations on the ground that he was unfit for society. As his daughter, Lucie, who was exceedingly fond of her father, later noted: 'Da is gloomy, I fear 'tis his normal state.' Sarah always liked to draw people around her, but when it was their turn to be invited he frequently was unwilling to meet others, and Sarah adopted the habit of going out alone.

John's condition undermined more than her social life: it threatened their basic livelihood. His difficulties as a lawyer were repeated in his attempts at writing. He held himself up to exacting standards that he could not meet; he was slow, diffident, perfectionistic, and in his choice of words precise, even obsessional. Yet when, after excruciating labor, he finally published an article, it was stilted and pedantic. Sarah, noting his inability to write in a popular style, explained that 'all he does must be profound, laboured, built for immortality, like an Egyptian pyramid.' It was not clear what employment he could or would accept, a circumstance that led Carlyle to speak of him as 'a hard case.' Meanwhile money worries were pressing; not that they were destitute, but Sarah had to pinch and scrape and practice the 'most rigid economy' while keeping house on a 'frugal, self-denying' scale. She spoke of having 'fought poverty single handed,' and with only some exaggeration could say, 'My own fingers and head sufficed to secure us from want.' A visiting American, John Neal, who was part of Bentham's circle, recalled meeting her; she told him 'with tears in her eyes [that] . . . all her husband could earn, together with the allowance from their parents, was not enough to make them comfortable.' Indeed, 'so straitened were they in their circumstances that they should look upon the advent of another child as quite a serious calamity.' They were driven to borrow, not from John's well-off father, but from sympathetic friends. Sarah was not exaggerating when she described these years as cruel.

A more gnawing anxiety than the shortage of money was her husband's health, which became, as she said, 'the mainspring of good and evil to me.' All other difficulties faded by comparison with his depressive episodes: 'The real irremediable *dreadful* evil is the state of his mind and spirits.' Resilient and energetic, Sarah fought to keep them afloat. Taking on her shoulders all the practical management of their lives, she kept house, educated Lucie, nursed and comforted her husband, and became the intermediary between him and the world—writing letters, apologizing for his lapses, and maintaining friendships with many persons who might become his patrons. To supplement their meager income she also took a variety of jobs. As she put it, 'I . . . worked for money that he might not be anxious.' Her dignity did not stand in her way and she was willing to do nearly anything that brought in a few pounds: she compiled a Spanish-English technical dictionary for Englishmen employed by one of her brothers in a Mexican mining venture; taught English to Italian refugees; reviewed books and gave language lessons to children. 'I have now, too, undertaken another trade, namely, giving lessons in Latin. . . . Lucy and I trot down to Bentinck Street with our bag of books, and quite enjoy it. I do not fancy myself at all degraded by thus agreeably earning a guinea a week, and if anybody else does, he or she is quite welcome to avoid my society, as I inevitably should his or hers.'

She also translated into English the works of French and Italian authors, including Voltaire, Stendhal, and Foscolo, without anticipating that within a few years she would become a professional translator with a reputation for skill, speed, and delicacy. In collaboration with a cousin she published a volume of medieval lyric poetry in translation. With reason she could claim to be 'the busiest woman in the world.' Her earnings, though small, were an important supplement to what Austin brought in and what their parents provided, and it was no empty boast when she claimed, 'I am the man of business in *our firm*.' Her friend Santorre Santa Rosa, in London as a refugee from political oppression in Piedmont, thought her far too burdened and urged leisure and rest, but Sarah's life continued to be one of ceaseless work and anxiety.

Holding the family together was an all-consuming struggle, but more painful by far, the circumstances of her life
eroded her assumptions about her marriage. Sarah's wish to
be the devoted helper to a noble-minded man contributing
to the public welfare made her vulnerable, should John fail
to live up to her ideal. Her self-definition depended on his
achievement, but now, only a few years after marriage, she
was dismayed to discover that his difficulties undercut the
ambitions they shared. As her high hopes rapidly faded, she
was forced to redefine her wifely role—her dream of being
the companion to a husband who would distinguish himself
serving the public had to be put aside as her activities were
dictated by harsh necessity. She explained how she was
forced to rethink her assumptions:

> Married to a man of the noblest character, the rarest
> talents, and the most extensive and profound acquire-
> ments, it will be easy . . . to believe that my ambition
> and vanity centered entirely in him and his reputation;
> and that it would have been more agreeable to me to be
> known as nothing but his wife and friend, which I regard
> as honour enough for any woman. Providence, however,
> did not see fit to indulge me thus.

In contending with her situation, Sarah became the per-
sonification of the strong, capable woman able to manage
her life; but her efforts were directed to upholding husband
and family and she thus earned praise from traditionally
minded men. To the well-known critic and judge Francis
Jeffrey she was 'the heroine of domestic life,' and to Carlyle,
who believed that a woman's fulfillment lay in domesticity,
she was 'a brave, true woman,' and he encouraged her by
telling her that 'friendly eyes and hearts are upon you.' Such
praise must have been double-edged, for the part she played

as nurse, comforter, and money-earner was a far cry from the vision of herself as intellectual companion and inspiration.

As Sarah took on more responsibilities, John withdrew from the activities of daily life. She would soothe and protect him from anything that might agitate him and try to counter his dark moods and nervous debility, but the price was increased dependency, as she acknowledged when she said that 'he leans upon me for support and comfort' and spoke of 'a husband habitually suffering, more or less, and with all the habits of dependence which illness produces.' While in his letter of proposal John had told her, 'in *me* alone is your hope and your stay,' now she was aware that their friends saw her as 'the stay and support of my husband.' John was quite accepting of Sarah's efforts as his sustainer and protector, and with a proud fastidiousness he left it to his wife and well-placed friends to solicit and arrange for the few positions he was to hold—at the University of London, on the Criminal Law Commission, and as Commissioner to investigate the government of Malta.

When not ill or despondent, he was anything but an agreeable companion. Often irritable and quite tiresome as the chronic invalid, he was preoccupied with himself, his symptoms, and his remedies. Meanwhile he also harbored resentments against the outside world for failing to recognize his talents and provide him with the professional niche he felt he deserved. As Sarah explained, 'He sees every crawling sycophant and charlatan preferred and promoted and himself with all his conscious powers and merits neglected, overlooked.' Nor was he inclined to appreciate her efforts to help him and more often than not was irritated by them. 'His least annoyance,' she revealed, 'redoubles itself on me.' Apparently he was not only demanding but exacting, and Sarah often gave in to avoid aggravating him, which led her to complain, '*My* will never passed for much.' Thinking of all the watchful care she had bestowed on her husband, she later recalled to a friend who had observed the course of her marriage that 'nearly the whole of my married life was passed . . . in rendering such offices, and a very small portion of it in receiving them.'

Sarah's assessment of her marriage was obliquely reflected in her comments on a fictional mismatch described in *Siebenkäs*, a novel by Jean Paul Richter. She described the 'sufferings of an ill-assorted union, and of the illusions which lead simple and virtuous hearts into that abyss of misery.' The fictional wife, Sarah noted, was 'loved and married, for her innocence, simplicity, agreeable person, tranquil temper, and for the possession of those arts and qualities most needful in the helpmate of a poor man.' Unfortunately the hero had 'in the housewife, forgotten the wife.' Consequently, this marriage had 'the dreariness and misery of [a] most ill-matched companionship.' Sarah condemned the husband in the novel for requiring from women 'the virtues rather of attached and industrious servants, than of equal, intelligent, and sympathizing friends.' She saw herself as also tied to a husband who prevented her from being all a wife might be.

Sarah's disenchantment was so great that in 1823, after only four years of marriage, she contemplated leaving John and returning to her parent's house. She felt martyred and dreamed of escape. Later she said 'his unkindness had alienated the passionate love with which I married him' and that she would have prized her freedom and 'gladly would I have separated from him!' To an unmarried acquaintance she wrote: '*You* are an independent woman, what a miracle!' While her expectation of being her husband's companion in a morally elevated marriage was blighted, even more intolerable was his irritability and indifference. It is possible that Austin's bitterness was intensified by a wife who seemed able to shoulder every burden. Sarah spoke about his 'inhuman neglect and unkindness' and called him 'unhappy and unloving, uncomforting.'

This crisis in her marriage coincided with her mother's last illness early in 1823. Mrs. Taylor was suffering terribly and Sarah went to Norwich to be with her. After a time, however, John expected her to return, and Sarah was left to choose between mother and husband. She revealed her dilemma to her confidante, the *simpatico* Santa Rosa, who wrote about her 'painful conflict of affections and duties' while encouraging her to rededicate herself to John Austin's care: her husband was an extraordinary man, and to make him unhappy would be doubly culpable, while to make him happy required great tenderness and was sublime work. Love for Lucie and a sense of duty to husband drew her back to London.

Outwardly Sarah maintained the appearance of a dedicated, loyal wife, but at times her distress seeped out, especially in letters to other women. To a friend with a problematic marriage she wrote:

> I have done with wondering at the injustice of men [i.e., husbands]—at what they exact, in proportion to what they are prepared to give or to do. To make any impression on them, armed as they are with power, backed by opinion . . . is hopeless. Would to God one could do any good by preaching to those women who have their destiny yet in their hands. Even *that* is hopeless.

Her feelings also surfaced in published work. In a note added to one of her translations she exclaimed, 'How many a heart-ache, how many a misunderstanding, how much disgust and alienation, how much secret and black despair . . . may be traced to the want of sane notions, chastised hopes, and rational expectations, at the beginning of married life!' And in another published comment she noted that marriage required 'moderate expectations, and a firm and humble preparation for evil and weary hours.' These generalizations reveal the extent of her bitter disenchantment.

Friends were aware of Austin's difficulties but were circumspect. Sarah, outgoing and gregarious, was always welcomed to a dinner party or a country visit; but when John, the 'incurable recluse,' did venture out, he was (as Abraham Hayward put it) *'agreeable* to very few.' Carlyle made a similar observation in even stronger language: Austin was an 'incompatible painful man,—whom it requires a great effort to love'; and on another occasion, 'so *acidified* a man he has grown; and *produces* nothing but acid.' Even so, Austin earned the respect and sympathy of some eminent and formidable persons, such as the economist Nassau Senior, Sir James Stephen, head of the Colonial Office, and John Stuart Mill, and though his relations even with them were rather formal, they were eager to help.

Those who were well acquainted with Austin recognized that he needed a protected niche to escape the competitive stress that was so destructive. Mill tried to get him an appointment at India House, where he himself was employed as a high-ranking administrator of the British government of India. It would be the 'sort of employment which probably would not knock him up, like writing,' he wrote to Sarah, 'and the improvement in his circumstances with leisure and freedom from anxiety, might give him a better chance than he ever had before of being well in London.' There was work to be done at India House, but the routine, as the novelist Thomas Love Peacock, himself employed there, described it, was leisurely in the extreme:

> From ten to eleven, ate a breakfast for seven:
> From eleven to noon, to begin 'twas too soon;
> From twelve to one, asked 'What's to be done?'
> From one to two, found nothing to do;
> From two to three, began to forsee
> That from three to four would be a damned bore.

This relaxed atmosphere was ideal for Mill, for whom leisure meant '*choice* of work,' and it would also have suited John Austin, who needed, in his wife's words, a 'harbour of refuge.'

The India House appointment never came through, but another refuge was arranged by friends—notably James Mill and George Grote—who in the mid-1820s were among those setting up the new University of London. The university was to have a professorship of jurisprudence, and in 1827 Austin received the appointment. This was not a case of George Bernard Shaw's adage, 'if you can't do it, teach it,' for Austin had valid claims. He had made a serious study of legal philosophy, was a spokesman for the new utilitarian school of law, and had theories of his own. This appointment seemed ideal, and the sun finally seemed to shine on him and Sarah. Since the university was not due to open for another year, he decided to move to Germany to prepare himself by studying Roman law and German jurisprudence.

They settled in Bonn—an attractive university town where their financial anxieties faded, for living was cheap and they had the peace of mind that came with knowing they could look forward to a modest but secure university salary, for three years at least and perhaps longer. The escape from London was a boost for John's self-esteem. He and Sarah were looked up to and fêted by distinguished scholars, including August Wilhelm von Schlegel and Barthold Niebuhr, and he flourished in Bonn, perhaps more than at any other time in his life. After enjoying the esteem accorded to learned men in Germany, he declared that the position of a revered teacher in a German university was 'the most enviable in the world' and that 'no life would suit me so well as that of a German professor.' Intellectually it was also a fruitful time: he followed a routine of reading and preparing his course of lectures and had the satisfaction of doing serious work without suffering his usual symptoms. Sarah taught English to a bookseller friend and to a young German who read law with her husband. Quick to improve her spoken German, she mixed easily with German women and became a confidante to some of them. Sarah puzzled some of her German friends: how could she be learned yet not dowdy, domestic yet intellectual? In the end she gained their respect and was pleased to discover that she was 'the object of a sort of traditional *culte*.'

Lucie, now seven, also thrived. She was remarkably precocious mentally and physically—'a monstrous great girl,' Sarah reported, with a shade of anxiety about her lack of feminine graces. In Bonn, Lucie was sent to school for the first time, and in no time spoke and read German 'as a second Muttersprache [mother tongue],' helping interpret for her father and even writing in the language. 'A herrliches Kind [marvellous child],' Sarah proclaimed, as she watched her grow 'tall and vigorous, with a rather pale face, a noble thoughtful brow, from which her hair is parted and braided like that of a German child.' She was learning Latin from Sarah but had little knowledge of standard school subjects, and her mother worried that she might be 'half-educated.' After returning from Bonn, Lucie was sent to a tiny day school where she took a fancy to Greek, something her father especially encouraged. Sarah occasionally was uneasy about the free and unusual manner in which her daughter was being raised and wondered whether she was 'too wild, undisciplined, and independent'; but fundamentally she doted on her clever, original daughter, who was 'handsome, striking, and full of vigour and animation.'

Sarah's greatest satisfaction, however, came from observing her husband in a healthier and more benign mood:

> He is quite satisfied with what his studies here have produced to himself. He goes on with the utmost steadiness and with unvarying cheerfulness and satisfaction. I believe with all my heart . . . that you will rejoice to see his excellencies come to view and my anxieties cease. If his health does but stand, I fear nothing.

On returning to London early in 1828 both were enthusiastic about Germany, especially Sarah, who spoke of being *verdeutscht* [Germanized]. The experience had an enduring effect on her career as a writer and translator, for it gave her confidence to translate German works and made her something of an expert on German literature and affairs. The 'pleasant days in dear Germany' were a period of contentment, and a few years later Sarah looked back on Bonn as 'the only place in which I had known a few months of tranquillity and happiness since my marriage.'

The comfortable months in Germany were only a brief interlude, and already as they moved back to London Sarah was 'oppressed with premonitions (too sadly verified) of what awaited.' John, under the pressure of having to start his lectures and prove himself, reverted to his former state of nervous debility. His friends intended the university appointment as a harbor of refuge, but it proved to be a maelstrom in which his old symptoms became more severe.

As the university session was about to begin, Austin delayed his first lecture for a week and then postponed it for a full year on the ground that additional preparation was necessary. When he finally began, he had a class of about thirty-two, a respectable size for lectures on a subject neither practical nor required. The hidden catch was that many of those attending were fellow utilitarians and friends of his most devoted pupil, John Stuart Mill. Those not tied by these loyalties found much to put them off. Henry Crabb Robinson heard the first lecture and noticed the same debilitating stage fright that he had witnessed when Austin was given the brief in court. 'I heard him deliver an inaugural lecture, but in so great terror that the hearers could not attend to the matter of his lecture from anxiety for the lecturer.' He was repetitious, and according to Carlyle, had a 'clanging metallic' voice. Although he was widely described as marvelous in conversation, at least when not dejected, his lectures were read from a prepared text and, consequently, had the formal, stilted quality of his written work. As Lord Melbourne was to say, Austin's *Province of Jurisprudence Determined* (which consisted of some of the lectures Austin had read to his class), was 'the dullest book he had ever read'—and this from someone who read theological works as a pastime.

A year later, in 1830, when Austin began the second course of lectures, his hopes withered—no students showed up. He expressed anguish: 'I waited last night in my Lecture Room from 6¾ to 7 o'clock but no pupil appeared. . . . If I shall have no Class during the present Session, I shall be somewhat surprised as well as discouraged.' Though disheartened, he persisted. When finally he had an audience, the word went out about 'John Austin's brilliant success, his having found two fellows to come to his lecture and stay till the end.' His four years at the University of London were marked by humiliating failures, intermittent illness, and deep dejection. He was 'so ill and nervous that nobody thinks of speaking to him about any thing that can agitate him,' and on another occasion Sarah reported, 'More calamities have fallen upon us. Another failure and breakup at the University—all last week he was in perfect despair. I must work and keep up *our* courage.' It was all too obvious that, as she said, at the University 'nothing is to come from that but suffering and disappointment, and the ground now fails under our feet.' In spring 1833, after four such years, he resigned, and Sarah spoke of 'that abortion the London University' and said that it was the calamity from which he never recovered.

The calamity was Sarah's also, but she met the erosion of their hopes with courage and resourcefulness. As ever, she was quick to take initiatives; she said of herself that she was 'always prompt and energetic when any thing is to be done.' When John's students faded away she insisted that he publish his lectures and negotiated with a publisher for what became his only published book in his lifetime, *The Province of Jurisprudence Determined* (1832)—the basis for his posthumous fame. As he sank, she once more demonstrated that unflagging energy and capacity which were legendary among her relatives and friends, and her easy domination of situations was visible to all. Francis Jeffrey called it her 'ethereal vitality,' and John Neal, one of Bentham's American disciples, concluded that 'she was altogether fitted for a commanding station.'

One dramatic example of Sarah's response to an emergency occurred in Boulogne late in August 1833, soon after John retired from his university appointment. They were staying at a hotel on the beach when a British convict ship, the *Amphitrite*, on its way to Botany Bay, ran aground within their view. As a violent storm broke up the ship, some of the bodies of the crew and prisoners, many of them women convicted of prostitution, and their children, were washed ashore. Sarah was not one to stand by and do nothing. As she later described the situation:

> I saw nothing, felt nothing, conceived of nothing but the present—the tremendous present; human beings brought into this house whom it might yet be possible to wring from the iron grasp of death. Had I been told that I should turn from one dripping corpse to another, tear off their clothes, think of every thing, order every thing, order every body, rub them with my hands, take their feet in my bosom nay once even *lift* a full grown man, and never once feel faintness, never lose my presence of mind for a moment and not ever suffer in health afterwards, certainly I could not have believed it—but it is true. I don't mind saying to you that I am still astonished at what I did—the promptitude with which I recollected every thing and did it.

She not only overcame conventional inhibitions, but along with a few other women she ignored a local taboo against touching the bodies of dead or dying persons.

Here my dear friend for once I recognized something superior in the characters of Englishwomen. There were four strong, highspirited lively, violent French girls, servants in the house, not ill-natured either, not one would touch the bodies, not one who could for an instant forget herself and her own sensations. Yet when 64 of these wretched victims were laid the next day in the hospital almost all the women in Boulogne thronged to see the sight. In the hotel was a little pale, delicate, quiet young English lady, so quiet that I hardly remarked her. She had a nurse maid and child with her. I had my good, faithful Elizabeth, my femme de chambre . . . . We four did every thing. Mrs. Curtis kept imploring the men to bring us more bodies. Something was said about the naked bodies of men. She said, we know no difference, we cannot think of those things. I looked at her with surprise and admiration. She was in all common things full of English reserve. The French girls kept pulling my clothes, entreating me not to touch their bodies. . . . we saved two men—they are alive and well.

The incident earned Sarah an award from the Humane Society and praise in the French press and from the poet Heine, who happened to be staying at the hotel. She also did not hesitate to give testimony to an official board of inquiry and to criticize the English Consul for delay in getting help to the foundering ship. With similar outspokenness she wrote a letter to *The Times* expressing outrage over her country's treatment of the victims. 'These 120 women and children were more kindly treated by the raging elements than by the Society that corrupted and then cast them forth. My poor offending sisters! it is not your death I weep for, terrible as it was, it is the bitter hours of shame and guilt that preceded it—the cruelty and injustice of man to you.'

The temperamental contrast with her husband that had always been striking now became extreme. Her qualities— self-confidence, ebullience, energy, resolution—were the very opposite of his. She was naturally optimistic, liked to challenge herself, and never gave up. Their temperamental disparity was even visible in their recreations. She liked to test herself by attempting any vigorous, challenging activity, and in keeping with the fashion of the day took up Swedish gymnastic exercises; she became quite proficient, while her companion, John Neal, attempting the same exercises, broke his arm. Neal reported that she also took lessons in the smallsword and 'might have been somewhat dangerous had she continued.' She relished sailing and intrepid riding, while John tended to avoid such activities and wished to go on walks. Whereas he was often withdrawn and silent, from Sarah words flowed as from a fountain— 'copious outpourings' and a 'river of talk,' according to Carlyle. At the time of the shipwreck in Boulogne, while Sarah tried to resuscitate those who had drowned, Austin was in his room. When a hotel they were staying in caught fire, she organized the firefighting, pushing a man with a pail into the thickest smoke and following him with another, while her husband stood by, 'teeth chattering, knees shaking, paralysed.' Yet on the following day, according to Sarah's irritated nephew, he 'had the face to use big adjectives, and talk of energy.'

As John's misfortunes multiplied, Sarah's disappointment and bitterness were strangely mixed with pride in her own achievements. In spite of their chronic shortage of money, she established a social position based on personal qualities alone. With truth she claimed, 'I owe *all* the consideration I enjoy (and it is not little) to *myself.*' It was not an insignificant triumph for her to 'go in an omnibus for six pence to a party and *say* that I came so and in five minutes see myself the object of more respect and attention than all the carriage ladies.' Reflecting on this, she confessed,

> It has been my pride and glory to make to myself a position in this haughty and slavish English society by dint of inward pride and courage—to spurn at their trumpery distinctions—to assert and proclaim my poverty and to force those who were affecting to be 'genteel' to give way to my real individual predominance and to the simplicity, good nature, liveliness and yet intrinsic superiority of my manners *which are* superior simply because I affect nothing and do not condescend to borrow consideration from any *body* or any *thing*.

She could not help noticing that wherever she appeared, all eyes turned to her. 'I cannot but see that I am valued, liked, admired and caressed.'

Among the talented men who admired her were Austin's students, who returned home with him after his lectures; her friends among the Italian refugees in London whom she helped and who considered her their 'protecting saint'; the young Benthamite radicals, such as John Stuart Mill, Sir William Molesworth, Charles Buller, and John and Edward Romilly, whom she jokingly called her 'Cavalier sirvienti [sic]'; numerous others in the London intelligentsia, including Edward Bulwer-Lytton, Thomas Carlyle, Abraham Hayward, and Henry Taylor; and also older dignitaries, such as Francis Jeffrey, Jeremy Bentham, and Sydney Smith. To a confidante she could boast,

Obscure as I am, I have made for myself, and by dint of character and conduct, *friends* of the elite of English *men*, and when I could find any worth caring about, women. The men with whom I live are such as Bentham, the venerable writer on legislation and morals, Mill, the Historian of India and writer on Political Economy; his son, the most accomplished creature I know of, and no less modest and liberal; Malthus, Senior, Whately (the Logician), the Romillys, the Lord Advocate (Jeffrey), Empson . . . and a host of younger men whose names are unknown to you, but who contribute a great part of the talent and political virtue of this corrupt and jobbing country.

The admiration from these 'persons of distinction' who were 'the wisest and the best that England contains' was a great boost to her sense of her own worth.*

That more than a few were more or less in love with her added spice to her satisfaction. This was perhaps inevitable, for men were drawn to her by her good looks and liveliness, and even more by her affectionate, open, warm-hearted personality. Young John Sterling, for example, was moved by her 'abundance of warm feelings and imaginative sympathy.' Sarah said of herself, 'When excited I am still the most vivacious person in company,' a statement confirmed by Carlyle's description of her as enthusiastic, eager, and possessing 'a warmth in her whole manner and look, which has

---

*All those mentioned are included in the *Dictionary of National Biography* and are still remembered for their achievements. Some, like Bentham and Malthus and John Stuart Mill (and another friend, Carlyle, not mentioned in this passage) are recognized to have been intellectual giants.

in it something feverish.' Though men were attracted, most
stopped short of declaring their feelings. Sarah insisted there
were

> no lovers in my *entourage* of young men. They are Mr.
> A's friends. Would to Heaven you could see and hear
> them speak with me or of me. John Romilly has a true
> and deep regard for me—for us—but he would as soon
> think of making love to the planet Venus. So of many
> others. Indeed I think no woman was ever so happy in
> *friends*. There are at *least* half a dozen men to whom I
> *would* trust myself, my child, every thing—*certain* that
> not by look or word would they ever ask for any return
> for all their kindness but what a sister might grant. Am
> I not rich? . . . I am free (I mean *franche* [natural] not
> *libre* [loose]) in my manners—cordial nay affection-
> ate—to a fault, but I am not coquettish and they under-
> stand me, as I am.

All the same, though most held back from open declarations of love, she was bound to notice that many young men
flocked to her house. And she recognized the unspoken
signals of love: 'The looking glass may deceive but one
thing cannot—the eyes and the voices and the manners of
men, and I can tell . . . I should have no want of lovers if
I chose.' While there was no breach of propriety, she understood that much was left unsaid, leading her to observe, 'I
think I know several who love me dearly and never
dreamed of talking or looking love to me.' She was not
merely imagining these things, for one of her friends, John
Neal, revealed his consciousness of her sexual appeal when
he recalled her 'in her glory—the glory of established wom-
anhood, and the full ripeness of something tropical that

needed translation.' Others reacted this way: her friend Santa Rosa, the Italian refugee, told her (probably speaking for himself), 'It was almost a fashion to fall in love with [her].'

Not all Sarah's admirers were reticent. Given her powerful attractions and her husband's difficulties, some were less guarded in revealing their fantasies of love. Francis Jeffrey appears to have felt a good deal more than esteem for her, for though she claimed he was not a man of gallantry, one is bound to wonder why he commissioned a portrait of her by John Linnell, and thirty years later she acknowledged that he had been *very adoring.* Sarah also playfully suggested that the distinguished barrister and judge Henry Bickersteth would be an easy conquest. And she recorded an older man's confession:

> A man for whom I have the greatest respect and regard—a man of sixty or more, a grandfather, whose wife and son are among my most dear and intimate friends, made a declaration of love to me. This you will find simply ridiculous. But if you knew the man—the noble, highminded, upright person he is—if you had seen his agony—how this confession came from him like drops of blood, the suffocation with which he spoke of his long and vain struggles, of his dreadfully hopeless and humiliated feeling of his age and of the absurdity I might see in such a feeling, I shall never forget it, never cease to feel that what Victor Cousin once said to me is true— 'He who has not seen an old lover cannot understand what is truly tragic about love.' So recognize that he must be a man of delicacy, sensibility, honour, tenderness—all that can inspire love—except youth. . . . What could I say? My only thought and wish was to comfort

and cheer him—but how? . . . I said all I could to soothe
his self love. . . . I am afflicted beyond measure at this.
To see a man I have revered and looked up to pros-
trate—in a sort of convulsion of agony shame and passion. . . . He once said . . . 'Tell [another man] not to
come near you, if he values his peace.'

Sarah resisted him, as she did the others, but such adoration
undoubtedly was a tonic to her soul.

The incongruities of her life were striking. She was
conscious of her strengths and aware of the bizarre circumstances that made her appear at her best just at the very time
John was low. In a letter describing his 'deepest despondency' she also explained that her 'gay and blooming face'
delighted Francis Jeffrey, who promised to return 'to sun
himself in my bright eyes and get into spirits.' After an
exhausting night trying to cheer her husband she could next
day talk 'on all subjects—and with all people—and seem
interested about all things.' At the dire time when it was
becoming clear that all was lost at the university, Sarah
noted that 'my *own* affairs are very flourishing.' Nor was
this something that only she observed. Carlyle sarcastically
described her as the 'celebrated Mrs. Austin' and as a 'London distinguished female.' During another sad episode in
John's disintegrating career, Sarah could say, 'my star (as far
as my personal position in society is concerned) has been on
the ascendant . . . never did I experience any thing like the
universal kindness and respect and attention which have
been bestowed upon me lately.' She reflected, 'I am always
to live in this troubled sea, however, I float on the tops of
the waves, waves that would submerge many.' She noted,
'what a piece of contrariety and contradiction is my life!'

Sarah's myriad qualities and achievements justified pride, but they also nourished her vanity. She 'felt a sort of triumph in the midst of circumstances other women would have found overwhelming and humiliating' and declared that she had 'borne up bravely against a world of misery that would have crushed and extinguished half a dozen ordinary women.' At a particularly dark moment she asked a confidante, 'If I were not truly an extraordinary creature, could I have still strength and courage to live and act?' This self-admiration can be discerned in her description of her ideal woman: 'Nature may now and then . . . endow a woman with all the qualities that become her sex, and superadd rectitude of understanding, a steadiness of purpose, and firmness of principles that any man might envy.'

In spite of triumphs and self-satisfaction, however, 'the drop of poison was always at the bottom of the sparkling cup.' More than a drop, it was a steady diet for much of the first decade of her marriage, and along with pride, she also felt a good deal of self-pity. She thought of herself as 'a poor unfortunate one overwhelmed by annoyance and cares' and spoke of 'long years of ceaseless anxiety and bitter suffering.' She wrote to her sister in 1829:

Many times . . . he has entirely despaired of being able to commence his public career, and I have held myself in a state of constant preparation for any decision he might take, and have accustomed myself to look steadily at the abandonment of all our prospects here for ever. Indeed, those who know what a life of prolonged uncertainty and suspense is, will not wonder at me for wishing that the worst were come and nothing left to hope or fear.

She indulged in a dirge of complaints. John was 'full of despondency and gloom, and I must do all and bear all.'

> My heart is very heavy—my poor husband is ill again—and very dejected, and on me falls the whole weight. . . . Yet my elastic temper and stout heart do not utterly fail me. . . . Come what may, I have courage to meet it.

Her resilience came to her aid; as she said on another occasion after she had cried for a week, 'That is over, and "Richard's himself again." '

She grieved not only about her day-to-day existence—money worries, care, anxiety, fatigue, sorrow—but also for lost opportunities to use her gifts. Initially she had been content to work only for money, but as she became aware of her talent there were stirrings of literary ambition, but she put this aside to continue the more humble translations that provided distraction from anxiety while bringing in much-needed income. Such renunciation also ensured that she would not upstage her husband with her ready pen and felicitous phrase-making. Yet if Sarah curbed her talent with her husband's sensitivities in mind, it was not without regrets and side glances at what might have been, as she revealed in a comment about 'voluntary abnegations of what I might perhaps have attained.' John Stuart Mill, John Sterling, and the poets Robert Southey and Samuel Rogers encouraged her to abandon translation for authorship; and Carlyle told her that while her translations in her 'fine clear-flowing English' were splendid—'I hear the fine silver music of Goethe sound through *your* voice, through your heart'—she ought to 'find a higher task one day.' Yet she continued to translate, and although she soon would be called 'our best living translator,' she knew she had a capacity for more independent work.

Sarah gave up more than a prospect of authorship. From the beginning she was driven—perhaps without being fully aware of it—by her vision of an ideal marriage. During the first few years of their life together her hopes for propelling John to usefulness and fame were sustained by her husband's intellectual promise and character; but as he faltered, she arranged his life to facilitate the achievement of ambition, hers probably more than his. Sarah became 'his secretary, man of affairs, and nurse and in short . . . managed the whole detail of existence for us all, leaving him to think and write—his sole employments.' When even this yielded no result, it became clear that she held the ambitions they had once shared far more tenaciously than John, and she realized that on every level her marriage was a tragic mismatch.

The dreams of what might have been were never far beneath the surface. 'Few women had a greater chance under what they call favourable circumstances of being a very brilliant and attractive person,' she reflected sorrowfully. 'Well, I have been called upon to forget all that.' She looked back on the decade since her marriage as 'one of labour, anxiety and constant self denial and self control . . . I have been disciplined to forget myself.' A strong sense of grievance ran through her complaints as she compared John's weaknesses with her own strengths, what she gave in marriage with what she received. She had come through cruel years and could not disguise from herself that the future looked just as bleak. 'I see nothing but anxiety, toil, suffering, physical and mental, before me—

ending in what I dare not think of. And this will have been my life!' Mourning the past and despairing about what lay ahead, it was nearly inevitable that she should dream of escape.

CHAPTER THREE

Secret Life

❧ ❧

Before you pronounce on the rashness of the
proceeding, reader, look back to the point
whence I started; consider the desert I had left.
CHARLOTTE BRONTË, Villette

I turn my heart inside out to you.
SARAH AUSTIN

THE early 1830s were bitter. A decade of struggle had
yielded little prospect of better days. Middle age loomed for
Sarah, and the writing on the wall proclaimed the end of
her husband's university career. As he taught his course for
the third time in the autumn of 1831 he still had a class of
eight students, and by means of a subscription raised by
loyal, like-minded friends continued to draw his inadequate
salary, but this improvised arrangement could not last. Soon
he would be without paid employment, and Sarah faced the
prospect of a retreat to some inexpensive city on the Continent, cut off from friends and relatives, with a defeated and
unoccupied man. In deep despondency she wrote to her
sister, 'We cannot live on air, but must go somewhere

where our little means will support us. Plan we have none.'

At this juncture a new epoch opened for her: she fell in love, first with a book and then with its author. It all began in pursuit of a business transaction. Late in 1830 the publisher John Murray asked her opinion about publishing a translation of two lively volumes (two more were to follow) of travels in England and Ireland during the late 1820s. The book, written by an 'anonymous' German, was creating a sensation in Germany, each edition selling out instantly, the sales stimulated by its title *Briefe eines Verstorbenen* [*Letters from a Dead Man*] and by the open secret that the mystery author was none other than the fascinating Prince Hermann Pückler-Muskau. From the moment Sarah glanced at the volumes she was determined to translate them, knowing that the English public would relish the flair with which the prince described places, manners, and people in breezy, journal-style letters to his former wife Lucie, called Julie in the book. He had natural advantages over most travel writers: his aristocratic credentials, good looks, elegance, and charm had given him access to exclusive salons, well-known persons, and the finest country houses. Using this entry ticket, he had taken a cool, appraising look at aristocratic society—its snobbery, shallowness, and plain silliness. Such a critique, Sarah realized, was bound to intrigue her countrymen, especially at a time when political reform was on everyone's lips. The Germans, meanwhile, delighted to see the mighty and arrogant British lion finally put in his place, were turning the German edition into a sensational best-seller. After years of struggling with marginal projects, Sarah was convinced this translation would be a winner.

While Murray vacillated, she stood her ground. It was

not in question whether the letters should be published in English—'nine people out of ten would say they *cannot escape* being translated'—so delay could be fatal, for the book would be snatched up by another publishing house. '*Vite* you must decide,' she urged, brushing aside his fear of publishing satire directed against his society customers. She told him that she would take the book to another publisher if he rejected it, 'which for your sake and mine, I hope you will not.' Murray, however, continued to drag his heels, unimpressed even by the fact that Goethe, the aged oracle of German literature, had given the book enthusiastic praise. Sarah sent him an ultimatum:

> I [have] seen enough of it already to be quite decided on taking instant steps to . . . translating it. . . . I shall take your silence not as consent, but the very reverse. If I do not hear from you definitely before Saty. next I shall take for granted that the scheme does not please you and shall consider myself at liberty to offer the manuscript elsewhere.

When Murray's caution finally got the better of him and he decided that the book was too risky to publish, Sarah, undaunted, lived up to her word and contracted with another publisher, Effingham Wilson. Her initiative paid off, for Wilson struck gold—and Sarah had embarked on the most significant emotional experience of her married life.

While Sarah the adroit businesswoman recognized the book's potential, the private woman was, from the start, intrigued by the man who wrote it. She praised the book's charm and cleverness to Murray, but 'a far higher charm, to me,' she explained, 'lies in the picture of the peculiar and interesting mind of the author, the philanthropy, freedom from all prejudice, and the gentle and somewhat melancholy philosophizing mingled with a strong sense of the ludicrous and a great power of describing it.' By the time she had completed translating the first two volumes she was under Pückler's spell.

After weeks of being steeped in his ideas and having his voice constantly in her ear, Sarah felt an overwhelming sense of intimacy with him. As she explained, 'Involuntarily I have written to the man himself with whose thoughts and feelings I have been occupied till they are become as familiar to me as my own,' for there was as much about Pückler himself as of the places he visited in his account. She had heard his views on society, politics, religion, social class, parks, art, high and low life, table manners, inns, and food, and in this kaleidoscope of descriptions and opinions she was astonished to discover how often his feelings and judgments mirrored her own. It especially pleased her that he shared her liberal political outlook, satirized the rigid English class system, and defended the poor downtrodden Irish and admired their leader, Daniel O'Connell. His heart was in the right place on so many issues, and she marveled that this astonishingly liberal prince was so enlightened, humane, and noble-hearted.

Pückler had an uncanny power to attract women. Like his hero and model Byron, he was reputed to be irresistible, and he was even credited with hypnotic powers. In writing these volumes he discovered that his charisma could be conveyed by pen alone. While he was in fact a perplexing, complex person, in this first work his most genial self prevailed, so much so that it has remained a classic of subjective travel literature. At a time when it was commonly assumed that German writers were deep thinkers and ponderous writers, Pückler was a virtuoso at the breezy tone. He gossiped with such casual ease and complete naturalness and let each moment speak so realistically that he seemed to address each reader personally. The lively 'Dead Man' sparked the imagination of his contemporaries, and he entirely captivated Sarah.

The man Sarah derived from his book had curiosity about everything around him and a keen appetite for life's offerings. He was the hedonist, the seeker of enjoyment, as he later called himself, who rejoiced in the world and asserted the right to pleasure. While he remained the grand seigneur, at ease, adroit and assuming privilege, he also pictured himself as akin to an utterly naive, light-hearted child—playful, full of vitality, enthusiastically reaching for every new toy, and always open to new experiences: the Weltkind—worldly child—as Goethe had called him. This master of enjoyment claimed at times to be afflicted by blue devils, but his dejection was soon cast off, and his gusto triumphed. 'The gloomiest horizon has no power to darken my inner sun,' he exclaimed. Little pleasures were as good as great ones. 'As a foreigner, and still more as an independent man, I take the liberty to seek enjoyment wherever I can find it . . . nor do I always find the most in the highest places.' He liked nothing better than to assume an incognito and to enjoy the freedom of the road. It was exhilarating to ride on the box of the stagecoach, or 'roll along in a comfortable carriage,' or put miles behind him galloping through the roughest country. 'I cannot describe to you how delightful this life is to me,' he enthused. 'I should most certainly spend the greatest part of my immortality on the high road, and especially in England.'

No mere passive observer, he threw himself into every

challenge. Undaunted by the foulest weather, he climbed to the top of Snowdon and emptied a bottle of champagne to celebrate; descended in a diving bell to observe the Thames tunnel excavations; and rode wildly, leaping hedges and walls in mad fox hunts. With the same zest, he observed the ways of the fashionable world, tirelessly examined the lay-out of park after park, roamed through London's prisons, docks, and warehouses, and explored its streets with their puppet shows, beggars, and prostitutes. Everywhere he was keen-eyed, open-minded; life was a feast for him. 'There is such an extent and variety of "terra incognita" in this illimitable London, that with no other guide than chance, one is sure to fall upon something new and interesting.' It was heartening to be in the company of his unquenchable, lively personality; his life-affirming message invigorated and spoke to Sarah's own pent-up vitality and longing for brighter vistas.

He brought fresh air and spirit. No severity or moralism darkened his horizon; he accepted himself as 'neither saint nor angel' and was tolerant of imperfections in others. As the distanced, amused observer of human nature, he held that sober virtues were fine, but only in limited doses: 'It would be the most terrible state of affairs if we all became entirely sensible here below.' Though he was given to everyday philosophizing, his outlook was, above all, artistic. He gloried in beauty of every kind; was fascinated by the unusual or irrational; pursued imaginative and fanciful ideas. What a contrast he presented to her austere, analytical husband, so fastidious and demanding of himself and others, his mind ever on books, principles, and his health.

Sarah's image of Pückler was warmed by the sentiments he lavished on his 'Julie' back in Germany. His capacity for

voicing affection and tenderness was vivid in the messages
he sent her during their long separation. She was his 'truest
friend,' his 'best comfort,' the loving woman who had
transformed his melancholy into sunlight, 'the most essential
element in his well being' with whom he had 'the most
perfect mutual understanding.' He recalled their 'years of
tenderness' together and constantly reiterated his gratitude
'for all your manifold love, kindness and indulgence.' In
spite of some puzzling ambiguities in his relationship to her,
he rarely failed to send her a stream of generous feelings.

Julie was obviously a confidante and cherished friend, but
unmistakably there was no bond of passion between them.
Upon reading the book, Sarah could have no doubt that he
paid court, more or less, to any pretty woman who crossed
his path. This Don Juan charmed the ladies at the races,
routs, balls, fêtes, and dances of the London and Brighton
social seasons and was ever ready to note the flocks of 'pretty
girls, against whom you are squeezed indiscriminately.' He
was not snobbish and had an eye for any pretty Irish girl,
flirted with the perky maid at an inn, and enjoyed a romp
on New Year's Eve with the foreign milliner girls at his
lodgings. 'He attracts and is attracted,' was how Goethe
sedately summed up the amorous Pückler. Sarah hardly
needed Goethe to inform her that Pückler was an experienced player at the game of mutual attraction, for his flirtations were a recurring theme. He was so obviously a
connoisseur of what he called 'sweet, forbidden chariots of
love' and of what induces tender thoughts in women.

There was no mistaking that he looked for women's
sensual qualities. In the little 'piquante' (one of his favorite
words) adventures he related to Julie, he appraised the
women he met for their sexual charms and described their

ankles, feet, and 'elastic limbs' and alluded to their lips, breasts, and sensuous bodies. His survey of the master paintings in the great houses gave him an opportunity for thinly veiled suggestiveness. He praised the supple flesh of 'a naked recumbent charming woman who laughed roguishly through the fingers of her hand,' and, at a time when Englishmen were said to avert their eyes from nudes in galleries, he rhapsodized in well-worn clichés about a sleeping Venus by Titian:

> clad only in her own charms and blissfully reposing on soft pillows; a dream seemed to thrill convulsively through her. . . . Her lovely limbs are as white as snow, not a blemish to be seen on that full, classical body over which stream luxuriant brown locks, affording stolen glimpses of the rosebuds of her virginal bosom. A lovely hand, an adorable foot . . . a mouth made for kissing and a yearning pearly face.

Then, imagining her eyes opening, he indulged his sexual fantasy and exclaimed, 'my senses left me.' Similarly, a painting of the Israelite Judith, who, according to his reading of the story, had sacrificed her virtue to the Assyrian general to save her people,* led him to fantasize about 'her arched sensuous mouth still expressing enchantment and tremulously revealing that against her will she had become acquainted with lust!' The erotic emphasis in his descriptions of women was usually not this blatant, but it was never far beneath the surface.

Unencumbered by middle-class moralism, he looked for natural passions beneath the veneer of conventional behav-

---

*Judith saved the Israelites by beheading Holofernes as he slept.

ior. Women who attracted him, Sarah could surmise, were high-spirited and revealed elemental, spontaneous sexuality. He favored roguish, teasing women who were seductively playful, 'lively as quicksilver,' and who only barely masked their 'wildness.' In contrast to every maxim of Sarah's youth, he asserted that coquettishness was captivating and 'women's greatest charm.' Most Englishwomen, he declared, had a hereditary heaviness and were prudish, pedantic, socially passive and utterly lacking in sexual attractiveness. Any spontaneity had been crushed by conventional decorum, and they were timid, graceless, awkward—unless by chance they were on a horse. For sexual naturalness and intensity he turned mostly to women who were not English and had, in another of his stock phrases, something of 'the fire of the South.' He was thus much taken by the exotic married woman, Harriet L——, the 'beautiful African,' so called by him because she had lived in the colonies. She was a 'teasing vixen,' an unburdened child of nature, who enchanted him. Irishwomen also showed the vitality that he prized, for they were of 'the wild genre,' with 'an inexhaustible fund of grace and vivacity' and sparkle in their eyes. Two such delightful 'sweet girls' he found irresistibly flirtatious in their 'Irish grace and gaiety'; of course, they were 'extremely un-English.' His general message, though overlaid by a decorous manner, was clear: he looked for seductive women who held the promise of being moved by powerful passions.

Though Pückler's humor, vitality, and natural tone are appealing even today, the way in which he insinuated himself into Sarah's imagination strains our credulity. For Sarah he offered a leap into another world suffused with the romantic sensibility and sensual appreciation she yearned for. Convinced that conventional preliminaries were out of place with one so unceremonious, she wrote to him as if she were just continuing a conversation—'for in truth I talk to my author; and cannot help it.' She was so permeated with his manner that she instantly adopted his impressionistic, free-associating tone, leaping from subject to subject, and like him, scattering foreign phrases along the way. Taking advantage of the private wavelength to which she had gained access through the book, she echoed its allusions and metaphors.* What is also striking is how willing she was to reveal her intense interest in him, and how eager she was to create an impression and start a dialogue. 'I have endless matter to discuss and controvert with you,' she told him right away in her earliest surviving letter, which accompanied her completed translation of the initial volumes. He had become a mental companion, someone with whom she had conducted a rich internal conversation that she intended to continue. 'Strange that I should think of you as I do so constantly, so affectionately and always as if I knew you and had talked to you.' Even her very first letters, which are lost, were apparently written in the intimate, flirtatious manner of those that followed, for she recalled them as 'my first mad letters—[written] so gaily!'

The tone between them was naturally not set by Sarah alone. Pückler, true to form, wrote in his familiar, insinuating, near-impudent way from the very start. He had played at anonymity in his book, pretending merely to be the editor of a dead man's letters, and now, tongue-in-cheek, as they began to correspond, he continued this game. When Sarah, at the request of the publisher, wrote asking for a

---

*She would continue to do this throughout her letters.

lithograph of his likeness to be included in the volumes as a portrait of the 'supposed author,' he replied, in his good but not entirely idiomatic English: 'To send you the portrait of the author is almost more as I dare answer for vis à vis the dead.' He sent it anyway, but made it clear that both in public and private, he was going to continue with the teasing if transparent disguise.

Sarah was delighted to pick up this challenge and demonstrate that she also had talent for mystifying and tantalizing. Falling in with the conceit of anonymity, she addressed him as the editor and later as 'My dear Original' (which is what he called himself in the book), even though she had little doubt about his name all along. Lacking his address, she directed her letters through an intermediary to 'the editor of the letters from a Dead Man' and simply signed her letter as from the Translator. Pückler, an addict of such hide-and-seek, was being invited to discover the sex of his correspondent. All this play-acting led him to suspect that he was corresponding with a woman, but he wrote, 'Madam or Sir (for I don't yet know positively . . . to what half of the human race you belong) one or the other,' and he addressed her as the 'Dear Translator of the Dead!' He did not have to puzzle long, for Sarah was not about to leave her sex in doubt, and in her first surviving letter she let it slip out. 'O cielo, my incognito—what has become of it? Well, sooner or later you would have found me out, and in good truth I could find in my heart to throw off all disguises at once.'

Disguises of other sorts were also soon cast off. She was hardly the professional translator addressing the author, but the attractive woman flirting with an intriguing man. Even crucial business matters were treated in a sexual context. Sarah had heard a disturbing rumor that he had encouraged another publisher to embark on a rival translation, and she had heard enough about his mercurial behavior to know that he had an unpredictable side. 'Just imagine if I have not reason to think you a traitor.' Having declared her sex, she used it to flatter his vanity. She would not be a passive bystander to an audacious attempt to set up a competitor, and had written an indignant letter to the other publisher. 'I *blasted* the wretch for his insolence, vowed that I was *your* Translator and that nobody else living was, or should be.' It was 'the letter of a tigress . . . I lay entire claim to you, swear I will tear out the eyes of any man or woman who disputes my claim, and will cause you to disavow, disclaim, and "utterly abjure and renounce" all translators on earth but myself.' If he treated her in this way, 'can I ever forgive you? Surely I was justified by your letter in imagining that you looked upon me as your sole and proper translator. Did you then know of and encourage a rival? It cannot be.' She would make him 'disown any rival, as men do naughty wives (in low life) by advertisement in the Papers—Dear Ghost, you will, won't you?' The mock tone of the betrayed mistress upbraiding the faithless lover was spirited and flattering. She was showing herself to be a woman who could pique his interest.

Sarah also challenged him by tossing a phrase into her letter, as if half-uttering an aside, suggesting that more lay beneath her playful manner—and this more held promise of submerged fires. Some time, she wrote, she would send him a different sort of letter, but at present she was oppressed and dejected, for she was nursing a sick husband and could not find the spirit to write 'such a letter as I would—and as I could, when I am un peu folle,' that is, in a wild, crazy mood. Pückler was not likely to ignore such an intimation.

Whatever encouragement he gave her, Sarah, it would seem, was not so much lured into the relationship but ran to meet it.

Meanwhile she made the rounds of her London friends, inquiring about him, only to find that his reputation was highly dubious. She was told he had come to England not so much as a traveler but as a fortune hunter in search of a new rich wife to replenish his empty coffers. This news could not have been a surprise, for in the book he had casually alluded to this rumor. Countless other tales circulated about him, sharpening her curiosity: a London newspaper, for example, reported that he had remarried his divorced wife. Her ears must have buzzed when she heard all the stories—his supposed liaisons, romantic intrigues, quarrels, duels, debts, eccentricity, love of ridiculing the conventional. Some saw him simply as the ultimate fop and dandy and discounted him as 'Prince Pickling Mustard,' while others clearly relished his company.

In a tone of mock disbelief, Sarah confronted him with the rumors she had heard. 'Do you know,' she wrote, 'that I have been told several times that the reported Author . . . was a person with whom no woman could safely hold intercourse?'

> You have not the least conception of the things they accuse you of. They call you, even to *me*, a liar, a swindler, an adventurer, a coward, they say you were compelled to quit England on account of the commission of an offense 'inter Christianos non nominandum' [not to be named by Christians] (the black-hearted wretches, the priests must have invented that). In short my

dear, je ne suis pas sur les roses *deinetwegen* [I am not on a bed of roses on your account].

An army captain had told her he was 'a perfect *roué*—tell me truly, am I to believe all this?' She also repeated the story that he had 'threatened to publish the letters of a married woman with whom you had an affair here, and had extorted two thousand pounds from the family as the price of . . . discretion. I of course exclaimed at the impossibility of a man with *human* feelings being guilty of such conduct, but was coolly told it was true.' The publisher John Murray, who heard all society gossip, had been told that Pückler was 'an adventurer "*not worth a shilling*," (the English *ultimate* of criminality) and his eyes popped out when I told him he could find Muskau on the map if he chose to look.' She had also been warned that her author was utterly indiscreet, and on hearing that she corresponded with him, a friend told her, 'write with the perfect conviction that every word you write will be made public if he thinks it will amuse anybody.' Then there was talk of his scandalous behavior at the Travellers Club, but another friend reported that 'he *knew* of nothing worse than your throwing an inkstand at a waiter's head; but that the *reports* were of some discreditable money transactions,' though her informant had found no evidence for them.

Pückler was unperturbed by these accusations. 'I am not conscious to have offended any one . . . I made it a rule to answer English impertinence allways by a dubble dose of the same.' He was pleased to have stirred up controversy.

Pray send me if you can get it, everything that abuses me. I am so constituted that nothing entertains me more and very often I have invented in former times horrid storys of myself only to have the pleasure to frighten good silly people out of their senses. I am no more young enough pour telles follies [for such nonsense] but I still like to be a little abused by indifferent people not by friends of course.'

Sarah also was content to disregard such stories. Her sense of excitement about him was not reduced by his reputation, and she had no intention of cutting this flirtation short.

It was one thing to pick up gossip about her author and try to piece him together from his book, but by no flight of fancy could she have conjured up the realities that had shaped him. His French mother was fourteen when she married Pückler's dour, thirty-one-year-old father, adding her sizable estate of Muskau, then part of Saxony, to her husband's far-smaller property at Branitz. A year later, on October 30, 1785, Hermann Ludwig Heinrich von Pückler-Muskau was born. There were to be more children, but the marriage was a calamity and finally ended in divorce. In the meantime, Hermann was shuffled from one servant to another, witnessing corruption and philandering all around. At age seven he was sent to live for four years in a nearby children's institute run by the Herrnhuter, an evangelical sect associated with the Moravians. By his account, he was sexually abused by one of his masters. Other doleful educational experiences followed, and Pückler acquired a fierce disdain for the clergy and a lifelong contempt for sham and hypocrisy. As he saw it, an imaginative, warm-hearted child had been tossed into the ice of the world and learned to survive, becoming deeply cynical about human nature.

The next decade of his youth was the predictable sequel, and he passed through more despoiling hands. He became known as the 'toller' [wild] Pückler—a daredevil rider, a crack pistol shot, a flamboyant charmer, and a womanizer, distinguished from other restless young aristocrats only by the scale of his sensational stunts and the magnitude of his debts. Then, suddenly, he veered in another direction and embarked on a walking tour of Europe, disguised as plain Secretary Hermann; but a year later reverted to a life of dissipation. His erratic path seemed to be leading nowhere.

Impulse and whim governed Pückler all his life, but an undercurrent of ambition drove him even during his wild notoriety-seeking youth. He had no taste for being one of the crowd or merely one more mediocre, impoverished aristocrat. As he put it, 'I fear nothing but the indifferent.' An opportunity for greater prominence came when, at twenty-five, his father's death left him master of Muskau, Groditz and Branitz, and forty-five villages. He was finally emancipated from a tight allowance and a sour relationship but instead acquired the burden of deeply encumbered estates. His financial woes were intensified by the devastation the Napoleonic War inflicted on his properties and by the drastic loss of revenue when his region was incorporated into Prussia. Pückler remarked bitterly, 'God turned his face from me when he had me become a Prussian.' The need to ally himself to a rich wife, which his father's agent and others had counseled for years, now seemed most pressing.

This brought him to England for the first time. For a while it looked as if he would marry the widowed Marchioness of Lansdowne, but the scheme fell through at the last moment, and he returned to Muskau empty-handed. He had more luck closer to home. In 1817 he married Lucie, daughter of the powerful liberal Prussian chancellor Karl von Hardenberg, quite undisguisedly for her money, compliant nature, and useful diplomatic connections, but with no pretence of conjugal interest. Lucie, a divorced woman with a grown daughter and a stepdaughter, Helmine, was a cultivated member of Rahel Varnhagen's free-thinking Berlin intellectual salon and shared Pückler's interests and taste for extreme luxury. She was also forty-one, nine years his senior, and growing stout. Even so, they formed a close partnership, with cascades of sentimental gush to smooth its way. Lucie had accepted him on his terms with open eyes and he had not lied to her—on the contrary, in spite of his emphasis on sentiment, he was given to unsparing, often brutal candor. When his marriage began with his falling in love with his beautiful stepdaughter, he ceaselessly pressured Lucie with his 'Helminomania' and demands that they might live 'à la Turk.'

Lucie's devotion to him survived this and similar strains. She was his 'guiding angel' and protectress, his 'other I,' to whom he could say anything, but who always gave him unstinting devotion. It was entirely appropriate that he addressed her as his 'Schnucke' [lambkin] and signed himself as 'Lou' [a derivative of loup, i.e., wolf]. Lamblike, in spite of warnings by her property manager, she set no limit as he poured her wealth into transforming prosaic Muskau into one of the most harmonious, imaginative parks in Germany. She fully understood that her money and support combined with his artistic vision would establish him as one of Germany's most gifted landscape architects and create a lasting memorial to them both. As Pückler put it, the park 'would compensate for many errors' and would prove for a hundred years and more that he had not 'merely vegetated.'

While Pückler's marriage was an ambiguous combination of attachment and calculation, there was no doubt about his passion for beautifying Muskau. As Lucie signed away ever more of her fortune, he and an army of workmen engaged in a titanic struggle to satisfy his 'parkomania' and turn Muskau into an unsurpassed splendor. No labor was too great or detail too insignificant for him. 'I have thought out everything without exception myself. There is not a tree, nor path, nor flower bed that has not been carefully measured and marked out by me and altered ten times until it has been successful, regardless of cost and time.' He was driven by a grandiose poetic dream as to how nature and art, landscape and buildings, could be harmonized. Already during his engagement, he planted hundreds of trees; and in the years that followed, undertook elaborate drainage work; fertilized and changed the sandy soil; shipped tons of grass seed from England to establish velvet lawns and picturesque meadows; and constructed paths that led invitingly into new vistas. The river Neisse was deflected to enliven the grounds with lakes, streams, ponds, and fountains, and he built bridges, orangeries, pheasant houses, a riding arena, and stables, and raised the economic productivity of the estate by improving the alum works which employed a hundred workers. Not to be outdone, during his absence Lucie created a spa—Hermann'sbad—for paying guests who, under the care of a physician, took mud baths, drank mineral waters, and promenaded in a special pavilion.

The exterior and interior of the castle, of course, could not be ignored, and he engaged a gifted architect, rebuilt extensively, and also had furniture, art, statues, chandeliers, porcelain, crystal, silver, coaches, and horses brought in from Paris, Brussels, and London. The estate became a sensation, a fantasia, the creation of a romantic imagination and inspired landscaping.* The park became breathtaking, but so did Pückler's debts. As he put it, 'Money with us is like water on a hot stove.'

As his vision became reality, creditors began to haunt him. To make matters worse, Lucie's father died in 1822, disinheriting his daughter and leaving all his fortune to his mistress, crushing all hope of financial rescue. Pückler was driven to capitalize on his remaining great asset—his attractiveness to women. A new rich wife seemed to be the only solution to his financial woes. So, in October 1823, as a birthday gift, Lucie declared she would release him. When the divorce became absolute in 1826, he sold his jewelry, horses, and carriages to raise money. He made over his other possessions to Lucie, left her and his supervisor with detailed park plans and instructions, and with much wavering and pathetic leave-taking left Muskau and set out for Britain to look over more parks and try to trade his title for a magnificent dowry.** He was forty-one, still handsome in his peacock-colored dandy outfits, tall, with a slim figure and penetrating blue eyes. By dyeing his hair, he claimed, he looked not more than thirty. Everything seemed set to land a rich catch.

Pückler found no lack of British fathers willing to sacri-

---

*The park, divided by the German-Polish border, remains well-known in Europe. The part on the German side is open to the public and until recently was maintained by the East German government as a national monument. As in Pückler's day, there are severe anxieties about future sources of funding for the park's costly maintenance, though various schemes for its financial development are under discussion.

**His head gardener joined him for the park-inspection part of his trip.

fice their daughters to Muskau's glory. There was Miss Gibbins, for example, the daughter of a Brighton doctor, young, available, and with £50,000, but she insisted on not being parted from her dear parents, and they were more than Pückler could stomach. They so appalled him that he got no further than drafting a letter of proposal. Then there was Miss Harriet Bonham, a seventeen-year-old—but naturally he had his eye on her unobtainable married sister. 'To love and to seduce this woman would be a delightful sin,' he sighed, 'virtuously to marry the sister, a bitter medicine.' He brought himself to make an offer to Harriet, stipulating that her family would have to increase her meager £10,000 to £50,000, the absolute minimum he required for Muskau. The family, however, felt unable to '*approach* in any way that unfortunate sum.' With the help of a matrimonial agent, he met a rich jeweler, Mr. Hamlet, and his daughter, another Harriet. She seemed to take to him but suddenly changed her mind when she heard about his strange divorce. Pückler crafted a long and irresistible letter explaining everything, but Harriet, an 'incurable Englishwoman,' in spite of her father's pleading, refused even to open it. 'The father took leave of me with tears in his eyes,' wrote Pückler to Lucie, 'as I did from his 200,000 Pounds.' This matrimonial minuet went on for some time.

As rumors about the details of Pückler's divorce spread, prejudiced, prudish, insincere Britishers, as Pückler judged them, hesitated, for arranged divorces like his were illegal in England and a remarriage could even be considered bigamous. His insistence (true enough) that his relationship with Lucie was like that of son and mother, and that 'a sum of ten million and Venus herself' could not tempt him to jettison 'Mama Lucie,' who was to continue to live on the estate, did not help matters. Nor did it further his cause that he broadcast that Lucie's picture stood on his desk. As the Prussian ambassador told him: 'Prince, this sentimentality is doing you more harm than you think.'

Pückler was his own worst enemy. Whenever he came within reach of his prize, panic seized him. As he correctly diagnosed to Lucie, 'It is my pride that chiefly suffers in this wife-hunting, and this insuperable feeling may prove a great hindrance to me.' Meanwhile he dutifully continued to send Lucie day-by-day accounts of the looks, character, and, above all, the likely dowry of his prospects. On April Fools' Day, 1828, he joked, 'Schnucke, it's all over, I am married. I have an income of £20,000 and two children.' All too frequently, however, he felt oppressed. 'It is a bitter medicine that I am obliged to swallow sooner or later. In theory it all goes down easily but in reality it is terribly nauseous.' Visions of piles of English gold to ensure Muskau's glory faded as he faced the terror of losing his freedom to 'a devil of a marriage.'

Pückler returned home without a bride (and without having run into Sarah) but with magnificent new park plans and hopes for a book, for Lucie had already shown his letters to the Varnhagens, and they were enthusiastic about publication. To his considerable surprise, it was to be his best-selling account of his travels, not a rich wife, that would transform his life. From now on he turned to travel and authorship, and although he was still improving his estate in the years 1831–1833, when the correspondence with Sarah was at its height, he was largely occupied with writing. Above all, he was absorbed with composing a now forgotten, satirical, semi-autobiographical novel, as well as a notable book about his landscaping principles and how they had

been applied at Muskau.* The years during which he corresponded with Sarah were an interim period for him, before
he set out on new adventures. He was passing much of his
time in his hunting lodge amidst forests of immense pines
which, as he wrote Sarah, 'resembled church steeples.' In this
favorite rustic retreat with only deer, horses, and his five
dogs as company, he divided his days and nights between
his four desks with pen ever at hand for professional writing
and corresponding with his translator.

From the start, however, the book that had brought them
together threatened to cause a rift between them. The bold
correspondent was transformed when she took up the translator's pen. While Sarah the private woman was sending
beckoning signals, Mrs. Austin the official translator was
prudishly blue-penciling his text, removing anything even
remotely suggestive out of fear that it might offend propriety and cast a shadow on her reputation. Pückler aimed to
be satirical and hard-hitting about the aristocracy and titil-
lating and insinuating about women, but Sarah was determined to prune the personal attacks and scrub out most of
the sexual allusions. The final volumes of his book, with
their descriptions of society notables, caused her the most
anxiety. She feared they might contain 'many a picture
which a woman's pen could not gracefully touch.' According to the proverb, she told him, Dead Men told no tales,

---

*Andeutungen über Landschaftsgärtnerei verbunden mit der Beschreibung
ihrer praktischen Anwendung in Muskau*, with 44 views and 4 ground
plans (Stuttgart, 1834). The beautiful plates by Wilhelm Shirmer depict
the romantic harmonious landscape of Pückler's imagination.

but 'this Sprichwort [saying] I fear you will belie.' It was ungentlemanly to ridicule persons who had been his hosts, and she feared that his portraits might raise a storm and that she, as his intermediary, and perhaps her family, would be exposed to the blasts of indignation that might follow in the press. 'The wife of an honourable man has no right to give her name *(which is his)* to a thing which *can* be censured— and the mother of a little girl has other and even more tender reasons for not braving public opinion. My name does not appear, it is true, but all my friends know that I translated.' Yet if what he had written in the final volumes was 'not too bad,' she would also take them on. Sarah intended to distance herself from him in public while seeking his friendship in private. Her extreme caution was evident in her unsigned preface to the last volumes: there she was merely the translator and not responsible for a work that made 'no pretension to any higher character than that of chit-chat letters to an intimate friend.' She was aware that he might not relish such maneuvers: 'Don't go in a rage at my Preface. It is most important to *us* (for I care as much for your credit as my own) that I should appear to stand quite neutral and indifferent. Otherwise all I do will be imputed to be mere bookselling interest in you.' Not surprisingly he was inclined to fly into a temper. Translator and author were set on a collision course that threatened to nip their flirtation in the bud.

Sarah set about reshaping the Dead Man, unaware that he had already suffered from considerable remolding by Lucie and himself; for when it came to publishing his uniquely candid letters about his fortune-hunt, even Pückler turned squeamish. As he told Varnhagen, he could use only 'a few of the original letters from this period and had to write more than half entirely anew, or rather to resmelt them entirely.' Sarah, even more determined to placate bourgeois notions, now resmelted once more; by reshaping with seamless joins, she would save her reputation and his.

She removed his fanciful introduction, portions of the personal satire, political harangues, and economic arguments she thought faulty. Some dreams, accounts of prostitutes, a suggestive bathhouse massage, a visit to a well-known courtesan, some crude doggerel, and anecdotes she found in bad taste were also cast out. Assignations were censored, no matter how cautiously he tried to tell the tale. In her version he no longer paid a visit to a woman 'with a foot like a zephyr that I have often kissed when I paid her a brief evening visit while the others were dining, and she allowed me to pretend that the unfamiliar punch had gone to my head.' Sarah's purifying went well beyond such stories, and she excised the slightest nuances that might be construed as indelicate. If a woman offered a 'rendezvous,' in Sarah's translation she merely became 'less cruel.' If Pückler had taken a high-spirited, very pretty married woman to a ball, Sarah made sure that she was merely good-natured and sensible. A recumbent naked woman in a painting became simply recumbent, and the voluptuous Venus vanished entirely.

Predictably, accounts of flirtations with married women (and clearly he was drawn to these) were deleted. One such story that fell to Sarah's editing was his description of an outing to Greenwich with the lovely Henrietta Sontag, a German singer who had taken him and all of London by storm. The hint of amorousness in his account of their idyllic May Day ride to Greenwich and supper in a private room at an open window overlooking the river was too

much for Sarah, especially as Sontag had somehow managed
to forget that she was secretly married to a Count Rossi.
In similar fashion, Sarah retained only seven lines of his
ten-page drama about his infatuation with the fascinating
Harriet L——. Her jet black hair, intense, dark blue eyes,
tomboy ways, and sudden soft glances had disturbed his
equanimity; and though he never put it to the test, he
evidently found her most seductive and open to temptation.
Sarah at first glance knew that Harriet would have to be
banished. She even got Pückler's agreement to this deletion,
for initially he was anxious for her to tone down what
might be unsuitable for the stuffy English. He had not,
however, reckoned with the degree of his translator's delicacy. By the time she had completed her work not only had
the barely perceptible ambiguities in his relationship to his
wife been obliterated, but so had even the most innocuous
little encounters with the opposite sex. She had mercilessly
transformed the bohemian prince with the roving eye into
an approximation of an English gentlemen whose adventures could be read aloud in a Victorian drawing room.

Pückler felt betrayed by the extent of Sarah's 'changes,
omissions, timorous translations.' How could she 'cut his
wings so dreadfully'; she was a traitor, 'a little coward'; he
was incredulous at her timidity. 'I really don't conceive
your terrors.' She had pretended that she was not one of
those conventional, moralistic Englishwomen whom he despised, but now he knew the truth: 'You must be a prude,'
was his cry.

> Really Signora, your womanly fear to offend one or the
> other insignificant person, and still more the conscious-
> ness your sex being known to the public, makes you such

a little coward that you are taking away almost every 'sel' [spice] of my book. But a translator ought to be of no sex at all. The German letters offered a consommé to the public, and you think of course that you ought to change it in[to] a breadsauce for your English. I am in a rage and should quarrel most furiously with you if I could reach you, illnatured destroyer as you are of all the best things I have written. . . . Banter aside, if you won't do me better justice I shall insert a fulminant article against you in some of the papers of the other world, and have it afterwards translated in English, giving the real text of all the beauties you circumcised like a Jewish High priest.

Perhaps he would have to look for a more faithful translator.

Sarah defended herself roundly: 'You, mon cher, you have outraged all common decencies, and even your warmest admirers lament over those passages, which your enemies exult and delight in. . . . Those passages which you are pleased to call the 'sel' . . . I take leave to call the dirt of your book.' She had acted only for his name and glory and had labored

to get justice done to the noble the true and the beautiful in your book . . . J'enrage [I'm in a Fury]. I have been a guardian angel to your book, and you abuse me. You seem unconscious of having offended people here, and you have not the least conception of the thing[s] they accuse you of. . . . it was in the most anxious and tender regard for *you* (and not for those creatures [society figures] *you* talk of) that I wished to take out all that might be thought disloyal or disgusting.

He was to stop hounding her about her caution. 'Only believe one thing. I have it at heart to make you appear in as attractive a guise as I can. I know . . . what my English do not like. . . . Every body here says you ought to adore me and bless your stars that sent you such a translator.' He was displaying abysmal ignorance 'of what really are the merits and defects of your work—at least in the eyes of others'; without her the book would not have been allowed into decent houses. One of the proprietors of *The Times* had told her, '*It was you who saved the book*. But for your judgment, the shameful treachery and personality [assassination] would have damned it.' One disreputable newspaper had printed some of the indecencies of the German text, but 'they do me the honour to say . . . my "fastidious taste" will lead me to exclude these. Oh Heavens that these crawling nasty reptiles should be able to do me more justice than you.'* As for the threat to replace her:

> Another translator, lieber Herr, oh by all means; tant que vous voulez, ingrat que tu es [as many as you wish, ungrateful as you are] I shall be trop charmée to be rid of you and to see you delivered over, with the aid of your *faithful translator*, to all the rage, scorn and vituperation of the whole press of England, . . . to hear myself congratulated by all decent people for having washed my hands of you.

Her ironic tone softened the indignation, but their differences were real enough.

As Pückler surveyed her changes line by line, his irrita-

---

*She was purposely misreading since, in fact, they were mocking her decorous editing.

tion increased. 'What the devil are you to that stupid Lady Farkhard [Farquhar] to be so anxious [not] to hurt an old fool like her.' Her timidity was ridiculous.

> O heaven! my beautiful portrait vivant, so successful! effaced as with a sponge. Indeed I hate you. And even the innocent Chancelier [chancellor] has been expulsed, but the silly Mistress Baring carefully saved. . . . Why did you not rather omit the tedious descriptions of country seats quite nauseous to English readers.

In fact, the 'Chancelier' had not been all that innocent, for Pückler had insinuated that this member of his household staff had been his wife's lover during his absence. Sarah claimed that the point of the story had eluded her, but she 'had an *Ahnung* [presentiment] of something wicked,' and so had removed it. Pückler persisted in his accusation that she was merely protecting her society friends. He was in danger of losing 'all my little reputation for a spirituel vaut rien [clever good-for-nothing], and if the book is no more sold, it is only the fault of your cowardice.' Sarah vehemently denied his assumption and explained: 'I have a numerous and respectable and affectionate family whose opinions are dear and sacred to me. Here you have some of the reasons of my "fright," my fastidiousness, my "prudery" . . . not the favour [of] your trumpery Ladies . . . I am not a Prince, and I cannot afford to sport away all that.'

Pückler recognized that he faced not incompetence but high-handedness. 'You can do much better if you like. Nobody *can* [translate] better, but you won't. The philosophical objects are smartly translated and yet they are the most difficult.' He also warned her, 'Beware to add to the text. It may be a great deal better as the original but it is not genuine, and [it can be] directly seen that it flows out of an English not a German pen.'

Their confrontation was short-lived, since the first volumes were already in print by the time Pückler saw the translation, and the edge of his indignation was blunted by the book's instant and phenomenal success. He might with justification complain of the unappealing English title, *Tour of a German Prince*, he might exclaim against the unflattering reproduction of his portrait, or fret that she had mangled and muzzled him, but he could hardly complain that his volumes had not sold. As soon as the first volumes were published she could announce: '*We* have been out only a fortnight and already we are talking of a second edition.' His irritation was thus drowned by the general acclaim of him and his gifted translator. Even Varnhagen, whose word was decisive for Pückler, was pleased and told him that the English version, freely translated or not, was agreeable to read and he had no reason to be angry with his translator. Pückler did not have to wait long to discover that the English critics agreed with this verdict, for he received from Sarah a huge bale of newspaper reviews (many of them written by her friends) that eulogized not only the book but the translation. In no time he became a literary sensation, earning more from world-wide sales than any German author of his day, except Goethe. 'Things are quite changed to what they were formerly,' he told Lucie. 'I have become a distinguished person.' Sarah, in turn, was 'instantly crowned Queen of English Translators.' She did not fail to remind Pückler of her contribution. 'All persons agree that this was the best translation from the German that had ever been made into English . . . do you hear that?' She had 'naturalized' him so perfectly that a rumor circulating in

London stated that an Englishman had written the book and even named him. Eighteen months after it came out, she could also report, '*Our* book . . . has made unspeakable *furore* in America; I hear there have been eight editions! There's news for you! Of course the Yankees are enchanted at your picture of the English.' With such a runaway success, what was the point of their squabbling, especially when their personal relations promised to be so diverting?

Though Sarah's editing rankled Pückler, he was not going to overlook the hint of submerged passion, and from early on he explored the mystery of the prudish yet beckoning translator.* While he claimed, 'I am in a rage and should quarrel most furiously with you if I could reach you, ill-natured destroyer as you are of all the best things I have written,' in the very same letter he addressed her as 'the amiable, dangerous Sara,' 'the lovely woman, the dear unknown,' and sent her love messages written in his experienced manner. He told her she was fascinating; her letters were his delight; he wanted to know all about her; she was to describe herself candidly; he felt he was falling in love with her; and, presumably to stimulate her imagination, he sent her a portrait of himself and pleaded for hers in return. Meanwhile he established his credentials as a man of great physicality and tested her by making allusions to his erotic exploits:

> I am really a spoiled child and have been so the greatest part of my life, perpetrating colossal follies but always more or less getting by in the world. God has had pity

---

*Apart from one very early note of Pückler's, his first surviving draft of a letter is from *c.* February 1832, but some of the content and tone of his early letters can be surmised from Sarah's responses. By January 13, 1832, Sarah wrote of having received love letters.

> on his children, show the same and love me a little as if
> I were a mad Turk to whom everything is permitted and
> who is never punished.

He left her in no doubt about his licentious ways and assumed he would be forgiven.

Sarah confirmed her willingness to move into deeper water. Though she protested, 'Don't fall in love with me, Primo, because il n'y a pas de quoi [there's no reason for it]. Secondly because it would be of no use—unless indeed you have a passion for writing love letters, no matter to whom.' She also confessed, however, 'I have not been occupied about you so long without feeling an extreme interest in you.' Yes, she could satisfy his curiosity, not by describing herself but by giving him names of German friends, all of them eminent persons, whom he might meet in Berlin. There was the famous composer, Felix Mendelssohn-Bartholdy; the theologian Friedrich Schleiermacher, who had called on her in England; and finally there was Louise von Kottwitz, a friend from her Bonn days. Though Louise was 'not the least capable of understanding or appreciating your translator, neither morally or intellectually . . . she can tell you that I am not horrible to look at.'

As for his talk about his affairs with women, she replied:

> I do not think it necessary to be offended at your letter,
> nor disgusted by your frankness. . . . but you cannot
> conceive how utterly foreign all such adventures are
> from my way of life and my belief of what is really best
> for women. You know it yourself. What "Roué" does
> not? How soon we lose our value with you as mistresses.

Yet she was eager to continue the correspondence and in scattered asides continued to acknowledge her interest in him. She revealed that she had imagined them together, with him at her side assisting with the translation, and the direction of her thoughts was clear from such asides as 'To me you are the Verstorbener [Dead Man] and no other—for it is only spiritually that I can ever know you.' Then she threw out a wisp of promise. 'I will tell you when I have time all about myself,' and hinted significantly, 'I almost fancy I should understand you, and perhaps, you me.'

Pückler continued his encouragement. 'You make me quite happy by telling me that the tedious task [of translation] once over, you have a great deal to write to me. No correspondence, depend upon [it], can be dearer to me, and no body will ever see your letters.' Then he threw down the gauntlet of completely unguarded intimacy. She was to 'forget all your English tricks and anxious principles' and write whatever came into her head. She was to think aloud, drop all disguises and reserves, sweep aside all conventional restraints and write, he implied, with no blushes or fear of confessing to erotic thoughts. 'I am sure you are born with good and genial Disposition but english education spoiled you.' Now she was to claim her imaginative rights as a blameless child of nature. 'Au reste, you must not take me for an immoral being. I part only of a different point de vue with you, and I think many things we have made principal virtues of are in fact but deficiencies.' She was to imagine herself as 'speaking to a dead person, we were in Paradise, soul and body naked, without all the stuff of clothing nonsense for one and the other.' Meanwhile he sent a sample of one of his uncensored mental flights of fancy—an ecstatic dream of her.

You get into a terrible passion with me, but I can't help it. Last night I had a dream of you dear Sara—a rapturous dream—oh it was life itself! I dare not say more, but, indeed don't be angry—I believe I was your husband, at all events you were mine, fantastic charming vision. I pressed a lovely form in delicious madness to my heart, and sought to feel her burning kisses on my thirsty lips. It was but a dream—but with all the sensation of reality. O heaven! if I could by enchantment give you an equal one. Don't think all this as mere mauvais plaisanterie [bad joke]. It would be then only impertinent et de mauvais goût [in bad taste]. *But it is true.* Truth justifies all. What magnetism [is] in Nature! One can thus not only love an unknown being but can even own her and sink with her into a sea of bliss—breast pressed to breast. Please, please, [do not be] angry. I cannot do otherwise than say in childlike fashion what I feel. I must have the privilege of thinking aloud with you, or no more write at all.

In talking love to Sarah, Pückler, master of the language of sentiment, was following his natural talent, for he had genuine interest and insight into the romantically minded women of his day. He saw himself as the conjurer of fantasy in his park, his books, and his love letters. Letter writing to women is 'basically my best genre,' he concluded when surveying his work toward the end of his life. To correspond with a cultivated and expressive woman was a testing of himself as a man, an outlet for his constant urge for self-expression. It had not needed many hints for him to grasp that Sarah longed to fill an emotional void. His clever and flirtatious translator offered a novel situation, an irresistible challenge. He was intrigued by wooing her mind and releasing her imagination.

Sarah accepted the invitation to think aloud with him and let her emotions flow onto paper. The conventional reticence that her mother had counseled was abandoned as she dropped self-protectiveness and avowed her love with entire openness. She was swept by a force of passion that at times frightened her and wondered at herself as she ceaselessly thought about him. Pückler had unlocked a floodgate. The words of the heroine in Charlotte's Brontë's *Villette*, written two decades later, describe her state of mind: 'I spoke. All leaped from my lips. I lacked not words now; fast I narrated, fluent I told my tale; it streamed on my tongue.'

She poured out confidences and incessantly longed to write, to reveal herself to him and explore everything about him: 'every incident that concerns *you interests me—how deeply*.' In long letters (one of twenty-one pages) she recorded what came into her mind as the pen flew over the paper to keep up with her thoughts. 'I write to you a thousand things I should never say—nay even never write were I not certain we should never meet'; 'I do nothing but think of you and write to you. Je me ruines [you are my downfall].' Yet more poured out. In the early months of 1832, Hermann entirely filled her days. Pressure from the publisher to finish the final volumes drove her to work long hours translating and in the late evening even though her eyes were tired with 'scribbling,' she continued her communion with him by letter. 'Good dearest, shall I never have done?' she wondered. 'I am really afraid of wearying you. But every day something fresh arises, and if it is pleasant, how shall I not tell it you.' At the end of the letter she added, 'That I think of you continually and with the profoundest interest, what need is there to tell.' Then she picked up her pen once more, and this time in French added: 'Here I go once more my love—(unfortunately for me) for I lose my existence in chatting with you.'

'Plaudern' [chatting] with him about all subjects became
a compulsion. She grudged the hours she was supposed to
spend on translation, for she coveted every minute so 'that
I may write volumes to you. . . . Every day something
occurs that I want to tell you, I deposit it in my memory—
but even now, the heap frightens me.' But she was driven
to continue. 'I cannot write, yet I cannot leave it alone.'
When he failed to reply promptly, anxiety seized her. 'I
would not write to ask you—*I shall never do that*, and I said,
after all *I* am the fool—what else could I expect? Think
then of my joy when on Monday Mr. Wagner [an agent
Pückler employed in London] brought me your package.
How impatient I was till he left me alone to devour it.'

It was a high-risk enterprise to lay herself bare in such
correspondence, for one misdirected letter would have top-
pled the entire edifice of her life. She had no illusions about
her imprudence and disloyalty, and her refrain was, 'I have
written 20 times as much as I meant—as I ought.' Initially
their publisher served as letter drop, and then Pückler con-
veniently arranged for the diplomatic couriers of the Prussian ambassador to London to carry their letters to and fro
in the ambassador's bag; Pückler's young agent undertook
the final lap between Sarah's house and the embassy. This
relay system not only permitted speedy exchanges but also
allowed Sarah to indulge in long and frequent letters which
otherwise would have been out of the question because of
high postal charges.* The links in this long conspiratorial
chain between Muskau and London and back again held
surprisingly well.

The possibility of some mischance was always there,

---

*Sometimes they both supplemented the courier system by using the
post.

however. Sometimes she feared that the diplomatic bags might be opened and asked Pückler whether her letters always arrived properly sealed. At other times she worried about his letters and implored him, 'Pray tell me, are you *certain* of the safety of this conveyance. Think of what *I* risk. Indeed I am in terror about your letters. Mr. Wagner left them here with the servants and they might have fallen into other hands.' To guard against such risks, Sarah thought of a protective screen that would make Pückler's letters illegible to her family and to most other curious readers. She asked him to write in German and, more important, in the old German script. 'I can read it though slowly, but I shall soon improve.' At first Pückler pretended to be affronted: why was she spurning his English? She rushed to explain: 'it is only *fear* that makes me prefer the German characters.'

> I doat on your English, which is excellent, and often remarkably idiomatic—there are only just little blunders enough to make it piquant and individual. Nevertheless, I am so convinced that the Deutsche Handschrift [German handwriting] is the only perfect security I have, that I must forego your pretty allerliebstes [most charming] English. Schade [What a pity].

He obliged, and she applied herself to deciphering the ornate writing. 'I can now read it through much practice very easily—at least *your* hand,' but when his secretary transmitted messages, the challenge was too great. To maintain the appearance that their exchange was merely that of author and translator, she urged him not to drop English entirely but to continue to use it for business matters or subjects of general interest, so that she could disarm her family by reading passages to them. Any words of endearment or anything intimate or amorous he was to disguise by writing in the old German hand. It was an elaborate subterfuge, but she carried it out with bravado.

She became so addicted to this confidential exchange that a crisis loomed in the summer of 1832 when she and her family were to spend the summer with Charles Buller at his house in Polvellan, Cornwall, for the courier chain would not stretch that far.* Sarah could send her letters through the post, but letters from Pückler would excite attention. She wrote to him anxiously: 'I am in great distress and perplexity about the suspension of our correspondence which must I fear be the consequence of my stay in Cornwall. I can write to you, and dearest, shall I not? But how am I to hear from you?' She decided that during her absence he should not write through the embassy but confine himself to writing by post and then

> not more than *once* as it will attract notice and mind not a word of English or French except what I may read aloud. The letters arrive at Polvellan at breakfast time and are laid on the table before a score of people all eager for 'news.' I know my treacherous face and the rush of blood from my heart to it, that will follow the sight of your hand. Perhaps, indeed, you had better not write, unless you have some *manifestly* pressing reason. *I will write to you*, and bear the privation as I may.

Then she recollected, 'Our young friend John [Stuart] Mill joins us at Polvellan early in September and will bring

---

*They had stayed with Buller the previous year also. It was from there in late summer 1831 that Sarah had written her first letters 'with so gay a heart.'

anything. On the whole this is safer than the post, as I may receive and read it *alone*—but for once be cautious what you write—confine yourself to pure friendship.'

Her own letters were anything but cautious. There was one topic, however, that Pückler told her he was not anxious to hear about—her husband—yet the subject was bound to come up now and then. Sarah left Pückler in no doubt about John Austin's inadequacies, though she did not indulge in a diatribe against him. She depicted him with compassion as a gifted, flawed man with a 'sickly frame and a wounded mind.' His physical and mental health were so precarious that in the early 1830s he was often on the point of total collapse. As he lectured to ever fewer students, expecting that soon he would hand in his resignation to face an unpromising future, his mood plunged to suicidal despair. Sarah confided, 'This gloom amounts really to the deepest despondency. . . . My nights have been dreadful, for that is his darkest time, and how can I leave him? I lie down worn out and ready to sink with exhaustion and then till two, three, or four have to try—always in vain—to soothe and cheer him. This has been my life, dear friend.' Often she had 'neither rest by night, nor tranquillity by day,' and she herself was close to breaking point. 'My own heart is nearly broken and yesterday I could not even write to you. I cried nearly all day—a torrent after long long self constraint.'

John's suicidal mood was not an isolated one. Under the strain of his roller-coaster career, as he was assisted by friends to highly visible but short-term public appointments, external and internal pressures mounted and he again became disabled. '*How often* has this extraordinary man told me,' Sarah reported, 'but for you I should have blown my brains out a hundred times.' She had kept up his courage and he had learnt to endure, but his mental balance was precarious, and in desperation she wrote, 'God give me strength for what lies before me, I see nothing but clouds and darkness—unceasing, unremitting toil and care, watching and weeping for him and with him and at last perhaps—in vain.' Her circumstances were beyond comprehension to those accustomed to normalcy: 'There are calamities, like death or loss of fortune, or others which people can appreciate,' she later told Julia Smith (Florence Nightingale's aunt), 'but I *feel* that *nobody* can conceive the slow torture of this. However it must be borne.'

John's condition blighted everything, including small everyday pleasures. He was repeatedly in wretched health or 'incapable of enjoyment.' She, like Hermann, had the gift of extracting pleasure, that 'Genussfähigkeit (charming word)—Yes—I have that indeed—from the most maddening rapture down to the simplest, smallest pleasure, and that has all my married life been crushed under a load of lead.' Despite her resilience, she felt so oppressed that she 'could resist no longer.'

Ill fate pursued her to the marriage bed. After John Austin's death she hinted about this to François Guizot, a leading politician in France and a close friend. John, she told Guizot, 'had not always been a very tender husband to me, nor easy to please. Ill health, disappointment, and anxiety had naturally enough made all things distasteful to him.' To another friend she revealed, 'I have thought all society even his wife was indifferent, almost burthensome to him.' To Hermann she was less oblique: 'I have all your tastes . . . for loving and being loved au suprême degré, and in that one, the life of my life, and the spring of my whole being, oh how I have been disappointed!'* Her former passionate love had been 'dead for years—*he would have it so*, or it would have been eternal.' John was too consumed by unhappiness to have love or comfort to spare, and she was 'ground to death, worn down with care and sorrow, all the animal part of me mortified more than with weeks of fasting.'

Incompatibilities of another sort can be inferred, for earlier in their marriage when John Austin was not so seriously depressed and showed interest, it was unaccompanied by the sentiment and love that meant so much to her. In response to some unknown comment from Hermann about repeated love-making, she explained that her experience with this 'very often . . . was a torture, not from any personal disgust, but for want of preliminary commotion de coeur [stirred heart],' for she needed 'fondness, endearment—*love*, in short, to make me care for it.' Usually, however, she was far less explicit about their difficulties and merely hinted at what she called his lack of kindness and tenderness. Referring to this deficiency, she reflected, 'you will tell me it is not in man's nature. Alas, do I not know it?'

While Sarah's marriage left her with cruel deprivations, the wounds to her self-image were as painful. Since girlhood, men had confirmed the potent nature of her sexual

---

*Was her feeling of marital disappointment mirrored in the following passage of Jean Paul's novel *Siebenkäs*, which was among the few from this book which she chose for translation? The hero of the novel 'could never raise his wife to a lyrical enthusiasm of love, in which she might forget heaven and earth, and all things.' (SA, 'Specimens of German Genius,' *New Monthly Magazine*, [May 1830], *448*.)

and personal appeal, and only her husband seemed blind to it. Nor could she lessen her distress by applying the partial balm of insight: the dynamics of depression eluded her, and at best she had only a flickering notion of a link between his condition and his turning away from her. The tangle of circumstances at times eroded even her habitual self-confidence: 'I think you [Hermann] would love me dearly. Most people I think find me loveable—*so I have reason to think*, and to you whom I should live for, could I seem less so? Heav'n knows.'

Hermann, the connoisseur of women, who so readily showed affection and had understanding for submerged longing and fantasies, offered emotional nourishment and was the affirming, nonjudgmental intimate, the foreigner to whom it was less hazardous to reveal all than to one of her countrymen. Though she was to write with longing for physical closeness and sensual fulfillment, he provided the solace of understanding and the tranquillity of affection that had eluded her. To him she could divulge her feelings. 'Your image is a sweet and dear companion, that I turn from my griefs to look at you and am, for a moment, comforted that your letters and consciousness of your love sustain me.' She was often overwhelmed—'heart, passion, imagination, gaiety, all crushed under this weight of care and anxiety,' but she sought consolation in dreams of mutuality. 'My heart is oppressed and what I want is a loving breast to lean and weep upon and when that April rain were gone a loving face to smile upon me.' She offered such comfort to him. 'Would to Heaven, dear one, I could sit . . . at your feet; my head on your knees, my arms clasped around them and yours around my neck, or better, would I were laid by your side, tranquilly, your head upon my shoulder, or my face in your bosom and that you could tell me all you wish or hope; all that troubles or annoys you.' Such visions of intimacy were compelling. 'But I think I could so dearly love and so entirely understand you that you would return to me for that sweet repose of affection and confidence which a heart like yours must sigh for, when the transports of passion are over.'

By spring 1832 she had completely surrendered herself to him. After more than a decade of drought, her heart filled and overflowed. Hermann, his affectionate interest and her confidential talks with him transformed her inner life. His portrait was in her private dressing room: 'I always have it before me, the first thing and the last— When I am alone and while I am undressing at night I talk to it. 'Tis very handsome, that I must say though 'tis *against my principles* to tell *you* so. How German too it is! It is the very face in the world I like.' She was sure that, in contrast to her husband, who rarely smiled, the portrait always looked on her benevolently, 'with its grave, thoughtful, sweet, generous smile.' At the end of the day, she bade it goodnight and kissed it 'with full eyes and a full heart.' On one occasion, exhausted by translating, she turned to it and reflected, 'I *can* write no more. I shall fall off my chair. "Oh Jupiter, how weary are my spirits!" One moments rest for my head on that dear shoulder—one kind look from the blue eye, one long soft kiss, and I should forget it all.'

Her gift for words enabled her to voice a stream of passion and tenderness. 'I fold you in thought to my heart,' she told him. 'Thank God you do not yet know how ceaselessly my thoughts are with you—how tender, how passionate my longing for you.' She declared her love in ever-varied endearments. He was her 'unknown Divinity';

her 'secret and unknown idol'; her 'beloved shadow.' She addressed him as 'my dear Vision,' 'the loved and honoured one,' 'sweetest and dearest,' 'my heart,' 'my life,' 'Mon Prince.' Four languages helped express her feelings: He was her *Bester, Liebling, Geliebter;* her *caro, carissimo, idol mio;* her *bien aimé, coeur de mon coeur, mon âme.* Her letters carried with them a most loving kiss (accompanied by a sketch of one), a shower of kisses, an Italian kiss, a long kiss, hot kisses, *mille mille baisers*, and statements such as, 'I kiss your eyelids.' When she did not hear from him, all her tranquillity vanished. When she did, it was 'delicious to hang for hours' over his letters. At one time she called it 'sheer madness and raving' and added, 'I will go out and see people and forget you,' but more often than not she was swept up by her erotic imagination and could only marvel, 'Strange, strange how I love you.'

CHAPTER FOUR

Desires and Desirability

No one who looks at my slow [calm] face can guess the vortex sometimes whirling in my heart, and engulfing thought, and wrecking prudence.

CHARLOTTE BRONTË, *Shirley*

The tacit agreement to ignore the subject of sex, whilst in reality it occupies the thoughts at least twice as much as any other subject, both in men and women, especially men, is childish folly.

HARRIET GROTE, 1859

THOUGHTS of her 'secret and unknown idol' consumed Sarah, but there was always the nagging worry that his feelings hardly matched hers. While she felt she understood him from his self-revealing book, his image of her seemed clouded by misconceptions. '*I know you* so much better than you know me,' she lamented. 'I must write volumes . . . to make you know me and then—I think you will at least think of me as worthy to be your friend.' To which he, nimble and detached as always, responded, 'I doubt not that after knowing you more and more, I shall find you, as you say, worthy to be my friend, though I fear that in your sense, I should like you unworthy, as I am myself.' His teasing was elixir after John's seriousness, but his light tone did not still her anxieties, and he would needle her with his wrong-headed notions. To put these right she interspersed the gossip of her letters with a persistent self-presentation, shaped to demonstrate the powerful affinities of their minds and spirits.

There was, for example, their compatibility of outlook. No matter what he might think, she shared so few of her country's attitudes that perhaps she had been *verteuscht* [sic; exchanged] at birth. She emphasized their similar political, social and aesthetic judgments, but above all she made it clear that she admired Germany more than anyplace in the world and despised the money-centered English values as much as he did. England was a 'corrupt and jobbing country,' its people were 'shopkeepers to their core,' 'sordid, manufacturing creatures . . . our souls are in cotton and steam.' What a contrast between philistine England and high-minded, civilized and enlightened Germany, where sentiment still counted, where there was less worship of wealth, less class hatred, and far more respect for cultivation. The spirit of his country was revealed in its sublime literature, and to make this better known to her mundane countrymen she had recently translated some of its gems. She could hardly have been more emphatic in demonstrating her leaning toward all things German, but it was by no means a pose struck merely to please Hermann. There was no need to stretch the truth, for as Carlyle noted on her return from

Bonn, she was 'a true Germanised spiritual *screamikin*.'

There were other more compelling sympathies between them. 'I have all your tastes—animal, social, and intellectual,' she declared, and it was perhaps significant that animal tastes now came first. Demonstrating such compatibility on paper was a bold undertaking, but how else could she convince him that they were right for one another and 'should pass blessed hours together' and 'live together in a sort of oneness (Einheit) such as is not to be found twice.' To prove how well-matched they were, her self-revelation became ever more audacious. 'I talk to you as you bid me, without reserve, for I think I may. I love you. I wish to have you for a friend. I wish to be yours.' In defiance of distance and every practical circumstance she set out to let him know that she was just the kind of woman he had admired in his book. She was all energy and spirit—passionate, infinitely loving and trusting, tolerant in her sexual attitudes, eager to serve—the perfect companion for one so demanding and blasé as he.

She embarked on her self-portrait by lightly sketching the warmth of her feelings. While she felt sympathy for everything German, her temperament belonged to the south, which both of them assumed was endowed with human warmth and unusual sexual vitality. 'I have heard the poor Italian Emigrants say as they passed me on the street, "Ecco una compatriota" [there goes one of our countrywomen]. ... They say I am *really* from Albano [a town near Rome]. Heav'n knows. I never was there. But this I know—in vivacity, passion and energy I am very little like an Englishwoman.' Nor was she an intellectual woman of the sort that made him uneasy. How could he taunt her with being a sedentary, book-bound bluestocking? 'I have not a tinge of

Blue, I assure you. Ask anybody.' Learning was the least distinctive thing about her. True enough, in Germany, given assumptions there, it had been hard at first to shake off her reputation as a learned woman, but she had surprised them:

> When I first arrived at Bonn and they called me 'Frau Professorin' thinking to do me honour, I screamed and said (to the men), 'call me so again and I'll turn you out of my house.' How I puzzled my poor co-Professorin-nen! First I was *ausserordentlich gelehrt* [extraordinarily learned], and of course *must be* a pedant and a dowdy; then I dressed as they thought, poor things, far too well for the corps—went to all the balls, plays, and concerts, loved dancing, rode with [the] 'Militair Frauen,' as they call them (what an expression), rode the 'Militair' horses.

Elemental drives moved her, she implied, and, like him, she loved speed and challenge and the release of her abundant vitality. Nothing suited her better than to abandon herself to wild riding or sailing, and evidently she relished these sensations in 'a pagan sensuous way,' as George Eliot described such feelings. She was never more in her element than when visiting Cornwall and riding almost every day 'over rocks and down precipices or [sailing] on the top of white waves' or breaking in a friend's filly. 'Is this not schön [delightful] for a Professorin?' The resilience Pückler claimed for himself was also hers. Though she might have been up all night, next day she could run around with spring and jump and with what a friend called 'a foot of fifteen,' for there was in her 'heart and mind and body an elasticity I never saw equalled.' Indeed, she was precisely one of those vibrant, lissome women he had admired for being able to 'leap around like deer.' Nor was her buoyancy, given her circumstances, mere acting or thoughtless levity, but 'the bursts of a full, overflowing, loving heart and the spring of a glorious animal organization.' How incongruous that one with such surging energies should be confined to a scholar's existence: 'I ought to have been born the wife of a *Norseman*, a sea king—or else of an Arab chief. . . . Anything wild and adventurous, and here I am, ye Gods, a Professorin!!! of all tame animals.'

Her work was misleading him. Beneath the veneer of the accomplished translator, she was far more woman than professional. Not even in jest was he to call her 'Schriftstellerin [authoress].' The search for professional fame, she claimed, is 'no part of *me* or of my life,' for she had 'never courted notoriety nor sought the reputation of an author.' Authorship, she insisted, would 'always be an *hors d'oeuvre* in your existence as well as mine. . . . But for different reasons [work] is good for me.' Her work was often grinding, but it had helped to 'deaden the capacity for love' and was a blessing in disguise. The 'necessity for labour, the endless petty cares and distractions of my life have stifled the craving of my heart, which in ease and leisure would have sometimes been intolerable. A character so strong and energetic as mine—feelings so warm and acute must be employed somehow.' She explained:

> There is no such cure for this as constant occupation of body and mind, and those small carking cares which, more than all things, destroy romance and voluptuousness. Were I a nun, God help me. I can imagine that it would go hard with me in the hours of leisure and contemplation: for religion such as I feel it softens rather than hardens the heart, and tranquility, opportunity of

thinking on oneself—one's own being, state and affections,—as I can imagine that I should die of it, or go
mad. But you who know human nature well under some
aspects, you perhaps know it not on this side, how the
active business, the reiterated small cares and occupations
of a mistress of a family in narrow circumstances effectively divert the mind from all such thoughts and weary
the body too much to leave that very importunate.

She was equally forthright in asserting that she shared his
belief in the life-enhancing force of erotic fulfillment. He
was not to assume that she was one of those phlegmatic
women for whom sexual experience was something only to
be endured:

> Don't fancy now, that I am going to faire l'Anglaise [act
> like the English], and protest to you that these transports
> are vile and '*shocking*'—or that they are unworthy to our
> wishes—Dieu sait! There *is* something vile, shocking,
> degrading, disgusting in *enduring* caresses—as most En-
> glish women would have you believe (perhaps truly)
> they do, as an act of duty and obedience—but the delight
> of giving and receiving equal rapture—nay, rather of
> enjoying one undivided, indivisible rapture made up of
> the most intense sensibility both of the physique and the
> affections—none but brutes, who cannot understand
> [sic] this . . . . But my hand shakes too much to go on
> with this topic. Here is a kiss—an Italian one if you like,
> to conclude it.

A sketch of a kiss followed.
As Sarah dwelt increasingly on love, joy, and visions of
sensual pleasure, she expressed the depth of her feelings by
recalling the passion in Goethe's famous climactic passage in

Faust. She gazed at Hermann's portrait—'the forehead, the clear eye, and the mouth. Oh! the mouth,' and asked,

> Do you remember poor Gretchen's song . . . That cry of rapture always seemed to me the very triumph of poetry. The way in which she enumerates all the perfections of her beloved, gradually ascending till at last the whole tide of passion bursts forth from the heart of the loving *woman*.

> > The touch of his hand
> > And Oh, his kiss!

> I never read it without a sort of spasm of the heart that I cannot describe, for I can conceive all that too—combined with the most heroic, the tenderest affection, and I could be as mad as you say you are.

But drawing back, she added, 'But Heaven be thanked, the temptation is far from me and is indeed a mere idea—*une manie sylphe*.' Yet her thoughts continued to return to Gretchen's 'perfect gasping of fond longing.'

The message of sexual promise was combined with statements implying that she was anything but a slave to bourgeois sexual assumptions. Hermann could infer that her ties to conventional morality were, if not as loose as his, at least capable of accommodating many of his ideas. She appeared to take a good deal of his cynicism about marriage and the infidelities of married women and his allusions to affairs and flirtations with this or that woman in her stride, and, in spite of some qualifications, seemed most understanding of his creed of sexual radicalism.

> I fancy dearest and best that I can see the peculiarities in your character and manner of viewing things which have

brought censure and doubt upon you. . . . You my dearest have chosen in theory and practice to run counter to the current opinions or prejudices of men. I will not say you were always right . . . but I can see that on many matters it is prejudice alone that you have offended against, not sound morality.

At least he was no hypocrite. 'I am not—as you must have already seen, prudish, nor do I value very highly the parrot morality of my dear *routinière* [ordinary] country-women.' She knew how to look coolly and critically at accepted moral opinions to distinguish between those that were socially beneficial and those that were mere conventional accretions. 'As a trained Utilitarian—looking only at the evil consequences of actions and not regarding the antipathies of bigotry,' she judged actions without prejudice by their effects, and this, Pückler could infer, gave her fresh, unbiased sexual attitudes. She did not enter into any systematic criticism of the sexual ethics of her day, for she was concerned not with ethical theory but with letting him know that she was a broad-minded, liberal-spirited woman.

His contempt for notions of chastity and sexual restraint did not provoke her into moral outrage. 'To be frank with you, I do not attach any very great value to the ascetic virtue of chastity and I can quite believe that a man or woman either who is not at all chaste may be a most noble, honourable, benevolent, intelligent creature.' She went further:

I shall dare to say to you that chastity, except in as far as it is essential to preserve a delicate sensibility, moral and physical (without which pleasure itself must soon be lost in satiety and dullness), seems to me as little condu-

cive to the good of the human race or to the design of
a kind creator as the most ascetic fasting or self castiga-
tion. . . . But if I were free and chose to live with you,
bringing the consequences upon no one else, be assured
my conscience would never give me a single twinge.

In spite of the provisos, she seemed to be open to unconventional arrangements.

The extent of her broad-mindedness was most marked in
her attitude toward sexual practices such as homosexuality,
with which Hermann was rumored to be familiar. 'My
moral liberalism goes farther,' she explained. 'I never could
understand the enormous evil of those strange Greek loves
which, in this country, it is necessary to scream and faint
with horror even to think of. I do not exactly imagine the
sort of pleasure, but I do not wish to limit the enjoyments
du voisin [of another] so they hurt not me or others.' Her
endorsement was not without qualifications: ''Tis true that
the opinions of society being *what they are*, I do despise a
man who has not sufficient self command to avoid incurring
(and inflicting) such enormous evil for so slight a good and
would certainly not trust him.' All the same, such experi-
ments did not affront her; 'if men [i.e., everyone] thought
sanely about good and evil, they could let such diversities
of taste alone.' The 'eccentricities,' of the kind she assumed
Byron had picked up in Greece, 'would never separate me
from any man I liked or was bound to for an hour.' Once
again she was anxious to point to their compatibility. 'I
think dearest Hermann you will see and see with pleasure,
how much we agree.'

As for marriage—here also she had unconventional
views: the promises and vows 'given in our marriages are

so impracticable of observance, that what *man* does observe them? Like all overstrained attempts at compelling virtue, it defeats itself. This institution (of which au reste [otherwise] I am an ardent admirer) wants entire remodelling.' No elaboration of this declaration of fundamental dissatisfaction followed, and she confined herself to some very personal reflections on marriage. Far too much emphasis was placed on the importance of fidelity: 'That single abstinence is made the substitute for all high and generous and active virtues.' She did not have 'the common stupid notions of conjugal duty—as if it consisted in nothing but that senseless coldness they call virtue here.' Fidelity, falsely regarded as the mighty cornerstone of the marital code, left both partners free to violate their more important obligations. A man or a woman could be sexually faithful and yet violate the entire spirit of the union by being cold and unaffectionate. 'Is not neglect, unkindness, indifference as much a violation of the vow as infidelity? Can a man be said to "love and cherish" a woman for whose comfort, advantage, happiness, he shews not the least solicitude and whose devoted efforts to please him he receives with sullen apathy, or worse?' she asked. 'Yet this, or corresponding conduct on the part of a woman, is *censé* [accounted] no infraction of the treaty!' The implication was that since her husband had violated this fundamental understanding, she was no longer bound.

Despite intimations that she was not rigidly constrained by conventional morality, Sarah was not as emancipated as her statements suggested, for her criticism of marriage was accompanied by the assertion that 'the breach of promises and engagments . . . must always and under all circumstances be a great vice.' She in fact underplayed their differences about marriage and only the parenthetical phrases qualifying her strong language revealed the extent of her ambivalence on this touchy issue. Meanwhile she encouraged Pückler to see her as a frustrated wife whose liberal principles permitted her to indulge in this overture to an extramarital affair.

Sarah's self-explanation did not take place in a vacuum, for Pückler continued to promote her fantasy and orchestrate her self-revelation by offering sensual dreams, suggestive cues, and by provoking her to jealousy. He echoed her emphasis on their compatibility: 'That you and I, sweet friend, are bound to be well suited in the most extraordinary degree is demonstrated by the mere existence of our present relationship.' He wrote of his longing for her, and confirmed that he reciprocated her love, not forgetting to refer to his sexual reputation: 'I am a great libertine, but I truly love you—body and soul.' Above all, he repeated that she should abandon herself to fantasy: 'If you have the power of imagination to imitate me in everything,' he instructed her, 'we can conquer all the disadvantages of our separation in a truly unusual fashion. But you must utterly banish every womanly reticence, for since ours is merely a written exchange, it demands intense belief, and you can give yourself over unreservedly.' He urged, 'Confide in me, give yourself to me entirely, even if only in sweet dreams; it is surely the most certain way to possess me entirely.'

He followed his own directives and wrote with unembarrassed openness about his personal life. One disclosure fostered another, as in an exchange about their marriages. Sarah was naturally curious about his, but she embarked on the topic cautiously, with a preamble about her principles:

This brings me to a subject I have thought of much and often and painfully. I think a woman base and a traitor who does not respect the claims of one of her own sex to the love, the faith, or the thoughts of a man with whom she may be connected. . . . Infinitely far from my heart is all impertinent desire to pry into your domestic circumstances. But it seems to me there is someone—and one whom you yourself have made me love and re-spect—to whom this wild, mad correspondence of ours might give pain. . . . I know not—perhaps I am wrong—quite wrong, in mentioning it—if so, beloved, only forgive me. All that is yours, all that you love and respect is sacred in my eyes and it would be *cruel* in you to let me run the risk of committing an offense I would hate myself for. I am guilty enough *here*.

His reply was blunt, even if a fraction short of the entire truth:

On account of my Julie [the name given to his wife in his book] you need have no conscience. We are since a long time on terms of the closest friendship and nothing else. She calls herself just about my mother and no mother could love her son more faithfully. She is ten or twelve years older than I am [he exaggerated by a few years] and when we married she was, in truth, a little in love with me, but I not the slightest bit with her and told her so in plain terms and that I reserved every liberty for myself. In the course of the years we have learnt to care and love each other, and our bond of friendship and confidence has become insoluble. . . . This no doubt is above your English horizon dear Sara, but we Germans are odd people.

Sarah responded that such a relationship was by no means incomprehensible to her. 'I can perfectly understand and appreciate the nature and value of a connection which you say lies beyond my English horizon. You might know from what I have said of my own history that I can— But enough of that.'

Pückler's encouragement went beyond confidences and general exhortations to indulge her imagination, and he sent provocative letters expressing his own erotic fantasies in unrestrained detail, as some tell-tale and only partly legible passages reveal. He wrote: 'I kiss your bare feet gently up to the knee and [beyond?],'* and then, supposedly overcome, cut himself short with, 'Oh Heavens, I perish.' On another occasion he depicted a scene to Sarah in which he seemed to fantasize about himself as an eastern potentate and her as his slave-like concubine. 'You would have to love me to an extraordinary degree and be my true slave, body and soul, giving yourself without reserve.' She would have to be like a chameleon, obediently adjusting her mood to suit his wishes—sometimes charming, at other times shameless, or, if he desired it, displaying 'the ravishing glow of wild voluptuousness.' Other attempts to stimulate her imagination appear to have been better attuned to their situation. 'I like women whose first bloom has faded,' he wrote, 'they have for me something more voluptuous . . . and add more mental spirit to friendship.'

Sarah's appreciative responses to his letters hint that he sent a good deal more intense emotional and erotic suste-

---

*Sarah, aware of Pückler's admiration for small feet, had boasted to him of hers. His reply in German, copied by a secretary in an ornate hand is only partially legible.

nance and lived up to a maxim he quoted to her that spoke of 'unlocking joyful things.' She wrote that it was 'delicious to hang for hours over your letters, and to catch the "thoughts that breathe and words that burn"* one by one.' His letters were so delectable that she spoke of feeding on and being nourished by them. After reading them she was as 'mad and love drunk as you darling.' Yet few such compelling messages remain in Pückler's surviving letters. Most of his potent erotic words were probably destroyed after his death by the caretaker of his papers, Ludmilla Assing, or by his family who, fearing scandal, burned, among other things, a box of secret papers. All that remains is Sarah's response to his offering—the intensity of the feelings he aroused and her move to explicitness.

Hermann had not mistaken that Sarah would be a receptive pupil, eager to exchange sensual fantasies and erotic 'pillow-talk' with him. 'I cannot *imitate you* in all, dearest, but ah [in] *too much*,' she confessed. Her 'images of joy and volupté,' as she called them, were often cast in intensely romantic language. 'You ask me if I would not admit your shadow if it came hovering to my bedside at night. Surely I might as safely as a snowflake or a polar breeze. But no, your very shadow would scorch my bosom like a burning and perfumed gale from Araby. No, dear one, write to me of other things; not of this madness—your thoughts, feelings, opinions, every incident that concern you interests me—how deeply.' Soon, however, she was once more encouraging him, 'Your fancy is herrlich [wonderful] and I love you for it and did from the first. I would *fantasiren* with you to the limits of possibility, and beyond,' and she

*Thomas Gray, *Elegy Written in a Country Churchyard* (1750).

went on to do so. His book contained dreams of meetings, flight across the sea, reunions in other spheres, and in harmony with such ideas, she speculated about flying to him and being able 'to float down softly and fold my wings and nestle by your side on the couch in that boudoir. Then if you chanced to be dreaming of me, how sweet to be just in time to catch you in my arms and receive all your raptures.' She spoke of devouring the English part of his letters, 'the other did indeed cost me *much effort* but don't pity me for that, my beloved, since it is only being compelled to "*savourez lentement*" [savor them slowly], as Rousseau exquisitely says of kisses.' Another time she asked, 'How are you—you, with your ardent heart, your boiling blood, your "kisses—sticky and greedy."*' She regretted that she could only experience these imaginatively by way of literature: 'for me you would be a book. Good God, why am I not there to cast off this *cold* pedantry? How I would make you do penance, Monsieur le Prince.'

She stepped well beyond erotic passages from literature in the early summer of 1832 when she was stung into a frenzy by a reference Hermann made to her 'little moustaches'—a blemish that had been reported to him, she assumed, by his London agent. In fact the agent was not the only one to make this observation, for one of her great admirers, Francis Jeffrey, spoke of her as the 'Barbata Bellissima,' [the bearded beauty]. Sarah faced her accuser boldly. 'As a matter of fact it is true enough. You can draw what consequences you wish from it, but be assured that whatever my beauty, it is of a kind that [children ?] like Wagner [the

---

*Sarah mentions the French author of this passage, but the name is illegible.

tattling young agent] do not understand.' She offered compensating attractions: 'You, my love, who are, I believe, a connoisseur, you will find something perhaps, above all, as you say in the dark.* I am tempted to write you some lines that come to my mind.' Then, giving in to the temptation, though first saying 'you will not despise me,' she recalled a passage in Latin from the *Satyricon*, a novel written by Petronius during the reign of Nero and well known for its erotic content. 'Ah! gods and goddesses, what a night that was, how soft was the bed. We lay in a warm embrace and with kisses everywhere made exchange of our wandering spirits.' Finally she added, 'It is you, you always you that I think of, when I think of such things. Alas, I must try to forget them. How I would love you! Beautiful or not I would make you love me.'

Later that summer she gave in entirely to her abandoned mood: 'I carried but too many thoughts "of love and you" to bed with me, and did not sleep the better for them. . . . You tell me beloved that your hand and mouth are appetizing. I do not doubt it. Why cannot I savour them? and tell you if I find them good.' In a crosswritten and only partly legible passage about breaking in a young horse, she seems to glide into sexual innuendo; she imagines him reborn as a young scholar with whom she plays the part of Mme. Warens—an allusion to Rousseau's patronness, who introduced him to sexual experience and the art of love. She suggests that there would be 'singular pleasures' and promises, 'I will teach you everything I know,' though 'you know more than me already.' Also, in response to his ques-

---

*'Tois, mon amour, qui[?] je crois connaisseur tu y trouverais peut-être quelque chose, surtout wie du sagst im Dunkeln.'

tion whether she had good teeth, she told him, 'yes, my heart, they are regular, strong and white. I have lost only one. Be assured that I would make you cry mercy if we were at that point. You *would carry* the mark on your shoulder, as [Ponsé?] always carried the toothmarks of his mistress Flora. Oh my love, let us talk no more of such things!'

It was perhaps inevitable that her self-revelation would escalate as she was swept into a whirlpool of sexual fantasy, and he tested how far she would go. Her feelings were intensified by her insecurity about a lover held by the power of words alone, and over and over, disarmed by her passion, she rose to his bait. Thus when Pückler speculated about what they could do in the dark, Sarah responded in kind. She assured him, 'I would humour you in your wildest vagaries and desires,' and though she would not allow herself to be regarded as a mere sexual object, beyond that reservation, she felt only eagerness to please. 'And yet if you knew what rapture it would be to me to minister *in any way* to the pleasures of a man who loved me as I desire and deserve.' Often she resorted to French to express such thoughts; what came into her mind seemed unutterable in English, and the foreign words added distance from her everyday self.

To demonstrate their devotion and keep alive the hope of erotic fulfilment they exchanged tokens of love—most with a decidedly sentimental period flavor. Apart from his portrait, so treasured by her, Hermann sent, in response to her request, a lock of his hair and thoughtfully had it framed in a locket in such a way that her lips could touch it. Of course, she explained, 'I must wear it when and how I *can*, not as I *would* or it would never quit me'; only on the rare occasion when she slept alone did she dare to wear it at night. When he expressed mock surprise at this, Sarah countered: 'But do you find it astonishing that I should be afraid to wear in my bosom, especially *at night*, a lock of your hair, or would you, in *his* place have thought that *tout simple*?' She also had Lucie's alert young eyes to consider. 'My child and I have no separate existence.— She has been always with me and sees all I do and all I wear. I would neither conceal . . . nor lie to her (*you* don't like the word—*I* hate glosses and palterings with what one means.)'* A ring, surprisingly, posed fewer problems. 'I wear [it] constantly, and ever shall,' she wrote. "Tis very pretty. I only wish it were plainer.' She declined, however, to accept some earrings for herself and Lucie, 'for we do not share this barbaric taste. My ears are intact.' Since Hermann ordered most such items from a London shop, she told him: 'I shall change them for something which will be equally *yours* and which [Lucie] shall wear.'

Sometimes his gifts led to effusive little dramas of love and self-mocking submissiveness, as when he sent a necklace. The French word *collier*, which could mean either a necklace, a chain of a knightly order, or a training collar, permitted an elaborate play on words. 'Thank you most tenderly for the books, the bracelets, the extremely elegant chain of the order of what?—of St. Hermann of love?—of anything you wish—what do you wish? villain, that I should carry your chains. Oh, well, I will wear them, but take care, for if you enslave me, I think I shall be the most [supportive?], sometimes, and sometimes also the most submissive, the most fervent [and] devoted. But————'

---

*Apparently this maxim did not apply in the case of John Austin.

With her smaller purse she sent gifts that were less costly but equal in symbolic value. She sent him some of her hair, that essential Victorian symbol of devotion; a cravat she had worn for riding; a measuring tape from her work basket for him to carry in his waistcoat pocket, every inch of which she had kissed; and, at Hermann's request, an old shoe. 'What a gift!' she wrote, though she knew well enough that feet, ankles, and by association, shoes, were assumed to be sexually charged. 'Du schwärmest [you gush] like a boy of 18—How I love you for it. Happy, happy you who can indulge in such fantastic visions.'

She also sent flowers. 'I send you from my garden what I would I could [sic] press upon your lips and feel in your heart—"Burning Love." But alas all the fire in me will be extinguished before I can see your dear face.' Violets, the favorite blue flower of the romantics, were another offering. 'Tell me, have you kissed the violets? If not you are a deceiver, for I kissed them a thousand times.' Hermann wrote in a similar vein, 'I have already pressed a hundred kisses on the blue violets . . . they still have their scent and I seem to be inhaling your breath and still feel your lips. See what imagination can do.' The exchange of hair, how-ever, had the deepest meaning for her, and her pleasure was untarnished by her knowing that it had been dyed. 'I shall not love the hair a whit the less for its tinge of silver,' she told him soothingly, and kissed it and his portrait secretly before going to bed. They also exchanged gestures of devo-tion to mark their birthdays, and Pückler, who later placed commemorative statues of some of his favorite women in his grounds at Branitz, created a special 'Sara Walk.'* In

*Sara's Walk and Sara's bridge can still be found in the park.

gratitude she wrote, 'Thank you for all your kind thoughts of me, for your pretty fête—for *my* path where I shall ne[ver] tread, for your flowers, in short for your love, source and spring of all.' She reciprocated, at least in thought. 'Tell me your birthday, I can fê[te it] if only by silent love and the tenderest wishes for your happiness shut up within my own heart.' Their erotic exchanges were cushioned by such love duets. After John Austin's sparse show of sentiment, Sarah's appetite for demonstrative gestures was insatiable.

After months of declarations of devotion, their intimate relationship was threatened in the summer of 1832. Driven by vanity and curiosity, Sarah imprudently set the scene for a romantic triangle that put her at a bitter disadvantage in an intrigue of the sort Hermann relished. When she first fell for the prince she was so eager to know more about him that she wrote to an old friend from Bonn, Louise von Kottwitz, an attractive, flighty, not too scrupulous, aristocratic woman ('vain, false, frivolous, and coarse,' Sarah said of her later), now remarried and living not far from Muskau. Sarah had been a motherly support during Louise's intricate, stormy love intrigues that entailed 'schemes of marrying, unmarrying and marrying again, her dying of love for one man and marrying quite another six months after.' Since those Bonn days, Louise had been Sarah's sworn and effusively affectionate friend, so much so that she had asked Sarah for a lock of her hair.

Now Sarah wrote to Louise, explaining that she was the prince's translator and had received droll letters from him as well as his portrait, which was most handsome. Then she asked for Louise's help. 'I beg you to tell me all you can learn about him. . . . He has made many inveterate enemies who tell all imaginable horror stories. I who know nothing am in a strange situation and don't know what to respond.' Did she know about his mysterious relationship to his wife? Was it true that he had remarried? She was most anxious to know about these matters. If Louise could not help, then perhaps her husband knew something. Louise was to reply at once. Sarah further told Louise that Pückler wished to 'interrogate you about me, for he pretends he wants to know what sort of woman I am. Thus my dear you see what awaits you.' Sarah also conveyed, though for once not very adroitly, that Louise was to speak about her in flattering terms.

'I know the hero of these Letters [from a Dead Man],' Louise replied. 'He is tall, his portrait you already have, but it greatly flatters him, for he has false teeth, uses rouge and powder and wears a wig . . . He affects English manners . . . he is by no means fond of Society; has little good to say of anyone but prefers to ridicule and mock.' As for the women of his family, 'His wife is twenty years older than he,' and both she and her daughter had equivocal reputations. The princess 'likes men to an incredible degree and needs every day at least two; one says appalling things about her.' Pückler, she implied, was well-suited to this ménage. 'One says he loves the beautiful sex; in short, he is a libertine, and strange tales are told about him.' This report was hardly encouraging, even for the most blinded devotee.

Yet Sarah chose to believe the better accounts of his looks she had heard from those who had known him in London, and her interest was not cooled by Louise's words. She had learned that her informant did not know the prince personally but only from hearsay, having merely seen him at some social event in Muskau, where he had overlooked her in the crowd. Louise's description of him, Sarah felt, was colored by this offence. Meanwhile Louise, whatever her pique, was eager to make use of the introduction that Sarah had arranged for her. 'I hope to go there in a short time,' she wrote, 'and am preparing for the examination. . . . I will not forget to excite his curiosity.' During her visit to Muskau, the prince made up for his former neglect—he set out to charm and succeeded.

Louise's tune to Sarah now changed entirely. 'He is so good, so amiable, the more I talk to him, the more he pleases me! He has a sparkling spirit.' She also wrote about the 'delicious visit,' the evening spent among an intimate circle of congenial people. She had enjoyed the great pleasure of listening to Pückler's agreeable brother sing in Italian in his superb tenor voice. And she had danced so much, she explained, that she was becoming quite thin. 'Do come to Muskau, dear friend, it is too beautiful here, one thinks one is in an enchanted place.' It did not take feminine intuition sharpened by jealousy to perceive that at the very least a flirtation was in progress. In fact, Louise promptly succumbed to the enchantment. Hermann's charm, a romantic carriage ride, and his 'sweet whispered words', the affectionate look of his dear eyes, the warm clasp of his hand turned her head in no time and there was some intimacy between them.*

More salt was rubbed in Sarah's wounds when the prince

---

*Sarah later wrote to Pückler that she had been told by a visitor, 'Louise's husband is an Ochs [Ox]—delighted to see you make love to his wife or rather by *his* account, she made love to you. Hélas.' Louise, in a letter to Pückler, confirmed that her husband was initially flattered that the prince took so much notice of his wife.

subsequently reported to her what Louise had told him. He had been informed that his London correspondent was forty years old, far too tall, and the worst cut of all—a masculine-looking woman. Pückler all too obviously was relishing the opportunity Sarah had presented him to stir up passions, and he sat back to watch them boil. From Louise he received streams of vapid love letters pleading for a reunion and scheming how to further deceive her husband. From Sarah, stung into a frenzy of jealousy and goaded especially by the accusation of masculinity, he received a list, a near cata-logue, of her feminine assets as proof of her desirability.

Up to now Sarah had mostly resisted his insistent pleas that she describe what she looked like. On one occasion, however, some comment of Hermann's about her appear-ance, as reported to him by his agent, had led her to succumb to boasting. 'I hope he had not the insolence to eulogize my leg, though I will tell you in confidence that it is most praiseworthy . . . in all its length. This much I must indulge my vanity by confessing, for having drawn from casts and statues I know what a *good* limb is, which is more than every body can say.' Then she pulled herself up with: 'Enough of this. Let us try dearest to love each others souls and to forget the "mortal coil" wherein they are wrapped.' This time, however, her terror of being thought masculine over-whelmed her. The same fear had haunted her earlier:

> I am afraid from my wild way of writing and from several things I have said, you may fancy me a masculine woman, which you dislike as much as I do. If you saw me only once, you would not think *that*, for if I do not deceive myself, there is not any part of my body or mind, that is not truly *woman*, far, far too much so for my own

happiness . . . Never for an instant imagine me eine männliche Frau [a masculine woman].

To put this false impression to rest forever she now expounded on her physical appearance and sexual promise.

The portrait began with a pretense of modesty. 'I told you I am not pretty,' for evidently she felt that this adjective was too weak for someone with her intensity and expressiveness. To call her pretty, a friend had pointed out, was as inappropriate as describing Giuditta Pasta, a notable Italian opera singer with a dazzling voice and personality, as merely pretty. Nor did she claim to be beautiful, for, as she explained, she lacked regularity of features. Louise Kottwitz 'could not understand my sort of beauty such as it is . . . indeed very few women can, though many as I have reason to know call me very handsome—but it requires either to be a *man* and a man of considerable intellect and at the same time strong voluptuous tastes . . . to admire me.'

In describing the features of her face, she seemed to strive for detachment. Her forehead was 'very good.' Her nose was 'quite irregular, only the upper part—the juncture to the brow and eye—is good. My mouth is I believe handsome.' 'My eyes are very dark grey with a very large pupil and of course dark eye lashes.' They had 'none of the restless glancing fiery brilliancy of . . . French eyes. They are extremely quiet, soft and thoughtful, though, as my sisters [sic] tell me, *awful* when I am displeased. Mr. A. tells me I ought never to laugh, that anything beyond a smile disfigures my face which is naturally grave and passionate. Yet I *do* laugh and heartily too without respect to my beauty.' Very dark, full, not very arched eyebrows shaded her eyes. They were remarkable enough for a well-known artist to have commented on them, and she felt they needed explaining. 'They are indicative of *thought* rather than any more feminine quality and may truly be called *männlich*. Yet he who ought to know them best always said and *says* there is extreme repose and softness about them.' She conceded that her jaw was 'square and somewhat massive.' It had 'a form not common in women nor in ordinary men' and was of a Bonapartean mold.

> They say this is an index of great eloquence. Cicero and Demosthenes are both remarkable for it. My mother who was very beautiful and certainly eloquent too, had it, and men of peculiar tastes and cultivation admire it. But I can fully understand that to an ordinary minded woman [i.e., Frau von Kottwitz] with no such associations it would appear a deformity, and if I were very thin might almost be so. Altogether I think you will perceive that poor Mme. de K. is justified selons ses lumières [according to her lights], in calling me *männlich*, though men who understand these things tell a different story and say that nothing can be more perfect *woman* from head to foot.

In the heat of her jealousy Sarah entirely forgot Hermann's preference for the oblique, light touch. She plunged on: 'I have confined myself to my face,' she wrote, 'though, to tell you the truth, that is precisely the part I pique myself on the least.' Then she resorted to her favorite device for self-advertisement, reporting someone else's comment. 'A man who had seen all that was most beautiful at the courts of Italy, France, Russia, and Berlin . . . and who was a profound connoisseur said of me . . . [that he had seen] "more beautiful faces, certainly, but a more beautiful woman never." ' She then described some of her other attractions:

> I have studied and drawn from sculpture, and I think I know what a beautiful body and limb is and that is my real and true beauty. As to my colossal stature, I am exactly 5 feet 6 inches. If what I hear and conceive of you is true, I am, as Rosalind says, 'just as high as your heart—that is for my head to be there.' My throat is too small and always was so, my shoulders wide and well formed and my waist extremely slender in proportion to the expanse above and below. My bosom is not extremely large and prominent but round and firm. But I tell you the rilevati fianchi [the hips] and all below them are singularly handsome, I believe I might say perfect. An old medical friend of mine once came behind me in the street and said, 'there can be but one such back as that in England. I knew it was you.' From my usual good health too I have a remarkably fine elastic muscle, 'clean-limbed' as jockies say, knee and ankle sharply turned, and calf and thigh firm, round and accurately formed.

Her self-description was more revealing of her state of mind than her bodily charms, and Hermann was soon to tease her with comments such as, 'in my thoughts I embrace your beautiful limbs.'

She went on to confess that she dyed her hair, which had begun to turn gray when she was twenty-five. Now she was thirty-seven (understating her age by two years), yet she declared, 'I must in all sincerity declare I believe myself to be not at all less desirable *as a woman* than I was at 20—perhaps rather more so—being plumper and more developed.' The description she gave lent support to that ultimate claim: 'In truth, my love, all that is beneath the petticoat is worth one thousand times the rest.'* She summed up this total self-exposure with some Italian lines that promised: 'I'll be the one who pleases you more; that which you wish, I'll do.'

Before long, Sarah felt thoroughly ashamed of her fit of jealousy and boasting:

> Ever since I had the *bêtise* and the *bassesse* [the folly and baseness] to be piqued with a sort of defence of myself from the representation of my 'fair friend,' I have been ready, as Hotspur says, 'to divide myself and go to buffets.' That *was true woman*. I confess it. I see you despise me for it. And you are perfectly right. *I* am indignant every time I think of it. *I* to think it worth while to remove impressions made by *her*! oh Cielo! And doubtless my charming zeal has had the effect of convincing you that she was right . . . What a fool I am.

She was hardly comparable to his retinue of women. 'I hope you don't expect me to say a word to take myself out of the category of your beautiful Luise [sic] and your Forester girl etc. etc. etc. etc. etc. etc. etc. Not for the world would I.' Hermann, in turn, wrote that he was 'fed up with Louise who bores me horribly with her stupid letters,' and a week earlier he had written with a wisp of contrition: 'I am really a bit ashamed of my behaviour with Mme. v. K.' Then with characteristic acknowledgment of his faults, he added, 'This vanity is my most fundamental failing and I will earnestly try to improve myself.'

---

*'te dire vrai mon âme tout ce qui est au dessous du jupon vaut mille fois le reste.'

This was a mere passing thought, for he instantly reverted to his habitual tone: 'The description you sent me of your voluptuous charms merely increase my Tantalus agony. It is fortunate in the circumstances that you did not nurse me after my accident [as she had wished to do following a carriage mishap]. The presence of such a body would have cost me my life, since any benefit of this sort would be linked with the greatest dangers. Now this is long past and I only suffer from a longing for you who, however, gives me no sign of similar longing and only translates books instead of translating pleasures as I do.'

Sarah recovered some poise, but not before she sent him a great bundle of Louise's old letters to her filled with professions of lifelong friendship. She also included a bunch of letters from other Bonn friends to demonstrate that her own reputation there was entirely different from that of her treacherous friend. Having evened the score in this small way, she determined that from now on she would not let herself be pulled down to such a level. Louise was too far beneath notice. 'Don't tell me more, my dearest friend, about poor Louise—that total want of all principle, dignity, and feeling makes me melancholy. You may laugh at it— for you are moquer—but, as I told you, I am grave and loving, and don't want to despise any body.' It was humiliating to recall that she had spoken of her as a close friend: 'Judge me not by her, I conjure you.' Louise was 'vain and uninstructed—not even *understanding* what principle means least of all. It would be pitoyable, beloved, in you or me to be angry at such a display of what is in character. . . . she never could in the slightest degree understand me, how should she? her mind and mine live in a different element.' It was 'ludicrous to talk of jealousy on my part towards a thousand such as Mme. de K.' Anyone who could think of them as subjects of even a comparison was not likely to have her respect. When speaking of Louise, she now strove to be magnanimous, and she counseled him to show restraint and prudence. 'Let me at least entreat, nay command you to be careful of her reputation. You will laugh, and ask me if *she* is?—That is nothing to you unless you intend to take her level. . . . Above all offer to *me* no triumphs or victims of this sort—I am humbled when my sex is degraded and can only weep over their disgrace and yours.'

While she appeared to forgive Louise 'her weakness and shame,' the episode left a residue of doubt and disquiet about Hermann's part in the intrigue. Louise, it would seem, had been the victim less of Hermann's passion or even of his passing fancy than of his wounded vanity. For what Louise had not suspected as she danced with Hermann was that her letter to Sarah with its damning description of him and his wife had come into his possession. Sarah, on receiving it, had felt obliged to warn him to be cautious with Louise. 'She is no friend or admirer of you, dearest.' Whereupon, to Sarah's dismay, Hermann had 'extorted' Louise's letter from her. Had he toyed with her just to even a score? Whatever the mix of motives that propelled Pückler into the episode with Louise, he had demonstrated that he was capable of the most elaborate scheming when crossed.

He was hardly that harmless great child that he liked to call himself, but could play at sordid, adult games with childlike irresponsibility. Though Louise, the 'beautiful blonde sheep,' as he called her, was anything but an innocent and was as well versed in intrigue as Hermann himself, her infatuation brought her unhappiness and humiliation. Her efforts to meet the determinedly elusive Hermann eventu-

ally led her to come to Berlin expecting an idyllic rendezvous, as Pückler had pictured it, only to find that he was
not there. She pleaded that he reveal whether he did not
mean well with her, and finally declared that 'the few
moments I spent with you on the Monday morning . . . have
had the most significant consequence for me. I swear by
Almighty God, I am pr . . . [pregnant] by you, for I no
longer live with my husband like that for over a year.' This
yielded the nonchalant response: 'I don't mind joining you
in intrigues against others, but will not tolerate nonsense
against myself. . . . It is very difficult to deceive me and I
assure you no one has gained by trying. . . . Be reasonable
my dear Louise and cease your little feminine tricks which
are pointless with an old fox like myself.'

Though Sarah did not know the details of these goings
on with Louise, the implications of his sordid manipulation
were not lost on her. 'All that shewing and sending of letters
is very low and disagreeable, c'est une cochonnerie [filthi-
ness] pardon a very vile word, in which I never ought to
have had any part. Where is it to end? Will she ask you for
mine? Vielleicht [perhaps]. It would almost serve me right
if—but no, Hermann. I will not impute to you even in jest
such a disloyalty.' Sarah had witnessed elaborate trickery
that might, after all, be directed toward her one day.

She did not conceal her disgust with his machinations.
'Poor thing—you made her think you loved her. It is an
unworthy game, dear friend—unworthy of your heart.
You know as well as I that it needed neither your person[al]
qualities, your rank, nor anything that distinguishes you to
accomplish this end. . . . Fie on your Valmonts!* Are they
men? Put all such out of your head and be you a man. *When*

---

*An allusion to the villainous seducer in *Les Liaisons dangereuses*.

you are one you will scorn such triumphs, and regard them as much beneath you as I should the devotion of a paltry dandy.' Sarah continued to voice her distaste: 'If however you thought you laid an acceptable sacrifice on my shrine by adding a mite to the degradation of a woman whose faithlessness to me is but the instinct of her kind, you did me wrong. Holocausts of such would not gratify my vanity and would wound my feelings of humanity and of respect for my ideal woman.' She claimed she was not angry, but she tried to cut him and Louise down to size:

I dare say you think I am convinced by this *succès* of yours that you are a very handsome, attractive fellow. Point du tout [not at all]! I don't even receive it as evidence of the non-existence of the perruque [the wig], the Schminke [the rouge], the false teeth—nothing. So you see my dear Hermann you take nothing (as the Parliamentary phrase is) by your triumph except the douce réalité [the sweet reality], which I dare say was worth something. But I know too well how little is necessary to complete the conquest of some women, to be at all on fire for poor Louise's heroes. Besides I have *seen Faldern* [a man with whom Louise had an intrigue in Bonn] who was a good amiable fellow but most astonishingly like a toad, in form and complexion and face.

Someone of his quality should not stoop to such paltry acts: 'For yourself dear Hermann I could have wished you above such small unworthy vengeance—but I know you too well not to see that you are not *yet* [what] I hope you will be. If I say more, you will think me jealous.' Later, however, she pointed to the shabbiness of playing tempter to human frailties. As a nobleman and a gentleman he should show 'something of the refined, respectful, sparing spirit towards women which may be called chivalrous. Let them deserve it or not—that is not *your* affair if they do not, too bad for them—you have done what is due to *yourself* and to them.'

Sarah did not need the Louise incident to remind her of the dangers of her own position, but at times it gave an edge of terror to her uneasiness. She knew all along that she had delivered herself into his hands, and early on in the correspondence had wondered aloud at herself:

> What induces me to write them [the letters]? Some strange fatality—often and often I wish I had never heard of your book, your name, never seen your face, never received a letter from you. Sometimes it hangs like lead upon my heart that out of this dream will come some too substantial, too heavy evils upon me and mine. If you think that possible—if you are not certain of your means of conveyance, of your discretion and care, I entreat you *with tears and on my knees* write no more except to say, '*God bless you and farewell*,' I shall understand and shall treasure those words till I die.

Yet there was no farewell, and the correspondence continued. 'I must be mad or stupid not to see the risks I run, nor could you, a man of sense, be flattered by such blindfold insane [assumptions of] security. Nevertheless I love you so dearly, and my nature is so frank and confiding, that I shall invent no pretexts to back out of my dangerous position.' Her fears were reinforced by a friend who knew that she corresponded with Pückler:

[He] implor[ed] me as I valued my peace and reputation not in any way to commit myself to you. Not that he guessed how far I was likely to commit myself, *indeed have actually done*, nor in what way. *That* he would never suspect me of. *But* he said 'take *great care* what you write. Tell him nothing that you would not *print*. Tell him nothing of any body, that he can injure or hurt them or you by repeating. . . . The universal impression he left [in London] is that though an agreeable, clever man, he is decidedly not a man to be trusted. That he is *indiscreet* and has no *delicatesse* about betraying to the world all he sees and hears, you yourself see and admit from his book; but more than this, I am convinced he is universally regarded as a slippery person.'

She recognized that 'for my own preservation (supposing it to be true) all this comes too late. If I broke off all communication with you tomorrow you have more than enough, (did you think it worth your while to destroy me).'

She used all her dramatic talent to picture what would happen should he allow her 'foolish letters' to see the light of day. She had described herself earlier as 'grave and passionate, courageous and resolute,' and told him that if their correspondence emerged to harm those close to her, she would put an end to her life within twenty-four hours:

Never, never will I live to see dishonour stamped upon my husband, or reflected back upon my child. Therefore, Hermann, know fully and distinctly that my life is as much in your hands as that of an eastern slave in his sovereign's; and that an indiscretion on your part—the vanity of shewing a letter or quoting a fond sentence, might as effectually kill me, as if you poured down my throat the poison I should swallow.

Sometimes, however, she managed a lighter tone to express her anxieties. 'If I should cease to write, assume that I am ill—that one has forbidden that I write, that one has seen one of your letters, that I am dead—assassinated.'

His inadvertent carelessness was by far her greatest fear. Did he realize, she asked, that he had in his power 'the sacred deposit of the life and happiness of three persons each of no common value.' Could he trust himself with such power? 'Hermann—as you are a man and a gentleman, if you doubt your discretion, your self command, your earnest sense of the solemnity of what I say to you—in the name of God— be frank and candid and save me, save us all from peril.' Aware of the imprudence of showing distrust in him, for if piqued he was likely to turn spiteful, she did not imply that he would expose her intentionally and stressed that she never doubted his good intentions. 'Cruel and treacherous, I cannot, will not, think you for an instant.' She had staked everything on his character as she had derived it from his book. The Kottwitz affair was a sobering reminder that she could have misread this mercurial man.

As if such suspicions were not enough, other things in his letters cast shadows on her vision of him. While exchanging tokens of love he requested something, it is not clear what, that led her to recoil. Byron's experiences, always relevant for Pückler, give a clue to what it might have been. In his affair with Countess Guiccioli, Byron had received some hair from her, and as he said, 'I shall *not* say of *what part*, but *that* is an Italian custom.' Nor was this the only time Byron received such a demonstration of attachment, for Caroline Lamb (the wife of a future prime minister) sent him the same offering. When Hermann made his request, a disquieting thought crossed Sarah's mind: she who was dreaming of erotic fulfilment, but only if suffused with affection and tenderness, might have fallen for a dissolute rake. The unusually intimate nature of the witheld gift is clear from her reply to him:

> I am not entirely satisfied with your last letter. There was very little coeur, very little tenderness in it, and *without that*, how would I like a request which it required a thousand folds of tenderness to envelop. Now you will cry out about prudery, Comme vous voulez [as you wish]. You would not find me a prude, dearest, but I should be profoundly wounded and afflicted by any thing that seemed like cold, hard sensuality.

Sarah promised, however, to consider the request, but quickly decided against it.

> Are you angry that I did not send you what you asked for? It was not prudery—for I cannot conceive the thing I would refuse you in the épanchement [outpouring] of fondness. But there was some thing, I can hardly define what, that wounded me in the manner of asking—some thing that looked like trying what you could make me do. Such a trial of your power over a confiding, enthusiastic heart I should *hate* you for. I should give you that, as I would a hand, an eye, my heart's blood, if we were once bound together in love, but in the same manner ... and not, beloved, in the spirit of a wanton. Whatever were a source of pleasure to you would be sacred in my eyes. It comes over me like an icy shudder, Good God, if I am writing thus, and write the tears gushing from my eyes, to one who does not, cannot understand me— to one whose heart is hardened and seared by debauchery! If that were so, miserable world it be for *me*,—more miserable for *you*. Sometimes I fear your Mephistopheles nature.

Then she dismissed the possibility that she was pouring out her soul to one practised in 'cold, hard sensuality,' but the specter haunted her periodically.

Sarah's misgivings surfaced here and there, as for example in their discussion of Hermann's hero, Lord Byron, whose manner and opinions he adopted. Like so many of his era and especially his countrymen, Pückler was swept up by the Byron cult. In late 1831 he read Thomas Moore's popular life of Byron with intense interest and sympathy and once more proudly declared that there were striking affinities between him and Byron. The surface resemblances were plain to see. Both swept women off their feet; had rakish, cynical, paradoxical attitudes; and spoke their minds with verve and stinging humor. Both were profligate with money, had to live by their talents and wits, and had great disdain for England's bourgeois values, preferring restless adventurous lives. To his credit, Pückler was realistic enough not to claim that his and Byron's talents were comparable, but Byron remained an inspiration for him and in his later travels he retraced the poet's footsteps. Byron, he told Sarah, was 'one of the most noble souls that ever lived. Unfortunately for his reputation he showed himself entirely as he was while everyone else was hypocritical. . . . I would gladly give years of my life to have known him and lived in intimacy with him. That the English generally put him down does not surprise me. His life put them to shame.'

Sarah did not mince words in letting him know that Byron's attitudes were abhorrent to her, and her sharp criticism of Byron became a device to try and turn Pückler away from his unsavory inclinations. In her eyes Byron was '*one of the many clear charlatans of our age.*' To venerate him was pernicious. 'Why the d[evi]l do you affect that byronic cant which is affected only because people think it *fine*. Simplicity is utterly destroyed by it. Do for God's sake rouse yourself and get out of that.' He was instead to turn to poets such as Burns and Shakespeare—'read anything healthy and get rid of hospital and bedlam tastes.'

She especially directed her fire against Byron's conduct with women—and Hermann was clearly on her mind. Byron 'habitually regarded men and still more, women, not as objects of benevolence but as *instruments* of power and pleasure. It is not on record that he ever behaved *tolerably* to any woman whom he had in his power. Those who were with him say that he tormented that poor Guiccioli [his mistress in Italy] frightfully, though she is the most gentle affectionate creature in the world.' Byron's behavior toward his wife was cruel and showed him for what he was: 'The truth is his object in marrying her was plunder; and he got it.' Admittedly his wife was 'a miserable prude and canter,' but was it right 'to subject her to things he [knew she] felt to be a sort of torture? Would any *gentleman* treat a prostitute so?' She had it from an eminent legal friend involved in the affair that Byron had 'offered [his wife] personally "outrages" [perhaps sodomy or a confession of incest] which no woman of the least honour or delicacy could support and that enfin she *ought* not to live with him. All this you will call English prudery.'

Genuine human failings she could forgive easily, but Byron's passions were not part of his inherent nature; they had been artificially induced, brought on by the sort of egoism, vanity, and search for excitement that by implication also motivated many of Hermann's sexual adventures. 'Your own faults incline that way. You are not above small triumphs,' she chided him, with the Kottwitz affair in mind.

'Voilà mon petit caesar—if you will confound honesty and truth and benevolence you will put me in a horrible rage.' Pückler replied that he was incredulous at her judgment of Byron. 'There you see what prejudices are. They are invincible. I give you up.' Byron and what he stood for remained, as he said, 'a subject on which they would never agree unless perhaps verbally.'

Her uneasiness about Hermann also emerged when he sent descriptions, quite possibly fabricated, of the sexual offerings of other women. On one occasion he wrote about one Victoire whose sexual prowess, he implied, included an unusual and wild, animal intensity that he traced back to her girlhood in a convent. Sarah responded with mingled feelings, 'sometimes wishing that I were Victoire—and dead.' She envied any woman who had pleased him, yet the sort of sexuality that he described was beyond what she considered natural. She was 'almost revolted' by parts of his account and disturbed that he seemed to find them acceptable. 'Your description of your life with poor Victoire frightens me.' She feared he had learned such lessons that 'I doubt if you would be satisfied with my *natural* tastes. . . . Yet there is something in those 'raffinements' you talk of that disgusts me. I do not know why. It seems to [me] to take the delicate bloom off love. I think of Suetonius and the monstrosities of Capreae and my stomach turns and I feel sick.' Hermann's description reminded her of the sexual antics performed at Capri for the aging Roman emperor Tiberius who, according to Suetonius, maintained a library of erotic manuals to instruct women and men in unnatural practices and had them 'copulate before him in groups of three, to excite his waning passions.' Although she had been momentarily put on the defensive about Victoire, she soon realized 'how little

I could supply her place to you.' She felt 'too good for this and that you would never be able to understand or value an attachment so different, or a character so unlike.'

Hermann's account of Victoire evidently included allusions to lesbianism. Theoretically, Sarah was open-minded, but while she could accept homosexuality between men, she found lesbianism objectionable. She realized that given her utilitarian training she was being inconsistent:

> I ought to feel that such amusements are as innocent as any other, for truly I can see no evil resulting, save one, that I think they must quite sensualize and unbrace the mind and all that does that is bad. Right or wrong, however, such is my *habit* of *feeling* that I could die before I could even hint to the dearest *friend* I have or ever had, that I ever felt the smallest tendency towards a desire that would make such a resource expedient. We Anglais of my class never talk of such things—and as far as my observation goes I know not one who would not turn me out of her house for such a suggestion and think me a devil.

For all her tolerance, she felt that 'what you speak of between women is utterly incomprehensible to me.'

She soon rallied and asserted that Victoire's refinements could not compete with her own natural, wholesome sexuality. He was not to expect from her what he found in Victoire. Their backgrounds were too different. 'Instead of the hot-bed of a convent I was reared in all the innocent and fine freedom of an English girl of the middle classes. The youngest sister of five brothers, I never heard an allusion that could make a vestal blush.' Until she was engaged and caressed by John Austin, 'I never felt that besoin [need] if so I must call it which seems so pressing in a cloister.' She could provide untold pleasures without resorting to extremes, and in spite of what he might conclude, 'I can swear to you I am not cold.' To prove her point, she offered an unlikely reference—John Austin. 'I can quote but one authority to you that you will not like to hear nor to think of (alas nor do I).' Her husband was more of a connoisseur than one might assume, for 'he has had but too much experience, having passed five years of his youth in the army and known the warm blood of Spain and Italy, and he amidst all his unkindness and neglect, has often protested that Cleopatra herself could not excel me as a bedfellow. . . . And yet darling, I think, were I with you, in your embrace in your bed, I should be more glorious if I could invent a new pleasure *for you* [twice underlined], that's if I could discover the longitude.'

Yet she unequivocally disapproved of the libertinism with which he challenged her. When Hermann implied that Heller, his agent, whom she had praised as an upright person, would no doubt be available as a lover, she replied, 'those jokes . . . are a little *fades* [tasteless], but believe that I *can* take interest in a promising human being without wanting to go to bed with him.' Lovemaking unalloyed with sentiment was abhorrent. The glow of 'the most heroic, the tenderest affection' always suffused her images of sexual passion. Women, she felt, were by nature more capable of this, and therefore a woman's love was, in that sense, more noble than a man's. Her experience with John Austin led her to think that 'men are capable of *passion* and of *friendship*, but not of that indescribable tenderness which survives the gratification of the one and is infinitely stronger, fonder, more sensual, if you will, but more devoted than the latter.' Frequently when she thought of Hermann, she indulged not in voluptuous dreams but in visions of a harmonious, warm conjugality, 'of the comfort of seeing your face, of hearing a kind voice;—of a walk in the evening to refresh myself in the calm and beneficient air;—of tears poured out in your bosom;—and, at most, of sleep on your shoulder or in your arms.'

It was the disjunction between sexual passion and affection that offended her in Goethe's *Elective Affinities*, a complex novel that especially fascinated her, since it depicted hidden desires and extramarital explorations. She admired its descriptions of nature, 'the poetry, the philosophy, the profound knowledge of the human heart,' and considered translating 'that wondrous book,' but as she told Hermann, '*I dare not*—the whole purpose of the book would be misunderstood,' for it was assumed to be utterly licentious in England. She had one major reservation about the story. 'Do you not find something very revolting in that double adultery, as Goethe calls it.' (The double 'adultery' took place when both partners in their lovemaking imagined they were with another person.) If she translated the novel, she would feel bound to omit this. 'Now you will call out about English prudery—but no—you are wrong. . . . I can neither imagine such a total divorce of the sensations and the imagination and affections, nor could I forgive it in another.'

However candidly she confided her love, he was not to mistake her. She was 'too proud to bear to be considered as the mere mistress of any man. I would not be that to Alexander the Great or Caesar if *they* regarded me as no more. . . . All that you can imagine and more I would do—but then—I must see *distinctly* that I was not valued for that alone, and I must feel that spite of it all I was treated as if I were a vestal and a queen, when I chose.' She would 'exchange equal love and equal respect but I would be the mere minister of no man's pleasures.' This was a persistent note: she was certainly no prude but neither was she a wanton.

Sarah thus countered Pückler's dark side by defining limits to what she would contemplate. Their disagreements and her periodic disapproval of him did not, however, lessen her interest in him or change her course. From the start, when she wrote her first impetuous letters and revealed her fascination with him, she had been well aware that he was a womanizer—a man known to be capricious and versed in worldly stratagems. Yet she had thrown all caution to the wind and been willing to take 'the simple word of an unknown against the most positive assertions of all England.' Beneath his vanity and egotism she discerned 'an honest true man, kind, cordial, generous, full of imagination and genuine feeling' who, in spite of his irresponsibility and taste for vengeance, had not lost a sense of good and would not inflict pain on those he respected. His all too obvious faults were mere aberrations, and her fond belief in him, though shaken at times, was not undermined.

While she condemned the influence that Byron's image exerted on him, she seemed unaware that she also was under the spell of romanticism, drawn to the idea of a compelling, unpredictable man whose better self would respond to the guidance of a tolerant loving woman with an understanding for less than perfect human nature. She thus was his ever loyal friend who spoke the truth to him, told him to throw off his unworthy inclinations, and assured him that 'what remains will be a glorious creature.' He was to live up to his true nobility and benevolence. In different formulations she 'preached' to him: 'If I lived with you sweetheart I should try and cast out that "mocking devil" from your noble heart.' Her investment in this idea of Hermann was so great and her confidence in her own powers so firm that she did not doubt that, were they to meet, she would be able to make him 'truly worthy of my heart.'

CHAPTER FIVE

Contemplating Adultery

We are the only women in the world who are
drilled from our cradles into government of our
feelings . . . If we *sin*, we do so with our eyes
open.

SARAH AUSTIN

The logic of passion is insistent.
STENDHAL, The Charterhouse of Parma

HOW, when, and where could they meet? The possibility
of a meeting threaded its way through Sarah's letters from
mid-1832 onward. As she let her thoughts dwell on a secret
foreign rendezvous, she made the notion of adultery acceptable by thinking of it in conjugal terms. Hermann's dream
of her as his wife was a most captivating idea, and she now
wrote of herself as his little *Weibchen*, shadow wife, and
petite femme and of him as her 'époux cheri' [dear husband].
He teased her as 'my dear and pedantic English little wife'
and signed himself as her 'absent shadow husband' or as

'your faithful husband in Germany.' When she was ill in bed with a fever she communed with his portrait, which 'looked lovingly and compassionately at your poor Weiblein,' and when she was better she described how 'I should like to have you seated here in my little house in that arm chair and I should sit there, on that little stool at your side . . . chatting.' In keeping with this domestic fantasy, she envisaged lovers' quarrels and submissive reconciliations in which she would ask his pardon, and 'then surely you would give me a kiss and take me on your knee, and I would embrace your dear neck with my encircling arms, and— and— Oh God, I cannot go on.' When she was irritated by his failure to pay promptly for purchases she made on his behalf in London, he spoke of 'the first marital troubles between us.'

Their fantasy of marriage went so far as to include a dream in which she was the mother of a little Hermann, and she wrote to Pückler:

> You have filled my poor head with troubling ideas. It seems as if my heart will melt in thinking of a notion that you, wicked one, beloved, have put into my mind. This little Hermann—if only you could send me the heart—more I would never ask. How I should look into his blue eyes to see if they were his father's—How [I should] talk to him of that being [Pückler] we neither of us knew and both of us loved. What a dream!— But this joy, the softest, purest, fullest of a woman's heart, how long it is that I have ceased to think of it as possible to me!

With such dreams she stretched the idea of marriage to accommodate two husbands. When writing to Hermann she depersonalized John by referring to him not by name but as 'he' or 'him,' and Hermann unknowingly may have helped to lift her out of her English setting by addressing her as 'Sara'—the German spelling of her name. Mentally, she lived a double life. 'Externally I am ever occupied with what is for *his* benefit, reputation and comfort or for my dearest child's—what passes in my inmost heart—in solitude and silence is wholly between you and me.' In her mind, Hermann, her 'true spouse in Germany,' coexisted with John. The conjugal setting in which she thought about Hermann helped to obscure the moral dimensions of what she was contemplating.

As Hermann's 'wife,' she became his shopper in London. The prince employed a young German for such commissions, but when he became dissatisfied with an inexperienced new agent he recalled Sarah's offer to help him and hinted 'I wish you would offer yourself as my Commissionaire . . . *you* my little wife would get everything for me.' Initially she was troubled by this: 'I could never have dreamt after I had once said I love you, that you could have wanted me to offer my services as your commissioner, and I take it as an ill sign that you want be told how charming it is to shop for all sorts of things for the beloved.' Yet while recognizing that he was not above exploiting her, she was delighted to take this on, declaring herself 'a capital *woman of business* (don't shudder) and shall no doubt get you every thing cheaper and better than poor little Heller [the German agent].' In fact, Heller would welcome her help, for, she explained, 'he speaks little English, doesn't know the shops or the prices, thinks he shall waste your money and not "give satisfaction"—in short, 'tis best as it is. I am willing and happy to do it and quite confident you will find me a better commissioner.' She was always hounded for time, but these additional errands were not unwelcome, perhaps because they allowed her to spend amounts not usually available to her, but above all, as she said, because they 'keep me before your eyes.'

As Hermann's agent in London she could play a domestic role in Muskau: 'I am delighted to involve myself in the details of your household. Let me arrange some more things [for you].' Since Hermann asked her to purchase curtain materials and furnishings for specific rooms in the castle, he sent floor plans so that she would understand his needs, but they also allowed her to visualize the place where she hoped they could meet. She explored London shops as eagerly as if she were furnishing her own house, submitting samples of fabrics and expressing decided opinions about which colors would blend well with his existing things. In keeping with the wifely role she also gave ample advice on matters ranging from the best hair for a shaving brush (badger's hair) to the intricacies of the quality, pattern, lining, hanging, and care of chintz and muslin curtains. While she showed concern with costs, she did not ignore considerations of quality appropriate to a prince. The young German, Heller, was not to shop on his own, as 'he will blunder or pay too much,' yet she was reluctant to skimp, as she wished to send things 'fit for your princely house and hand.' At first she was careful to consult Hermann's 'exquisite' taste and recalled his preference (also hers, she said) for the oriental. Gradually, however, she asserted her own opinion, adding small items that took her fancy: 'I took the liberty also to send an exquisite little teapot, sugar basin and cream jug of an eastern pattern.' As for curtains, 'I have decided . . . that the lining must be a rich emerald green.' Recalling his extravagance and heavy debts, she declared, 'Were I your wife or your steward, dearest, I would set you at your ease, make you rich and independent, but I must have absolute power.'

Under her supervision, cargoes of goods were packed and shipped by sea to Hamburg and then on to Muskau: shortage of cash had not cramped the princely way of life. On his orders she sent horsecloths and brushes, sets of china (including a Wedgwood tea service), the finest gilded writing paper, furniture and curtains, curry powder, fish sauce, India pickles, mustard, perfumes and sweet bags, vases and jars, rugs and mats, soap and sponges. Having assured him that she was 'famous for picking up odd and pretty things,' she purchased miniature replicas of the Elgin and Phygalian marbles and a bust of Byron, but she failed to find one of Gibbon, which he had requested. Sparing no effort, she undertook excursions to nurseries to find rare seeds for the park and enlisted help from a brother who was a member of the Horticultural Society. Hermann also had her search for a special chimney piece and make inquiries about the purchase of horses. She insisted on making all his English purchases except those from his tailor, telling him, '*You belong to me*, dearest Hermann, and your affairs are mine.'

Details of business were inevitably mixed with messages of love. When shipping some screens Sarah thought aloud, 'if only they were the shutters to enfold us. But I must stop this talk or I'll forget the business details.' When she sent curtains for his bedroom the idea struck her, 'Oh that I could be packed up in the bale of muslin and form part of the furnishing of that boudoir!' And looking at the large accumulation of goods that were to be sent, she playfully wrote, 'Let us hire a ship. I will come as super-cargo.' When

Sarah suggested that she might send him a dog, he welcomed the idea, noting that it 'would speak more to the senses than endless paper and ink.' A couch, which she had specially made to his specifications, led them both to flights of romantic extravagance. He especially asked that 'no wood should be visible. Everything [should be] done appropriately for you know what.' As it and other things were about to be packed, Sarah sat upon it, and with 'melancholy renunciation of hope . . . felt that these mute senseless things were going to where I should never go, to be under your eye, to touch you, to live with you. Had I been alone, I should have kissed them all.' On reading this, Hermann promised that 'since you have not kissed the couch but have *sat* on it, I will kiss it where the beautiful limbs have touched it, which will make me voluptuous.'

All this shopping nourished Sarah's vision of being with Hermann. Her intense identification with him and his interests, her intimate knowledge of the various rooms and their furnishings led her to speak of 'our castle of Muskau' and 'the rooms I have furnished.' He encouraged such talk by telling her that he would cover the mantel in his bedroom with things she sent and that they would be called the Austin collection. She reciprocated by asking him to send back some of the larger fabric samples: 'I shall make something of them that I may look and think of Muskau—that I may see what you see.' After her purchases were shipped she noted, 'How impatient I am to hear of all the things I sent you. To see your room, in my mind's eye. To be with my dear, dear beloved friend—to place all with my own hands. Oh heavens! What a delight.'

She adopted the same wifely role for Hermann that she had brought to her marriage. Once more she was the help-

mate arranging for favorable reviews of his book, negotiat-
ing with publishers, reminding him to pay his debts, and
promoting his interests in London. 'You yourself cannot be
so solicitous about your name and glory as I am. . . . I should
esteem no trouble and no *personal* risk too great to raise you
as high in everyone's estimation as you stand in mine.' Nor
did she neglect his moral improvement: he was to live
within his means and be self-reliant, not marry simply to
gain a rich wife, and act honorably with women. Above all,
she exhorted him to aim high, to contribute to public
betterment, to be industrious, and to recall his noble nature
and responsibilities. He was also to study political economy
and 'serve your country; do good and I'll love you a thousand times more.' She could have been talking to John
Austin early in their marriage when she told Hermann, 'I
feel that I could make *all* sacrifices for and with a man who
were capable of that lofty enduring benevolence which will
serve mankind almost against their will.' Such activity
'raises man into a God. You—you Hermann, might be this,
for you have a clear head and a loving heart.' As always,
she was the moral prompter eager to confer her love on the
worthy pupil; even with her lover she remained the managing, didactic wife.

When Sarah first indulged her imagination with visions
of felicity, she told herself it was innocent enough and that
she could write spontaneously to her heart's content, for the
likelihood that she would ever encounter Hermann was
remote: 'At all events, I am safe with the sea between us.'
As she slid into the realm of imaginary sexuality, she reminded herself that their intimacy would be confined to an
exchange of letters only: he was her 'dear soul, for you shall
never have a body for me,' and she was the 'invisible friend

who love[d] him.' This allowed her to give free reign to her lively fantasy: 'Oceans divide us, my heart, and I can but dream about you.' She would see him only in the next world where they would exchange 'lunar kisses, [for] . . . that truly is all I ask, but those I won't forego when I see you in the Elysian fields.'

Meanwhile Hermann was an intimate though invisible mental companion with whom she could share her feelings. As she explained to him:

> I shall never look at a mountain or a waterfall or hear the whisper of a wood or the tinkling of a brook or see a fine picture or read a touching passage or feel my heart stirring within me by the Great or the Beautiful without having you by my side fancying the pressure of your hand and the beaming of your eye. There I shall live with you but no otherwise.

She imagined even greater joys—'the rapture of a long passionate kiss' and, as she told him, 'a thousand times I have pressed you against my heart. A thousand times I have kissed your eyes and your lips. Alas, they are all shadows that I clasp.'

Their shared fantasy—the 'strange and überirdisch [unearthly] love'—became so precious that she cultivated and protected it, and his letters were tangible evidence of its link with reality. But what if he ceased to write?

> Whatever happens to me in this old and arid world—a world, dear, for which I am as little made as you—I have always one secret and treasured thought to fall back upon—one image that the world cannot mar or deface, nor see, nor know of, and I find an extreme luxury in

that. You are mine in such a way that nobody can rob me of you—nor interfere with you—nobody but yourself.

Repeatedly she confessed her dependence on him. 'You alone can break the charm,' she told him, and implored, 'Write write write. Tell me if your dream lasts. Every day I fear you will wake and seize on some more substantial reality near you.'

She was so immersed in her vision of her lover that when she was about to depart from London for a short trip—and therefore from his letters—she felt the pain of separation:

Do not laugh at me as I bid you farewell somewhat solemnly and as if we were parting. Here I have lived in a sort of half presence of what I love. Here I have received your letters. Here hangs your picture. Here are a thousand things . . . which remind me that you are not all a dream.

A fortnight after departing she wrote, 'my heart which is overflowing swears it is three months since it emptied itself into your bosom.' On returning to London and to his waiting letters she was overjoyed: 'I am home thank heaven and feel as if I were restored to you.'

Her imagination was vivid and it provided great comfort, but she realized it was a poor way of being loved. The emptiness of her dream existence gradually became all too clear. 'You have turned this correspondence which began so gaily into something half tragical; for between fear, longing, remorse, and despair of ever seeing you, the gaity is gone.' Only the unsatisfied desire remained: 'All that relates to you is but a dream, a vain imagination and fruitless longing'; and sorrowfully she added, 'one thing is no more absurd, perhaps, than another, when *all* is madness.' Fantasy alone no longer sufficed, especially not for Sarah, who was ever one to seize the initiative and to create opportunities.

Her dreams were so compelling that they soon shaded into more tangible plans to make a meeting possible even while she declared it was unlikely to happen. Sarah was well-known in London, so a visit by Hermann was out of the question, and whenever he suggested it, she panicked. A meeting in Germany was her hope; Muskau was her promised land; her heart was in Muskau; she would never be at peace until she was there. She gazed at his portrait and yearned for him, but concluded, 'I shall never see your blue eyes'; yet she also told him about a dream that left little doubt about her wishes. She was 'in an open boat on my way to Hamburg—whither bound God knows. I seemed to myself to have no ultimate object, but I suppose I had. Has one reticences from oneself even in dreams? All I know is that the wind was N.W. and that we blew over the waves like a bird—that I said the north is against us, 'tis true, but the wind is getting round more and more to the west—we shall have a dashing, blowing voyage.' Nearly every letter had some allusion to the longed-for meeting. She made half-jests about the house on the estate that would suit her best: 'I claim the English House.— It is de rigeur that an English woman should live in it. If I had no duties, no considerations but those I owe to *myself*, I am afraid not many suns would rise before I should be on the salt waves.' She would declare that she could only dream of him, and then in the next sentence write, 'Now for the proposition you make to me as to the *manner* of our meeting.'

The vista of her promised land, of being in Germany

within reach of Hermann, was uncomfortably linked to the failure of her husband's career in England. Sarah and Hermann could meet in Germany only if her husband chose to go there, which he was more likely to do as his prospects at home declined. 'Ecoutes, I think ... that I have explained to you the precariousness of our station here. The London University has been as poorly managed as one can imagine. More and more he inclines to go to live in Germany and you may be sure this inclination is aided by me and was so long before I knew you.' Sensitive to Hermann's insinuation that she was advising her husband with less than pure motives, she urged him to

> lay aside all your Mephistopheles nature and do not think I am labouring to gratify my own desires under the mask of consulting my husband's interests. I advised him to remain in Germany when we were there 4 years ago. I have never ceased to tell him it was the country for him, and I should equally persuade him to go to Berlin if you did not exist. That some selfish feelings creep in I do not deny, but never, never could I be base enough to counsel him to his disadvantage.

Since circumstances in 1832 were playing into Sarah's hands, there was a realistic prospect of a move to the Continent.

Such a retreat from the misfortunes in London would set the stage for a sexual adventure, and in spite of occasional qualms, she would seize the opportunity so as to satisfy, as she put it, 'all my claims to being loved, as a woman, passionately.' She did, however, set conditions for such a meeting, for she would 'risk nothing that may afflict others.' John, and of course Lucie, 'the one unhappy, and the other helpless,' had to be protected. The days when she had thought of leaving her husband were behind her, and she now expounded at length about her sense of duty to a man so profoundly dependent on her. 'I am the depository of the reputation of a most fastidious and sensitive man—a man to whom the world has turned its dark side. . . . I have no right to give this man pain. . . . I should be a brute to do so.' In spite of disenchantment with her marriage, there were still 'the traces of some few "natural ties" . . . connected as they are with the sufferings of one whom morally and intellectually I revere and almost worship.' Although the usual bonds of marriage were loosened, she admired, as she had always done, her husband's mind and character. While he lived, this would never change, nor 'could any thing on earth induce or force me to live away from him—*not even his own unkindness*—for I know that he could not live without me. I am certain of it.' One for whom she might have felt 'indifference in prosperity (though always admiring respect) is unspeakably endeared to me by misfortune.' Though all passion had drained out of her marriage, there remained her 'deep, solemn compassion and enthusiastic devotion to a man I revere and have sworn, to God and myself, never to forsake.' Sarah had not lost her sense of responsibility, however unusual the setting in which she deliberated about it.

Sarah hoped to meet Hermann on the Continent where she would enjoy the anonymity she lacked at home. John's reclusiveness would help to make this feasible: he was so self-absorbed and withdrawn that it would be easy to circumvent him. In her own way she would remain if not loyal at least considerate: she would shield her husband from the intrigue while exploring adultery.

Then there was Lucie—for her Sarah's feelings were

1. Sarah Austin, by John Linnell, 1834.

2. Sarah Austin, by John Linnell, 1840. 'I am not horrible to look at.'

3. *Above left*: Sarah Austin, by Wilhelm Hensel, 1835. The inscription, in her hand, reads: 'Sarah Austin, Boulogne-sur-mer, Sept. 8, 1835. Strangers in a strange land, may we meet as friends in our own.' She said of this portrait, 'I think of myself as a sad person, but perhaps this resembles me more.'

4. *Above right*: Sarah Austin, by Wilhelm Hensel, 1843. This was painted in Berlin at the time of her meeting with Pückler.

5. *Below left*: Hermann von Pückler-Muskau, from a lithograph by Friedrich Jentzen, after a portrait by Franz Krüger. This portrait was included in Sarah Austin's translation of Pückler's book; on seeing it, she told him that he was 'in every way perfect.'

6. *Below right*: Hermann von Pückler-Muskau, by Franz Krüger.

7. The castle at Muskau. Photograph taken in 1944.

8. The English Cottage in the park at Muskau. Sarah Austin told Pückler, 'Your castle is a princely residence. . . . I could not live with you *there*—but I claim the English house.'

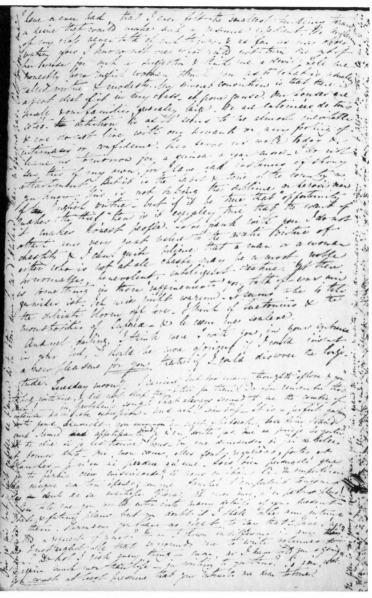

9. A page from one of Sarah Austin's letters to Pückler, dated August 27, 1832.

unmixed. 'Oh if you could see that darling child—the sun of a gloomy life—the hope of a heart in which hope for *itself* was nearly extinct.' Lucie presented no obstacle to Sarah's visions of meeting Hermann, on the contrary, she seemed an asset, another bond between them. Hermann had sown this idea. 'As to the persons dear to you, I won't know nothing of your husband, but speak to me of your child. A mother's love is so beautiful and it will make me even dearer to you, when you are sure that I always include your child in my fantasy picture of yourself.' Sarah, convinced that he and Lucie were made to enjoy one another, was happy to fall in with this. Lucie, she told him, shared his gift for fantasy: she had invented the cast of an entire fairy kingdom and like him had intense sympathy for animals and kept a menagerie of them. Above all, she was 'perfectly natural, and not in the least dressée [artificial]' or spoilt by wrong-headed social pressures,—just the child he would cherish. 'How she would delight to run about the fields and woods with you, to schwärmen [gush] with you.' While on a visit to the coast, Sarah was struck by a similar thought. As she watched Lucie, 'the happiest being in the world, fishing, riding, picking up shells,' she envisaged the three of them together; 'if you were but here, what charming Kinderspiele [children's games] we should have together.' Unaware of her mother's less than innocent games, and no doubt encouraged by her, Lucie wrote letters in charming German to the 'dear prince,' and he wrote back to her. In one of these letters she told him that she very much wanted to come to Muskau 'to play with you.' Harmony thus prevailed in the shadow family, and Sarah counted on Hermann being sufficiently a man of honor to keep the child insulated from her mother's secret.

The possibility of a meeting loomed large in early summer 1832 when it seemed John would resign from the university. They still received £300 from John's father and she could earn about £100 by translating and writing; on this they could live in Berlin more comfortably than on the £500 they had in London—and Berlin, Sarah well knew, was only about fifty miles from Muskau. There was a problem, however, for Austin's father disapproved of his son living in Germany without any regular occupation, and this led Sarah to wonder whether Hermann could arrange employment for John in Berlin: 'You would like me near you—that I cannot doubt, but yet be sincere, and if such ideas are quite wild, tell me so at once.' There was also a possibility of an academic appointment in Paris, and they toyed with the idea of Bonn, at least for a short stay, as Sarah had an invitation from Schlegel, the translator of Shakespeare into German, whom she had met there in 1827. At the thought of Bonn she closed her eyes and dreamed of 'the sweet villages on the Rhine and of you, and of what it would be to combine all this.' Yet Bonn had its drawbacks: 'I should never dare to receive you there, in that little place, where one's every movement is seen and known,' and she explained 'I take for granted you would not choose to see me always in the presence of others. *I* could not bear that.'

Hermann was encouraging, even beckoning: 'Basically I do not really care for the social world, and I want to live with you, Sarah, in pleasant comfort, quite unknown, without glitter.' He claimed to 'now feel the need, which was never the case before, to attach myself to one woman and be true to her.' He even specified the kind of woman: 'Only Englishwomen know how to manage a household for one's comfort. They are active with much grace and have a hundred fewer pretensions than others. Hence they love steadiness, order and the simple pleasures of nature, all things that appeal to me.' Finally he suggested they 'consider how we would find each other in the summer' and concluded with a little doggerel about what bliss it would be to meet his *Liebling* on the Rhine. All seemed set for the consummation of Sarah's vision.

Yet two months later, in the summer of 1832, these plans collapsed. John Austin, with his characteristic vacillation, decided to hold on to his university position and instead of going to the Continent for the summer he accepted an invitation from Charles Buller to visit Cornwall in August. 'It is decreed that we all go to Polvellan,' the place in Cornwall from which she had written her first inviting letters. Her summer plans were thus fixed. 'Till now I had some lingering hope that something might occur to render it possible for me to go to Bonn. But now all hope of that is over.' Even so, she continued to tempt herself with will-o'-the-wisp schemes: perhaps she could avoid traveling with John and Lucie and make the trip to Cornwall alone. Challenging him, she said, 'I would contrive to stop a day and a night on the coast. Would you encounter the sea and all its horrors for that? I would.'

The Bonn setback did not stop her from looking for alternative possibilities. With John lecturing once again, she now pinned her hope on what the following year might bring and wrote that her husband 'has nearly decided on going in September [1833] to *live* at Berlin.' Pückler had every reason to believe that Sarah eagerly, even if subtly, promoted such an arrangement, for during the summer and late months of 1832 her messages of love and desire were

especially intense. (It was during these months that she
described the declaration of love from the sixty-year-old
friend and, jealous of Louise Kottwitz and desperate to
assure Hermann of her feminine qualities, sent the elaborate
description of the attractive exterior that enclosed her passionate nature.) She made it clear that she expected to
receive and to give the joys of love. 'Were I happy—were
I with my Hermann, laid in a bosom that cherished me—
tranquil and confident that I imparted the joy I felt, I think
I should be the most joyful thing in the world. . . . I say
to myself, surely surely my beloved would love me and find
pleasure in me.'

Sarah left Hermann in little doubt about what he could
expect if she and her husband were to live in Germany.
Were they to meet, 'you know not half I could dare, or half
I could imagine, for the man I love. *I have thought and felt
it all. It should be as you wish.* I want not to act any reserves
or scruples. If I love you at all, I love you entirely.' She
alluded to the need to prevent pregnancy. 'The production
of children under circumstances unfavorable and unhappy
for them . . . [was] a deadlier crime than infanticide,' and
added, 'this is a point I should go into further if we were
likely to meet.' These observations must have reminded
Hermann of the way she explained the virtue and modesty
of middle-class English women by tracing it to lack of
opportunity. Their houses were small and families large,
making detection almost inevitable. 'This is not taking the
sublime or heroic view of English virtue,' she admitted, but
she drew the clear inference that 'opportunity makes the
thief.' A meeting in London could not be concealed, but in
Germany, whether visiting the vast estate at Muskau with
its spa and houses for visitors, or in Berlin, there were

opportunities for clandestine meetings. With the prospect of John Austin terminating his professorship in the summer of 1833, Sarah's arrival in Germany seemed imminent, and her ardent, erotic letters left little doubt about her mood and expectations.

As the year 1833 opened, however, a fresh, cool breeze blew in from Muskau. Only two weeks earlier Hermann made it clear that he expected her to '*actually come here*,' but as he began to address this reality he showed unmistakable signs of retreat. 'The first intoxication of our personal phantasy is over,' he wrote, and reminded her that they would have to begin to discover one another anew, this time in the real world. 'You are entirely right,' he explained, 'you deserve that I no longer seek to conquer you in writing but face to face.' He could foresee a difficulty, however:

> It is possible, even probable, that at the very beginning we will like each other much less than in the pictures we built up in the freedom of our imagination. But with familiarity this will change and we would, *I am convinced*, regain the present state of deep inclination, perhaps even passionate love, for our spirits are made for one another, and even in the worst case—if the outer covering leaves us cold—we would still remain the tenderest friends. Do not fear a tepid relationship with me. That is not in our and not in your nature.

There was no misreading this unusually tactful hint that there might be less in Muskau than she had expected.

This was not all. The man who had presented himself as vigorous and experienced now depicted himself in a different light: 'In the physical aspect nothing is any longer enough. . . . The greatest beauty no longer makes much of an impression on me. . . . I am no more so young, so handsome, nor a big hero in love. In addition to this I tend to a characteristic which you would never imagine—a great shyness of character inspite of all effrontery.' He also implied that his performance in the bedroom required a special psychological atmosphere that only a sensitive and accommodating woman could provide. It was important that he feel entirely secure with her, convinced that she had unquestioning love for him. There was, moreover, another difficulty. This boastful seducer of married women confessed that 'one thing bothers me terribly, and that is your husband.' As he tried to lower Sarah's expectations, Hermann revealed himself as timid and sexually defensive.

Had love and desire not blinded Sarah, she might have discerned earlier signs of Hermann's waning interest. His letters, never as frequent as hers, had become suspiciously rare. 'Why do you not write? I pay you at the rate of 6 for 1, which is disgraceful to me, to you. And you have nothing to do, while I . . .' Yet she continued to correspond, even on his terms.

> I begin to be so restless, uneasy at not hearing from him who is ever in my thoughts, from whom I would if I could hear every day and every hour, that I can bear it no longer. I had determined not to write again till I heard from you, but this womanish sort of *punctilio* is unworthy of me and of all true affection, and I disown it. That I care for you (oh how much) you know, dearest, and whether I give one proof of it more or less can do nothing to save my wounded pride, if you care no longer for me.

When he did write, he mixed inviting and affectionate observations with rueful comments that he no longer en-

joyed youthful vigor: 'I am un peu passé. I have perhaps had
too much experience and one is not a roué for 25 years
without feeling the effects.' He spoke with envy about his
youthful agent in London: 'Now that it is nearly finished
and I rest on my laurels, I would give a lot to be as fresh
as my new Chancellier [Heller].' Sarah's emotional investment in him was so great that she ignored these signals. To
give up her image of him was more than she could endure.

Early in 1833 she could not fail to recognize, however,
that he was trying to redefine their relationship. She acknowledged that he had invited her to accept 'a transition
the hardest to female vanity to bear—the sliding down
from vehement passion to a more sober and waking state,
in which the heart can question its own vagaries, and thence
perhaps into mere esteem and affection. You will not deny,
dearest Hermann, that something very like this is traceable
in your letters.' Even so, she had 'not one sentiment of pique
at the flight of those dreams.' She accepted that her 'image,
fancied as it was, should no longer have the power over
your imagination and your dreams that it had.' Yet she was
certain that if only they could meet—if Hermann were to
be exposed to her compelling presence—she would arouse
his interest and command his love. Even now she again
recommended that he get a confirmation of her attractiveness, this time from a Berliner whom she had met casually,
five years earlier, on a boat journey down the Rhine. In
spite of the passage of time, she assured Hermann, 'I am
worth what I was then—and perhaps more.' Her self-confidence, even when facing Hermann's discouragements, was
boundless.

Faced with Hermann's sexual defensiveness, Sarah wrote
less sexually charged letters and reassured him that she was
not put off by his being neither young nor virile: 'Boys I

never liked—beauty in men is of very subordinate and doubtful effect—a good person and the air of a gentleman, with a look of feeling and sense is all I ever cared about.' She went on to tell him:

> At no time of your life would any very astonishing achievements *sur le champ de bataille* [on the battlefield of love] have been any recommendation to me. I suppose it is an *idiosyncracy* of mine. Vehement, intense, mad as I have sometimes felt this enjoyment, I never could stand a repetition of it. . . . There may be insatiable natures— kurz [in short], mine is not one—very far from it.

When they met she would throw her arms round his neck and kiss him heartily, 'taking the risk of your turning your cheek to me. I would take some odds however that it would not be so bad as that.' Sarah was sure there would be no such outcome, for she had never failed to turn the eyes of men. Why should it be different with Hermann?

How little she feared indifference was evident in the spring of 1833 when a meeting was once more in the cards. John finally resigned his university appointment and his employment would certainly terminate in July, leaving Sarah 'to doubt whether he shall in a few months have the means of living decently.' Once again John pondered the possibility of life in Germany, and Sarah reported that 'we talk of Berlin daily.' For her, these dark days were filled with opportunity. 'At the end of July we leave this house,' she told Hermann, 'the next question is how, where, when are you and I to meet?' Their departure was delayed, however, when Austin's father, recognizing the seriousness of the situation, announced that he would visit in July to talk things over. But Sarah still looked forward to the move:

'We think we shall be very quiet and happy at Berlin. Unless something is done (which I don't expect or wish) to keep him here we shall be at Berlin next winter. . . . I must now say one thing to you, to my dearest Hermann. For the first time in my life it seems to me possible we may meet.'

Hermann seemed to encourage her: 'Do not assume that I have grown cold, for if I put the dream image somewhat in the background, it is only because of my longing for *the real being* is increasing.' He wished her to be a 'companion for always' and reflected, 'How sad it is that humans cannot be united as they wish, that they cannot fly through space as their thoughts can'; he also described the delights of his majestic forests with their luxurious undergrowth: 'We would not have to go far to find a swelling lover's couch, my sweet Sara.' His description nourished her eager imagination. 'The lofty massy pines are very enticing,' she told him, 'and the soft green herbage yet more so. Ach Gott! Do you understand all the force of that exclamation?' Hermann also made a gesture of hospitality: 'What saddens me is the uncertainty of your own fate. . . . Oh God, if it only were to me, with tears of friendship and goodwill I would receive you, for I am a true German heart.'

The pictures of the love they might enjoy, however, were now invariably accompanied by rueful warnings that he had grown old, capricious, and unattractive, and by fears that John Austin might make a meeting difficult. The latter concern Sarah ignored, but she responded to the warnings:

> I beg you to regard all that has been written by you as no wise binding on you to receive me (if I come) otherwise than as a person entitled to your esteem, and capable of appreciating your mind and conversation and disposed

to take no common interest in all that concerns you. I
have thought of this maturely and I will not have you
meet with the feeling of an obligation to make love to
me. If we meet, we meet, *mind*, as acquaintances, nay
friends, for I cannot be *less* than a friend to you, but free
as air. We may not be smitten with each other, and
imagine any thing so fade and ridiculous as to have to
affect it. *You* have had too much of enjoyment and
experience not to be very fastidious and *difficile*, and *I*
may have the caprice of not liking that de près [close at
hand] which I have been dreaming about de loin [from
a distance].

If she disappointed him, he 'would have nothing to regret—
but I—I should die of mortification and humiliation.' Until
he was sure about her, 'you shall not have me, and not then,
unless I am of the same mind. And if you do not make love
to me at all, don't think I shall be angry. . . . We shall discuss
and agree and disagree and romance and philosophize and
I, dearest friend, shall feel an unutterable interest in all you
say and do and shall never by word or look remind you of
the projects you imagined in the dark. Can you trust me for
this?'

Sarah's expectation of putting Hermann's will and her
own charms to a test were at their height in July 1833—
when, suddenly, the entire edifice collapsed. 'We do not
leave England,' she announced. John, unaware amid all this
scheming, prevailed after all, for a new position had been
found for him by his friends. The Lord Chancellor appointed him to the Criminal Law Commission for two
years, at £500 a year, which more than doubled his former
salary as a professor, though, fastidious as ever, he had 'a

thousand difficulties and scruples about accepting it.' In addition to the money, the post gave him an occupation 'useful to himself and the public' and 'an opportunity of shewing what he can do.' Undeniably this was great good fortune but Sarah mourned the cost to herself—'the Rhine, Germany, and the cherished hope of seeing the beloved Unknown are for the present gone.' The conflict between duty and desire was most painful. 'Whether to rejoice or not, I in my secret heart—know not, but *to all appearance* this is matter of great congratulation. So all our friends say and think.' Only to Hermann could she confess: 'If you think I am very violently happy, you are mistaken.'

She had no choice but to agree to the new arrangements, but they left 'the cravings of [her] heart' unsatisfied. The meeting, she told herself, was only postponed, and now that they were less pinched for money, she speculated about the possibility of a visit to Germany. She found comfort in the thought that 'at no period of our lives can we meet without finding in each other something that we have sought in vain elsewhere, and that the Wahlverwandschaft [affinity] will retain its power as long as we live. But alas, this is not all—I would like —————————'* For once she seemed to lack words to describe her sense of deprivation. The long blank line represented the great gap that she had hoped to fill. 'You fill this empty space as best you can,' she told Hermann, 'whatever you put in it will not prove to be an exaggeration.' Facing the dark future, she mournfully reflected, 'years pass and we cannot remain as we are.'

For almost two years Sarah had been sustained by an imaginary, secret life and by the hope that it might be

---

*In the manuscript the long dashes extend to this length.

transformed into reality, but now that hope quickly eroded. She continued to write affectionately, but her letters lacked their former animation. Her husband's new employment was not the only obstacle to their meeting, for Hermann was at a turning point. He made no secret of the fact that financial pressures were driving him to reduce his household at Muskau and that he was preparing to resume life as an adventurous traveler, this time beyond Europe. When the intervals between his letters lengthened in late 1833 and early 1834 she had no idea where he was—in Muskau, Berlin, Paris? In November 1833 she responded to a six-week-old letter. 'In it you say that in a month you set out for a long journey. Whither? Even now while I write you are gone— Whither, whither? . . . Adieu. We seem more severed than ever.' A month later she addressed a letter to Muskau 'or wherever else.' When he finally set out on his travels in mid-1834, he went to Paris, expecting to continue on to America, but he was delayed by a duel (his eighth) and missed the boat. His plans then changed, and he went to North Africa and the Middle East instead.* Sarah was left in the dark. 'Where are you? What are you doing? Have you had any of my letters? Why do you not write? In God's name let me hear something.' Plaintively she asked, 'Am I never to hear from you again? What is the reason you do not write. Have you forgotten your Weibchen or do you wish to forget me dear one, because I am sometimes too unhappy and oppressed to be agreeable? . . . My mind returns constantly to the dream of seeing you but with ever

---

*He expected to go to North Africa, Greece, the Near East, and Russia. His actual journey included Malta, Algeria, Tunis, Carthage, Egypt, Greece, Jerusalem, Damascus, and Constantinople.

less hope.' Sarah was desolate. 'We are half *dead* one for the other. I do not know how many months have passed since I have had news of you. I do not know where you are, what are your plans.' She for whom Hermann had been a living presence cried out, 'My imagination hunts about for you in vain. . . . Tell me where to find you.' She felt deserted: 'I have a sort of dread of it as if you were quitting me'; to which he candidly replied, 'My dear Sara, you are correct in feeling that in a sense I am also leaving you. For I have lived with *you* a lot in this castle.' Soon he would be in distant places with no adequate postal service, and she was forced to recognize that any pleasure or consolation that might still have come with his letters would be quite rare. To add to her distress, she discovered that while she had been in Normandy, Hermann passed through Paris, only 120 miles away. She was distraught, 'knowing that we have been within reach of each other for the first perhaps the only time in our lives and that the opportunity is gone—for ever.'

'The shadows of life fall around me,' she wrote in 1834. Her dejection seeped into letters to others. As the year began she told Julia Smith, 'how very little I go out, how very unwell and triste I am.' And to Henry Brougham, the ex-Lord Chancellor, she said, 'I am oppressed and dejected beyond description. . . . My courage which has stood him and me in good stead is breaking down.' The years 1834–36 were among the most unhappy in Sarah's life. More painful even than the thought of Pückler's departure was her belated realization that perhaps he had only shallow feelings for her, that perhaps he was incapable of strong attachment. She even asked him about this: 'How and why it is that *you* have this [fulfilled love] still to seek or to wish for.

What is it, dear one, that *can* prevent your being the object of all you wish to many a one within your reach?' He probably would have agreed with the implication of her question, for in his self-analytical way he had told another woman that his 'cool attitude to the outer world was not achieved without a cooling of the inner self.' He also admitted that 'something is missing in my heart. . . . I have little of it. It blazes up like dry straw and dies just as rapidly.' He had so little interest in Sarah's hopes and plans that, while she had been urgently pleading with him to contrive their meeting in Berlin, he was planning his long journey, considering a renewed search for a rich wife, and contemplating the sale of his Muskau properties.

Sarah's emotional investment in him would not allow the scales to drop from her eyes. She could have wondered, however, whether Hermann had elicited her self-revelations as material for a book that would combine fiction and reality in a genre that was distinctively his own. He had, after all, told her he was thinking of writing a novel about two persons who fall in love through an exchange of letters. As Pückler envisaged the novel, the correspondents meet and fall in love, each being unaware that the other is the postal lover. Of course, both feel guilty about their second falling in love and regard it as a betrayal of the postal love affair. Eventually they discover the circumstances and they embrace and are, so to speak, doubly in love. Hermann had even asked Sarah whether their situation might end in a similar fashion.*

---

*She also had an opportunity to discern his weaving of personal experience into ostensibly fictional work when she read his novel, *Tutti Frutti* (Stuttgart, 1834): E. M. Butler, *Tempestuous Prince*, 263. Sarah in

The possibility that her confidences might be used for one of his literary efforts could have crossed her mind again when, after corresponding with him for more than a year, she became aware that he kept copies of his letters to her. She had even purchased (at his request) his copying device. She was bewildered by his use of it: 'What in the name of all wonders can you want copies of your letters to me for?' His habit of keeping copies made her uneasy, but she did not suspect that Hermann was less a lover than an interviewer. Nor could she have known that he was a compulsive collector of letters from women and that at this very time he was pressing his Hamburg friend, Count Kasper von Voght, who had shown him letters from many well-known women, to explain how he had managed to elicit intimate revelations simply by correspondence. Sarah was also unaware that his fascination with the psychology of romantic women led him to amass letters, many of them love letters, from scores of women. By the time he was an old man his collection of such letters was so large that he alphabetized them, beginning with Karoline Apelt, continuing with Aschbrock, Beckendorff, Beltzer, Benlitz, and on to Marie de Zastrow and Caroline Herzogin von Zweibrücken. Few are likely to have been as forthcoming as Sarah. He knew why he addressed her as 'you noble delightful creature, good natured *foolish* Sara.'

---

reviewing the book flattered the author but offered some restrained criticism of the book. She made many allusions to themes in their correspondence, the most notable being her hope that in future works 'he will forget to remember, or remember to forget, whatever is not worth recording or ought not be recorded.' 'Pückler-Muskau's *Tutti Frutti*,' *Foreign Quarterly Review*, 13, (May 1834), 380–97.

Meanwhile in his infrequent letters Pückler continued to write in his habitual manner. When he announced that he expected to begin his journey in Paris, he mischievously suggested a diversion to London so he might meet the 'dear fantasy picture,' though he was entirely aware that such a visit was out of the question for her. He certainly had no intention of going to London to meet her, for in the same letter he lamely pointed to the danger posed by John Austin: 'If only your husband did not exist, that is so sad.' His real message, however, was discouraging, for he persisted in distancing himself from her and in depreciating his capacities as a lover: 'Soon I will have to bid farewell to the last rosy clouds of youth, and what a sad figure I will cut when you finally get to see me. My vanity fears this mightily.' He elaborated on this theme:

> I long for you so much but I fear that I will not please you. You think me still handsome, but the last year has aged me greatly, for, my child, I am 48. In five years I will be what one so grossly calls an old man. You still believe me to be strong, a fortunate man, living on velvet; but no, it is nearly finished! You think me gracious and good. But I am moody, vain, egotistical . . . Only an angel of love and sacrifice could get along with *me*, who has a hundred pretensions and tolerates none.

He rounded out this portrait by describing his dyed gray hair and wrinkles. 'You will be surprised to have loved in your imagination such a scarecrow, for I now begin to grow old. The spirit is still willing, but the flesh begins to grow weak.' As if such discouragement was not enough, he went on to disparage the shopping she had done for him. Sarah was eager to know if he liked the things she had sent, but he allowed them to remain at Hamburg for three months, and when some of the furnishings finally arrived he made deprecatory comments about many of them, including the couch. She also learned that because of his forthcoming departure, much of the large shipment would not even be unpacked.

As Sarah lost her German 'husband,' she might well wonder what kind of wife she could still be to her English spouse. Early in the correspondence with Hermann she noted, 'I am afraid I am imbibing poison while I suffer my thoughts to dwell thus on impossible events. My heart grows stranger to my house.' Now it was essential to come to terms with what remained of her marriage.

If her correspondence were exposed, however, her marriage would disintegrate even further. Now her nervousness about the letters—those from Hermann and hers to him—became a kind of torture. Occasionally she had burned a letter immediately after reading it, but the rest she had saved. In mid-1834, when she could no longer expect to meet Hermann, she acted decisively:

> Several circumstances lately have occurred within my knowledge to prove how vain are all precautions save the one—destruction. To this I am at last reluctantly and with a heavy heart about to resort in respect to your's. Till now—I have kept them—but I must do so no longer. In a few days I shall go to this melancholy work reading and burning—reserving all I dare and may.— Before I leave England again I shall do this, with what regret I need not, cannot say.

Her letters in Hermann's hands—at this time numbering more than seventy—were more worrisome by far. She had urged that he 'take good care to destroy all those crazy

letters' and burn them within a week of receipt, but that was
farthest from his thoughts. They were his greatest pleasure:
'How dreadful that I should burn them. Calm yourself
about them. They are safely locked in my desk, so stop
being so needlessly anxious.' But this was hardly reassuring,
for what if he were killed in one of his daredevil escapades?
Sarah pleaded, 'If you are truly and fully alive to the
consequences to me and mine—my darling girl—I know
you will take care that not even if you ceased to exist we
should be put in peril.' Her letters if discovered 'would
convert all to darkest night,' and gossip she heard intensified
her anxiety: 'Ever and ever am I disquieted by something
new that is said to me about your caprices, your want of
consideration for the feelings you wantonly wound, your
regardlessness of the honour of others so your own vanity
be gratified.' Though she had coolly managed the correspondence right under her husband's eyes, now she had
'nerves so taut that I can hardly hold the pen at this moment,
so much I tremble in doing something secret.' The letters,
she said, 'rise like demons before my eyes to torment me.'

Sarah's dream was shattered, and she was in danger of
being shattered with it. In 1834 she was forty-one and began
the year in a state of 'quiet desperation,' and matters rapidly
deteriorated. She who had done 'all the hoping of [her]
family' now was without hope. 'I am well nigh worn down
to the earth with care and sorrow, with ceaseless fears and
inquietudes and fatigues.' It was a low point in her embat-
tled life, and the usually energetic and buoyant Sarah suffered a serious collapse. She experienced the first symptoms
in late summer during a retreat to Boulogne:

> It was no acute or severe illness, but a feeling of being
> utterly and entirely worn out. Even at Boulogne, though

I was in health, though I grew fat and though [Victor] Cousin said I was 'embellie' [improved in appearance] I perceived in myself something unusual, a want of animation—a torpor and apathy of mind quite new to me. My English friends thought me dead, or at least could not explain my long silence. I wrote nobody—what is more I really cared to hear from nobody. I avoided all society—never went once to the theatre. All seemed to me a trouble and vanity of vanities.

The full force of the breakdown struck after she returned to London to retrieve her scattered belongings, rent a new house, and face an accumulation of invitations, letters, and bills that required her immediate attention—once more it was a case of 'mountains of business and seas of troubles.' She felt completely overwhelmed:

I broke down and for some weeks during which I did not write to you, I felt as if some spring within had snapped and that I was never again to be myself. The Lord Advocate [Francis Jeffrey] wrote to me, 'I cannot believe it . . .' But those who saw me *did* believe it and saw with alarm a look of settled depression and exhaustion which spoke plainly the state of feeling within. . . . I felt as if old age had suddenly grasped me soul and body, and I said my life is gone like a dream—a dream of care and sorrow and toil—and now what remains? But for my child, my darling, I should have been ready calmly to close my eyes and say let it end here. I have done all I could—I am spent—now let me depart.

Like her husband, she now became a recluse, suffered from depression, and had suicidal thoughts.

Sarah collapsed as she realized that her quest for love had failed and that there would not be another opportunity.

John's dependence on her was greater than ever, and she felt bound to him, even trapped. '*I can never more leave my husband*, even for a month. I must go not where I wish, but where he chooses. I must watch him and nurse him without ceasing. There dearest friend you have my resolution— rather my fate.' At forty-one she had not forgotten her longing, but she was entering a time of life when she would be 'too old to form new attachments [and] too young to have acquired the apathy of age.' She was no longer self-deceiving: 'If you reflect on *my own* age you will feel how little it is that of great pretensions, or of wild illusions.'

To escape her gloom, she plunged into translating, but the mind-breaking labor only aggravated her mental exhaustion. During the two years since the English publication of Pückler's *Tour of England*, she had translated two major scholarly works by Sismondi (*The History of the Italian Republics* [1832] and *A History of the Fall of the Roman Empire* [1834]); Carové's fairy tale, *A Story without an End* (1833); Victor Cousin's *Report on the State of Public Instruction in Prussia* (1834), and three volumes of commentary on Goethe (*Characteristics of Goethe* [1833]). These works, moreover, were not straightforward translations, for she also provided a good deal of selection, synopsis, and interpretation. She had gained a certain fame but had worked, as she said, like a galley slave. She also wrote articles and reviews and published passages from the Bible, which she had assembled while still in Norwich. She told Hermann she would send him a copy of the book, *Selections from the Old Testament* (1833), 'but you would die laughing,' perhaps referring to the passages condemning adultery. Such work brought in money but it also was 'diversion . . . from bitter thoughts and hopeless cares.'

Her husband's affairs hardly helped her state of mind. On the surface he appeared to have fallen on his feet, for his appointment to the important Criminal Law Commission brought him prominence and more than doubled his salary, but it also brought responsibility and all its consequences. Continuing to confide in Hermann, she wrote:

> I . . . begin to resign myself to the thought that my fate is wholly unrelenting, and that gleam of hope and joy cross me only to make the gloom that succeeds them the darker and the harder to bear. I told you of my husband's appointment on the Commission for the revision of the Criminal Law. This is a great subject of congratulation—but the state of his health is such as to inspire me with the most horrible fears of all sorts, and especially with a view to the present moment, the fear of his utter inability to fulfill the duties of his new office.

And what if he succeeded? This thought also failed to raise her spirits. Having such a disabled husband created unusual demands on her, and her many personal and intellectual qualities came into play as she rose to meet the daily challenges. She felt pride in her achievements acting as an unusual kind of wife. If Austin were to thrive in his new position, there would be fewer demands upon her. 'If once I am at ease, rich, and the wife of a prosperous and popularly distinguished man, all this is over. I share in the vulgar claims . . . I shall have no more waves to struggle with. However, this is a curious taste, and shews you the vehemence that lies at the bottom of a very gentle, complying affectionate gay nature.' With considerable insight, she recognized that this also contributed to her breakdown: 'Curious that after struggling so long—and constantly standing between my dear husband and despair, when at last he seemed landed in a safe harbour I should then sink.'

She need not have worried about the safe harbor. It took Austin not much more than a year to resign from the commission, having discovered that he disagreed with colleagues and that the work was uncongenial. He was even reluctant to accept the £800 owed him, as he felt he had contributed so little. The Inner Temple lectures, which he had been asked to give at this time, were another disappointment: he was no more effective here than he had been at the University of London. Sarah realized that he had an 'inability to go on with anything he undertakes' and 'that he must give up every profitable occupation'—that in fact he was unemployable. His misfortunes led to a renewal of all his symptoms, including the alarming moods of self-reproach and dejection. Thomas Carlyle called on him and after a long talk concluded that Sarah's gloom was justified. Austin was 'very unhealthy, little likely to be healthy, a painful, faithful, pitiable man.' Pückler was to put it even more starkly: in his unsparing way he declared that John Austin was 'neither fully alive nor dead.' Sarah expressed her dismay: 'What is to become of us I know not. I begin to give up all hope of his doing any thing. Never did I feel so entirely discouraged.'

Her acute depression gradually lifted but a deep melancholy persisted. With an uncertain future, the Austins began a wandering life. After only six months in the house they moved into in the midst of her breakdown, she and John were once more 'uprooted and cut afloat on the surface of the water.' They moved to her brother's house, to Hastings, then to Jersey, then to semi-furnished rented dwellings. 'I write to you in the midst of another *déménagement*, another uprooting—will there *ever* be a *last*? We go in a few days to Hastings where we shall occupy the house of a friend of ours who is in Parliament during the Session. At the end of June we return to town.' Sarah's mood is clear in her explanation to Varnhagen von Ense as to why she had delayed answering his letter:

> The clouds which have long hung heavily over me seem now to have closed around me, and I can see no ray of light, at least on earth. My husband's health is worse and worse. We have left London—we have given up our house—I have left home, friends every thing that helped to cheer me, and we shall soon leave England. The packing up books, papers, and all lesser moveables—then coming down to settle my husband, child and servant here [at Hastings]—then returning to let my house, sell my furniture, and wind up all our affairs—(all of which I did myself)—then hurrying back to my husband, who was worse—need I say these things have more than occupied me, and have nearly exhausted my strength and my spirits? Indeed, dear Sir, my heart is almost overloaded and I write with effort and difficulty.

Carlyle once more had an opportunity to etch the picture with his verbal acid:

> Mrs. Austin seems to be here [in London] again; half in secret; looking after the letting of her house. We are to go up and drink tea with her; and she promises Jane a chair; I and herself are to sit on stools or as tailors do, for the whole establishment is dismantled. It is truly sad to see how soon the place of the most popular public favourites is filled up: Mrs. A. had carriages by the score at her house daily, and you could not see her, or hear

yourself speak to her for the cackle of admiring lady-
visitors, and already it seems to be forgotten that she ever
existed.

While enduring this unsettled life, Sarah complained—this
time from Granville, in Normandy—'I have never known
from one week to the next if we would stay here or go on
to other shores.' In a rare moment of lightheartedness she
summed up her situation: 'I am now subject for the Vagrant
act, having neither house nor home.'

Once again, in 1835, after almost two years of this itiner-
ant existence, they headed for Boulogne, this time intending
to make it a permanent abode, as they could live there on
their small income. Although they would have a fixed
address, Sarah hardly looked forward to her 'banishment' on
the French coast. 'About the middle of July [we] go to
Boulogne, where we intend to reside, probably for some
years. I can hardly tell you that this change is caused by my
husband's illness, nor need I attempt to describe all the pain
and the toil, the losses and the sacrifice which attend it.'

In the isolation of Boulogne, Sarah's conscience, which
was never quiet, had ample opportunity to feed and flourish.
A brooding sense of guilt settled over her and permeated all
her thoughts. She condemned herself for dreams and intentions, and though she did not have an opportunity to act
on them, she had no doubt that she had come close to doing
so. In a mood of repentance, she wrote to her friend Anna
Jameson, who also had marital troubles, 'My view of life,
dear Anna, has long been growing more and more strongly
this, that it is a trial, a discipline, hard as any Spartan boy's;
which becomes tolerable and instructive exactly in proportion as we see it to be this, and *accept* evils as either chastisements or probations.'

Steeped in the Bible, she did not lack words to give theological weight to her sense of guilt. Life's difficulties were to be endured as divine punishments. To Heine, she wrote with uncharacteristic self-abnegation:

> We are worth so little! When I see dear Mr. Heine, how easy it is to inflict a wound, how difficult it is to heal it, what wisdom, what patience one must employ; what distaste one must endure; how many emotions of our lower nature one must suppress, I believe truly in the divinity of him who could pardon all, who wished to appease all, to purify all.

Nor was her conscience relieved when he tried to reassure her.

> This man [Heine] who esteems nothing, nobody, tells me that he has a quite extraordinary esteem for me . . . Oh if I had all the merit he supposes. Meanwhile, courage. I hope to be an excellent old woman. It is this notion that helps me sustain sorrows and God perfects me thus for the grave so as to be worthy to approach Him. I have so much to correct. It is perhaps a harsh schooling but would any other have sufficed? . . . I accept my education in its entirety with due submission.

The path to redemption lay in shutting her mind to love and performing the duties of a self-sacrificing wife.

To appease her conscience she developed an inflated idea of wifely duty, and, as ever, disdaining half-measures, she carried her new dedication to an extreme. To an impartial observer, however, it might appear that only after having been frustrated in her quest for erotic adventure did she discover this new devotion. Not that she had ever failed to express conventional wifely pieties, but she became loud and insistent about them after all hopes of a meeting with Pückler had vanished. Her husband's dependence elicited even more sympathy from her now. 'I am very necessary to him,' she explained.

> If more and more I withdraw from the least thing, a country excursion, an opera or a ball which may give him any disturbance or annoyance, what can I say to what would rob him of all his remaining consolations. No dear Hermann if you would come and see us—if you knew him—if you saw his sufferings and if you saw how entirely and absolutely he rests on his wife for support and assistance . . . you would say persevere to the end, fulfil your appointed task.

She made a pledge to 'sacrifice . . . *all* [her] tastes and pleasures' and declared that 'the path of duty becomes [every] day narrower and sterner.' In explaining her renewed devotion, she emphasized her husband's fine character—his conscience, his scrupulousness, his nobility—but was silent about anything intimate. Suddenly she could say, 'I am grown to him. I love and honour him indescribably and I feel that the freedom I should formerly have prized so much would now come too late.' She went so far as to declare, 'The ties that bind me here are no chains of convention. . . . not for all that the world could offer me would I leave my dear and suffering husband. Alas if you knew *how* he suffers you would never think that a woman who has lain in his bosom and born him a child, and who knows his great and good qualities *could imagine* leaving him.'

Alone in Boulogne with John, Lucie, and her conscience, she continued translating with greater intensity than ever. Driven by financial pressures and the wish to lose herself in work, she published book-length translations of works by Hase and Raumer. 'I must fag day and night,' she complained, as she rapidly translated two massive volumes of Raumer in order to achieve the planned simultaneous publication of German and English editions. 'I am nearly half dead,' she wrote her publisher, signing herself 'Your slave.'

She was also isolated from the circle of friends who gave her admiration and esteem. 'Burdened by misfortune, bowed by an agitated and anxious life that I have led so long, exiled from all on earth that is my consolation and sustains my courage, having neither family, nor friends, nor distraction, nor intellectual nourishment . . . bereft . . . of all the pleasures of objects of attachment, is it astonishing if all unsettling and fanciful ideas present themselves to me?' Sarah, the most gregarious of persons, felt utterly alone. Life, to her, 'was as tasteless as a tepid glass of water.' To Jane Carlyle she confessed, 'I never sit down to write a letter, or to sew, or to think, without rivers of tears which *will* come. . . . Oh, my dear, I feel as if I could clasp my hands over my eyes and die. But *that* I must not, and yet I am frightened at myself, for it seems to me as if I could never hold it out. Pray for me that I may.' Early in 1836 she told Hermann she was much changed: 'I have lost my gaity. I only seek to fulfill my duties and then to die in peace; if that can be. You will not love me any more. I have grown old.'

CHAPTER SIX

A Victorian Wife

Happiness, I should have known it, is not made
for me.

SARAH AUSTIN

Desire is chastened into submission, and we are
contented with our day when we have been able
to bear our grief in silence and act as if we were
not suffering.

GEORGE ELIOT, *Adam Bede*

WITHIN a year there was an extraordinary transformation. Sarah and John, exiled in Boulogne, were living mod-
estly and disconsolately among the fishermen, the genteel
poor fleeing costly Britain, and the less genteel fleeing creditors, when suddenly in mid-1836, fortunes changed. John
Austin was given a major government appointment as leading member of a two-person commission of inquiry into the
laws and constitution of Malta. Discontent on the island had
forced the British government to set up this commission,
and admirers of Austin, including the head of the Colonial
Office and well-placed friends of Sarah, secured him the

position. In Boulogne they were obscure, forgotten, pinched for money; but in Malta, an important colonial outpost and a military base for the Mediterranean fleet, John Austin would have a prominent position and be paid £1,500 a year plus generous provisions for living expenses. Their arrival in the great harbor of Valletta on the frigate *Vernon* gave Sarah a foretaste of their new status. She related their triumphant arrival to her sister:

> No description and I think no painting can do justice to the wonderful aspect . . . the way in which the rocky points throw themselves out into the sea; then the colouring, the points a rich yellow white, the bays deep blue, and both lying under a sky which renders every object sharp, and every shadow deep and defined. The fortifications which grow out of all these headlands are so engrafted on the rocks, that you cannot see where the one begins and the other ends. In the bright sunlight the shadows of all these angles cut the earth or the sea just as various as the solid walls do the sky. . . . Imagine these walls and bastions, this Barraccas, and every balcony overlooking the harbour crowded with people whose cheers as we entered the harbour rang across the waves and re-echoed from side to side, with an effect that to me, who expected nothing, was quite overpowering.

This welcome was only the prelude to the one that greeted them ashore. It seemed as if the entire populace was in the streets waving flags, singing, and shouting with joy. According to protocol, John Austin was out-ranked only by the governor-general and the archbishop, and Sarah took precedence over every woman on the island, a great change from having been 'la belle anglaise' to the fishermen in

Boulogne. She now was the official hostess, on one occasion, receiving as many as five hundred guests, including admirals, diplomats, and visiting notables.

To be the wife of a conspicuous public servant was Sarah's dream come true, and Malta was the ideal setting for her to display her energy and eagerness to do public service. Considering herself 'an equal member of the Commission' and regarding her time 'the property of the public,' she set up ten new village schools, arranged for the sale of Maltese crafts in England, and in every way appeared, as her friend Jules Barthélemy-Saint Hilaire noted, well-suited to be the wife of a diplomat. During a fierce cholera epidemic, her courage set an example for everyone. When many, even physicians and clergymen, were panic-stricken and took refuge in superstitious rituals to ward off the disease, she kept her normal routine of riding and bathing in the sea, the only relief from the oppressive heat. 'This feeble, abject terror, this inability to look death in the face, was always despicable to me,' she declared, making light of the danger and encouraging others to do the same. She opened her door to convalescents and commanded her servants not to desert their families; as usual, she was uncomprehending of the 'degrading and brutalizing effect of fear.'

She also displayed moral courage, making a point of befriending middle-class Maltese—receiving their visits, inviting them to balls, and attending their christenings and weddings—thereby violating the social code that frowned on such fraternization. Early on, during her first fortnight on the island, she asked, 'How will the English ladies bear this—so strong a censure, though a tacit one, on their conduct?' As she had foreseen, her actions irritated the resident English, who accused her of 'having skulked off among

the Maltese.' She told John Stuart Mill, 'If I escape poison-
ing you may rejoice. I think I have . . . reason to have a
taster. . . . I am sorry to be an object of hostility to any body,
but civility to the Maltese is an inexpiable offence in the
eyes of the English ladies.' Those she befriended, of course,
saw it differently:

> I am told, and I believe it, that I am extremely popular
> among the Maltese. Unaccustomed as they are even to
> decent civility, they must needs be pleased with a person
> who does all in her power to shew them, what she really
> feels, deep interest in their welfare, sympathy in their
> sufferings and a desire to place them in all respects in such
> a position as their rank, their conduct, or their talents
> merit.

Sarah was described by a Maltese 'as a mother to us all,' and
her conduct earned a eulogy in a local newspaper as 'La
Signora Commissionaria.' This success on the island helped
her recover a sense of capacity and inner strength.

As Sarah threw herself into her new life, she tried to gain
emotional distance from Hermann. She no longer regarded
him as a lover but as a sympathetic confidante who would
be glad to hear from her occasionally. Hermann, however,
saw things differently. Rather than act the compassionate
friend, he preferred to be a skeleton in her closet, emerging
unexpectedly to agitate her conscience and her fears. His
dangerous letters made Sarah feel more than ever vulnerable
to exposure and harassment. Her fear of being discovered
had reached nightmarish proportions even before their departure to Malta:

> Of all that the future could have in store for me, the most
> terrible, the most insupportable, and I mean literally, I

would know none comparable to that of mortally wounding an honorable and already saddened heart; to withdraw from the sufferer the cherished but unworthy hand that serves him as support and consolation, to tarnish the lustre of an unblemished reputation of a beautiful, precious child; and finally when she has lost everything except the esteem of decent people of goodwill, and hope of God's mercy, to see herself deprived of these as well. Such, dear Hermann, such are the thorns on which I lay my poor tormented head—whenever I think that my plight is of my own making. You will mock me as before. Oh you do not know me, neither me nor my sad circumstances.

Her high visibility in Malta intensified her anxiety, especially as Hermann, now in North Africa, continued to send compromising letters that seemed to play roulette with her safety. She pleaded with him:

I have tried to make you understand things I would prefer not to explain, given the risks of correspondence in such countries as you now are in. (*Your last letter was handed to me after having been opened*, fumigated etc. etc. [due to fear of epidemic diseases such as cholera] and necessarily read by any one who wished it.) I have told you that I can only receive letters that are agreeable for him to read, and that in effect he practically reads everything that I receive. Your letter, by a sort of miracle arrived during his absence. But once more I plead with you to consider what he would have thought in reading it, and the consequences for those for whom you profess so much friendship.

Her fears now dominated. 'It is true he [her husband] knows that I have never known you,' she explained, 'but do you believe that such letters are likely to make him think that it is good that if chance should allow it, I see you? He already has some ideas which would make the latter difficult.' She was even terrified that she herself might inadvertently reveal something and tried to show no interest when his name was mentioned by Maltese who had met him on his visit to the island during the previous year. Recalling her recent breakdown, she wrote, 'I had hoped you would put yourself in my place, that you had understood . . . that for me it is essential to seek tranquility; that I am exhausted, wearied with strong emotion; to live and die in peace with him is all that can remain to me at my age after my misfortunes.' She begged, 'Be more careful carissimo, I repeat, a true Knight would die rather than compromise his lady.' Yet showing consideration for others was not Hermann's way. He was anything but guarded and even suggested that he might return to Malta, going so far as to announce a visit, which was reported in the *Malta Government Gazette*. The prospect horrified her. 'I plead with you not to think of it while we are here. . . . You must realize that every word we say, each step that we take is examined, spied on, reported, scrutinized under every light, and I lead a life altogether diplomatic in its annoyances and its public visibility.'

She tried to meet the danger by never casting doubt on his fundamentally good nature; after all, he had declared that he was 'as soft wax in the hands of those who love me, but I admit, a stinging thistle for others.' In fact, it may have been to appease him that, earlier, while still in London, she continued to perform services for him: she had negotiated with publishers about the translation of his book about landscape gardening at Muskau and his proposal for publication of new travel books in England. In the same spirit she appealed to the better side of this most unpredictable and unmanageable man by urging him to 'give your many and great excellencies *fair play*.' She also recalled what Varnhagen had told her—that 'when people address themselves to your good side you are all goodness and generosity and kindness. I am sure of it. I feel that it is only by misunderstanding that one can fail to love you.'

These diplomatic attempts to steer him away from sending incriminating letters had no effect. 'If you *cannot* feel for me, or fear for me, words are hopeless,' she wrote. Finally she courageously met the danger head on. Following his suggestion that she need only indicate that he should stop writing, she wrote a letter that completely changed the tone of their correspondence.

> Listen now and accept the perfect sincerity of what I tell you. Not only do I not want to receive, but it is a real pain for me to receive your letters if you persist in writing to me in the tone you adopt. My friend, I have no choice—I dare not, *cannot* because without doubt he will see some letter, and do you think he would want others? He has found and with reason that I have too much correspondence, that this occupies too much time and spirits and costs me too much money. You have no idea how much I have renounced entirely. If you care for me, you will hear with pleasure that our [my husband's and my] relationship is very much changed—that we get along better, and each of us having made some concessions of one kind and another, and having talked together with perfect frankness, we [now] live in perfect accord—which is made possible by the fact that there is, dare I say it, recognition of a fund of qualities on both sides, that some faults would never alienate us from one

another. If only he would be well, I now do not despair
of spending the rest of our lives very tranquilly and very
affectionately together, and I am resolved to cut out
anything that could trouble that precious peace.

He should write only if it was worth his while to write as
to a friend who appreciated his letters, but 'if this has no
appeal to you, I have to renounce the great pleasure of
receiving news of you. Whatever be your decision, I will
always have interest and admiration for your talents and
zeal for your reputation and happiness . . . which I have so
often expressed to you and now express once more.' With
this, their correspondence came to a virtual close.

Ample cause for worry remained on other fronts. The
Malta position was a diplomatic tightrope, and Sarah knew
from experience how stress affected her husband. John had
regained his health while unemployed in Boulogne, but as
their ship arrived in Malta, Sarah became uneasy when the
jubilant crowds expressed their high expectations for the
commission. The ship's officers congratulated her on the
flattering reception, but she turned away to hide her tears.
How would her husband handle such intense pressure? She
soon found out: after eight weeks of intense work, he again
fell ill; as she put it, 'our usual misfortune pursues us.' She
was 'devoured by an anxiety the most terrible that I have
ever had to endure . . . Thus here I am once more exposed
to all the tortures of uncertainty and the fear which are all
the more sore after the hope that had dared to form of some
serene days.'

Her fears were justified. Not that John Austin failed to
accomplish a good part of his mission. He put in place
important and useful changes in governmental organization

and drafted a new law regulating the press which greatly reduced the extent of censorship. His intellectual qualities came to the fore, but he also left a trail of resentment, anger, and opposition. Some of it was inevitable, for his economies and reforms eliminated jobs, reduced salaries, and disturbed the complacent enjoyment of colonial privileges. He was not given to being diplomatic, however, and made little effort to soothe the feelings of those who suffered from his reforms; as a result he offended the entire establishment and quarreled with its leader, the chief justice, whose job he abolished. When he returned to London he stirred up more waves, disagreeing with the attorney general and solicitor general, who had criticized his proposals, and provoking the anger of a former lord chancellor, who then mercilessly ridiculed his work in Parliament. This humiliation was reported in all the newspapers. Although highly placed officials privately acknowledged his success in reforming the government in Malta, there was no official statement of appreciation for his services, and this embittered him further. The Malta appointment was one more debacle, the final one, for John Austin was not to be employed again during his remaining twenty years.

The return to London in 1838 after their twenty months in Malta once more meant unemployment for her husband and the drudgery of translation for Sarah. She took on the awesome task of translating the three thousand large octavo pages of Ranke's *History of the Popes*, working for eight to nine hours a day. Lucie, now eighteen, joined her mother in complaining about John Austin's dark moods: 'My father continues very poorly and much depressed, which makes me anything but gay.' She soon had further reason to be aggrieved, for she had fallen in love with Sir Alexander Duff

Gordon, an impecunious aristocrat, but her father refused to consent to marriage because of her youth and Duff Gordon's poor prospects. Within the year, however, John relented, and Sarah was relieved when (on May 16, 1840) he agreed to accompany his daughter to the church.

Austin now once more considered a move to the Continent as a liberation from London and its humiliating memories and as an opportunity for the stressless existence that suited him best. They could look forward to a comfortable stay abroad, as Austin had received £3,000 for his services in Malta, and they had fewer anxieties about the future, having learned that Austin senior had provided handsomely for them in his will. Sarah, although still lamenting the lack of a protected niche for her husband, accepted the prospect of life abroad. As she explained to her friend Harriet Grote, 'I . . . have been so disciplined in living *au jour la journée* [from day to day] that I have not even a place to hanker after; I go where the winds and waves drive, and try to make the best of the spot where I am.' After almost three years in London, in 1841 they set out for Germany, intending to settle in Dresden, only one hundred miles from Berlin.

Berlin! Only nine years earlier it would have meant the greatest hope and the greatest danger. Now Sarah surely approached it with more than a little curiosity, perhaps with some trepidation, but not with the sense of eagerness she would have felt earlier. She had become so cautious that when Hermann, who in 1840 had returned from his travels, made the first move—inviting her and John to Muskau—she subtly revealed her detachments. She explained that Lucie was married, indeed pregnant, telling him 'I feel very *grossmütterartig* [grandmotherly] as you may suppose; but this too I do not lament. I am infinitely more tranquil than formerly. My husband's improved health and my child's quiet happiness are enough for the rest of my life.' After some delay, in late 1842, she and Hermann met in Berlin. Unfortunately, we do not know what either of them thought about their encounter, but we do know that they exchanged books, including her scrapbook, which she offered 'in remembrance of our meeting.'* Some brief notes imply that there were a few such meetings, all taking place in the presence of others. The tone of these encounters seems to have been agreeable but not intimate, as Sarah indicated by signing one such note, 'your *old, new* friend.' With these words she reminded him of her former devotion and her new affectionate but distanced interest in him, and in another oblique statement she told him, 'I have not forgotten the kind interest you formerly expressed for a stranger.' The episode with Hermann—all but the memory of it—was behind her.

Hermann was no longer at the center of Sarah's emotional life, yet as he had told her, 'you will not forget me.' What about him? Did she remain in his memory? Some rather bizarre evidence suggests that she did. In a book about his travels in Greece, *Südöstlicher Bildersaal: Griechische Leiden* [Southeastern Picture Gallery: Greek Sorrows] (1840), Pückler created a novel-like fragment, a macabre

---

*She was in Berlin from November 1842 until the end of March 1843: Sarah Austin to Varnhagen von Ense [March 31, 1843], Jagiellonian Library, Cracow; Janet Ross, *Three Generations of English Women* (London, 1893), 185–90, 192. The few letters in which Sarah alludes to meetings with Pückler are undated and endorsed 1842, but as one of them seems to have been written just prior to departure from Berlin, she and Pückler also appear to have met early in 1843.

fantasy, 'a mysterious love adventure' about a beautiful married woman named Sara Namor (Sara as he spelled it in his letters to her). The love story (partly narrated through a correspondence), though veiled by an atmosphere of dreams and horrors, echoes their romance. The Sara of the novel, ambivalent about her husband, hesitates when a stranger (i.e., Pückler) speaks to her of love. While she invokes duty and virtue, the stranger insists that 'love knows no such dry duties, the duty of love is a necessity.' She parries his advances with 'teasing grace' but ultimately yields to her passionate nature and awaits the stranger expectantly, while her husband (assisted by some magic) is present but oblivious to what is going on. At the crucial moment of the seduction she is distressed to find that her lover 'freezes to ice, paralysed,' thus 'offending her femininity to its depth.'

Many of Sara Namor's characteristics, even words and actions, seem drawn from Sarah Austin's letters. Sara Namor has 'ample limbs' but a 'little foot'; full-blown black hair; and 'neck and bosom such as Venus might have admired.' She has an intensely passionate nature—'her eyes burned like coals'; she is ravaged by desire and is eager to experience 'transports of rapture.' In saying 'I will be yours' she promises him 'more bliss than he could find with anyone in the world.' Both Sara and Sarah proclaim, 'I am no ordinary woman,' and both talk about duty and virtue. The stranger sits with Sara Namor on a red silk couch and associates her with the scent of violets. Some mysterious *Wahverwandschaft* (affinity) draws Sara and the stranger together, and he tells her, as Pückler told the real Sarah, 'I think aloud with you.'

Sarah reading this could tell herself that she had left a mark on Pückler's memory—even a scar. Here she could discover how Hermann might have felt about his cold response to her eager wish to meet him in Berlin, for in a similar situation the stranger found this 'the most agonizing moment of his life.' He confessed, 'I knew . . . what the loving, yielding woman counted on, and how repugnant my coldness must appear. . . . How is it, I cried, that like a lifeless icicle, I have inflicted such deep injury to her femininity . . . and have abandoned her in the most unchilvalrous way at a time of her greatest need.' This may have been little comfort in the early 1840s, yet the overall message had to be gratifying, for despite Hermann's detachment and coolness, in this fictional account the stranger declares that the affair began as mere gallantry but turned to love. 'I love you Sara, with all the strength of my soul,' and he describes how

> my heart nearly ceased to beat . . . I felt only a great flow of love for this seductive woman whose marvelous being knew how to arouse every fibre of my soul. . . . Time lost its meaning and I thought I had known her since my life began. . . . Without thinking I wished to follow her . . . the loved one now filled all my senses.

It would seem that Sarah had stirred the imagination of this suspicious and cynical man. After seeing Hermann in Berlin, the Austins remained in Germany only briefly before moving to Paris for almost five years until driven back to England by the revolution of 1848. Sarah continued to be a social success wherever she went. She was a favorite in Parisian salons where her friends included Alfred de Vigny, François Mignet, François Guizot, Alexis de Tocqueville, Victor Cousin and Alphonse Lamartine. She also drew many notables to her small apartment where as Barthélemy-

Saint Hilaire explained, her animation was the attraction. The German writer Heinrich Laube described it as a place where French, German, and English guests conversed about European literature and politics in three languages. 'This tower of Babel,' he noted, 'the hostess dealt with admirably.' Her candid friend Sydney Smith was less impressed and chided Sarah for her Paris head-hunting. Harriet Grote, on the other hand, was excited by the prospect of meeting Sarah's famous friends: 'Mad. Austin has "let down her net" in honour of my advent, and I expect a good "haul." ' Although treated to conversation with Cousin, Vigny, and Tocqueville, Mrs. Grote came away disappointed. 'Soirée a comparative failure. Very few individuals worth laying out one's money upon. Bearded barons from Livornia, and scarcely a woman fit to look at. . . . The only feature of the evening I valued was a long confab. with Bar[thélemy] de St. Hilaire, on Grote's studies and life, and etc. which of course was interesting.' Her verdict on John Austin was no more charitable: he was a specter, marrowless, and though he talked a good deal, she accused him of being tame and languid.

When the Austins left Paris in 1848, John again refused to live in London. After having resided in at least fourteen different temporary dwellings in four countries during their thirty years of marriage, they settled into their first and last permanent home—a substantial house that still stands, with an attractive garden—in Weybridge, nineteen miles from London. The death of Austin's father that year left them with an inheritance sufficient to make them financially comfortable without either of them working. Lucie with her young family lived nearby, and Sarah looked forward to more tranquil times. In 1851, Pückler was only a few miles away, visiting the Great Exhibition in London; Sarah was not even aware of it.

Now, however, her family succumbed to ill-health. Lucie, only thirty in 1851, began showing the signs of what would be a long struggle with tuberculosis. John also became ill, no novelty to him, but on this occasion it was unambiguously not a manifestation of his hypochondria, although it is not clear what label would be attached to it today. Lucie described his condition as a threatening of paralysis, and though only sixty-one he suddenly seemed to age. During the same year the indomitable Sarah was struck down with a severe heart attack. She had grown enormously fat, according to her son-in-law, Alexander, who also explained that she was

> a very difficult patient. She sees too many people and I suspect eats too much, a natural failing in a person suffering as she does from the heart. She has a sensation of faintness which she attributes to wanting of nourishment instead of the feeble action of the heart. For two more dreary months she must remain a close prisoner. Poor old Austin is in despair about her, I see, and cannot manage her.

Her condition was so serious that it was thought she might not survive. The doctors, she explained, 'did me the honour to think I could bear to hear the truth, and I find the familiar aspect of death neither terrible nor saddening, tho' grave. I wonder indeed at people of my age [she was fifty-nine] who do not rather cultivate than shun this acquaintance.'

While she calmly faced the prospect of death, her son-in-law wondered how John, who had depended on her so much, would manage.

I can't think what will become of him if she dies. I could not, in justice to my children or to Lucy, have him to live with us. He is too depressing. It would be awful to have a black demon always sitting on one's back, and yet it seems so brutal to leave so helpless a man, and one endowed with such brilliant capacities, to his own melancholy company that I sometimes almost relent. But children's youth should be bright if possible.

The prognosis had not improved a few weeks later, nor had John's outlook. 'Padre Austin's black morose face and miserable apprehension make our visits there very dreary,' Alexander noted. Eventually Sarah showed some progress, but the doctors forbade every exertion, sentencing her to 'absolute *donothingness*'—and consequently she did not complete the book she had been working on (the closest she came to an autobiography), *Contrasts of Foreign and English Society; or, Records and Recollections of a Residence in various parts of the Continent, and England*. Alexander feared she would never be able to resume an active life: 'I think very ill of her. I don't mean to say she will die immediately, but that she will never again have strength or ease.' Of course, in the end she proved him wrong. The only one who did not surprise anyone was John. Sarah, her son-in-law soon explained, 'is very much better, is much thinner and now gets out for a drive. She felt the exclusion awfully. I don't wonder at it. Padre's blackface is unpleasant to sit under always.' With care and prudence the doctors thought she could live the usual three score and ten.

John recovered his health—such as it had been—but if *he* had died, it is not clear that Sarah would have been more welcome in her daughter's home than John. She who had organized a rescue from a shipwreck, led the efforts to subdue a hotel fire, initiated successful publication ventures, and dominated most social occasions had an eagerness for command and an expectation of being in charge that was not easily put aside within her own family. She was, after all, the 'man of business' in the family, and while there was clearly a need for her to take this part, the gratitude of those she served may have been alloyed with resentment. Possibly her husband and certainly her daughter and son-in-law felt this way, and in reaction to Sarah's 'maternal despotism,' as Lucie called it, she and her family moved from their home in Weybridge to another village four miles away. There was no quarrel with Sarah, but putting some distance between herself and her mother was 'an immense relief,' and she even spoke unkindly of 'Raven Sara.'

John was fifty-nine when they settled in Weybridge, but Sarah's striving continued to counter his wish for retired ease, and some of the crosscurrents of their younger days persisted. Her ambition for him and her habit of taking charge led her to press him to get down to work, to produce a significant book by which he could be remembered. She now tied her hopes to John's former wish to publish his ideas about the philosophy of law, and this did not appear to be such a difficult task, for Sarah was convinced that the notes he had used for his lectures at the University of London could be turned into a book without much rewriting. Taking matters into her own hands, as always, she conspired with friends, editors, and publishers to stir him to write. She wrote to the editor of the *Edinburgh Review* that she would be forever grateful for 'any stimulus or encouragement given to *him* to employ his great power.' John Murray, who had published Austin's first book at her instigation, was asked to 'urge [Austin] to go to work immediately.' She also asked Lord Lansdowne and Guizot to prod her husband by inquiring about the state of his work.

In spite of such manipulation, John Austin steadily refused to touch up his lectures and even declined to have his first book reprinted. Sarah's management, ostensibly to ease his way, may well have irritated him, making him resist her pressures. In retirement, during the last decade of his life, he left his old lectures untouched and wrote nothing except a political pamphlet. Gardening was one of his few diversions. When Sarah looked back on this period, she recalled it as the

> happiest period of his life; the only portion during which he was free from carking cares and ever-recurring disappointments. The battle of life was not only over, but had hardly left a scar. He had neither vanity, nor ambition. . . . He had no regrets or repinings at his own poverty and obscurity, contrasted with the successes of other men. . . . Long daily walks . . . were almost the sole recreation he coveted or enjoyed. . . . He wanted no excitement and no audience. . . . He never expressed the smallest desire for society.

After recovering from the bout of illness in 1851, John enjoyed reasonably good health, good enough that Sarah reported to a friend, 'you would hardly know *him*, nor *me*. He looks so well and robust and I am so *enormous* and look so weary and worn.'

Sarah, whose hopes for him had been so high, wondered why he had published so little and had given up his ambitions. As she speculated about this she did not conceal her irritation:

What reason can he give to me or to himself? Health?
But to *me*, he can hardly urge *that*. The truth is, that
many causes, and among them some very sufficient ones,
long ago conspired to disgust him with men and their
judgments and their affairs; and he, poor fellow, has
made this an excuse to himself for obeying his own
reluctance to set about work . . . It is true he was
shamefully treated; but you and I know there is another
way of avenging oneself on the injustice of men.

Instead of attributing Austin's unproductivity to poor
health or even to circumstances, she traced it to something
more deeply personal.

I believe that some people with the weakest frame, the
weakest health, the weakest nerves, *do* and *suffer* immense things, because *they will*, and that others either *do
not will* or *will not* (which are two different things). My
conviction is, que ce n'est pas plus fin que ça [there is no
need to look further] and that this obvious explanation
is the true one. I *see* it in my husband and myself. He
is and has long been, thank God, in perfect health, better,
I think, than 9/10 of the men of his age. I can discover
no impediment whatever to his doing any thing within
his competence. But he never *does anything*. He reads and
walks and eats and sleeps—a very good life for those
who like it, and who do not feel called upon to use their
faculties in any way.

She, in contrast, managed her house, kept accounts, wrote
letters, entertained visitors, cut out and made her own
clothes, and occasionally wrote for publication, despite the
fact that she was 'always ill, always uneasy and oppressed,
often so weak as to be incapable of walking ⅛ of a mile,

often utterly sleepless and frightfully nervous.' No doctor, she claimed, who knew their states of health 'would say that I were capable of a tenth part as much work and exertion as he. Yet to say I do ten times as much, does not express the case, since he does nothing.'

Harriet Grote confirmed her observations:

I found Mr. A. particularly well, and brim full of talk; Mrs. A. far less subdued by her malady than one could have expected. Locomotive capacity apart, she retains almost all her faculties, and exercises them more actively, even now, than many younger healthier people. Her spirits are wonderfully elastic.

Sarah's spirit was evident in her boast 'I am naturally *speranzosa* [hopeful], I do not give up' and in her confident assertion that 'even the frequent recurrence of pain does not impair the health. The vital force and energy remain unshaken.' With these qualities went austerity, evident in an October visit to her beloved Cromer, a seaside town in Norfolk, where she bathed in cold seawater: 'Thus I hope to season myself for the winter.' Her energies continued to flow into bookmaking, and in 1855 she edited a volume of letters written by her old friend Sydney Smith.

The ambition she brought to her marriage was put aside with difficulty, but finally she accepted John's apathy. 'For the few years we have to live I do not care to disturb the tranquility of mind he has attained.' She now regarded him as 'an immense, powerful, beautiful machine, without the balance-wheel, which should keep it going constantly, evenly, and justly.' He was, 'poor fellow, like a Titan chained to a feeble and suffering body.' She would make fewer demands on him and accept him as he was.

In my heart I continually commend him to God, and pray that his great and noble soul may find a sphere more fitted to its development. With this hope I am obliged to console myself for my *bitter* disappointment—not, believe me, that he has not coined his talents into gold or risen upon them to power or greatness, but that he will depart out of the world without having done for the great cause of Law and Order, of Reason and Justice, what he might have done. To enable him to do this I should have been proud and happy to share a garret and a crust with him. But God knows our ambitions, and checks them.

In the last decade of their marriage she no longer struggled against her husband's inactivity, but her bitter disappointment remained. He would produce nothing to vindicate her faith in him, and she had to watch him 'wearing away his life without devoting any part of his great power to the service of mankind, or leaving behind him any but the faintest trace of what he is.' All her trials and sufferings, she said, 'shrink into insignificance compared to the *despair* of contemplating day by day and year by year my husband's *resolute* neglect or suppression of the talents committed to his care, especially since he was one to whom the *ten* talents were given.' It had to be accepted, but she never made her peace with it: 'tho' resigned I was never reconciled to it.'

By ceasing to struggle with John's limitations, Sarah allowed for some harmony. Whereas 'the midday of our lives was cloudy and stormy, full of cares and disappointments . . . the sunset was bright and serene.' A friend spoke of the last years of their marriage as 'a deferred and long honeymoon.' Sarah also noticed a change in John's state of mind; he became

> so gentle and noble, so without all alloy of unsatisfied cravings, or vain repinings, or harsh passions, or low desires . . . In this blessed frame of mind all his youthful and passionate love for me seemed to return, mingled with a confidence and intimacy which only a life passed together can produce.

Now she appeared to have forgotten her complaint that during the first decades of marriage he had been selfish, insensitive, and incapable of tenderness. She went further:

> It is necessary for the safety and repose of one's soul to have been heartily in love, and with whom, but with one's husband? I allow for all *contretemps* and disappointments; spite of them all, there remain the embers of the *sacred fire* which the breath of misfortune, illness, or a thousand accidents can always wake into fresh life.

She even made the extraordinary assertion that in spite of everything that had occurred, her marriage had been worthwhile: 'Much as I have suffered and still suffer from what is called adversity, were I to begin again, I should choose the same lot.'

Late in 1859 the whole tenor of Sarah's life changed. John developed acute bronchitis and after seven weeks of illness, on December 17, 1859, left her a widow. As ever, she dramatized her feelings. Experiencing 'convulsions of sorrow' and wallowing in grief, she felt as if she had 'lost more than half herself.' She made a shrine of his study—everything remained as he had left it—and she used the widest black-bordered paper for her letters, the ultimate in Victorian mourning stationery. Harriet Grote ridiculed her demonstrative mourning, calling her Artemesia, after the widow renowned in ancient Greece for mixing her husband's ashes in her daily drink. Guilt seemed to drive her: 'I think it is not possible for grief and desolation to be deeper and more settled than mine.'

She now reshaped the past. Suppressing memories of the conjugal desolation that had helped breed her fantasy with Hermann, she insisted that

> every link in our early love had been rivetted by common adversity and suffering, by mutual cares and services, by profound humble reverence on my part, and tender indulgent approbation on his—lastly by a community of thought and feeling more rare than all the rest, and enjoyed in an almost unbroken tête à tête for years. You may understand that the void is *entire* and incurable.

There were those, however, whose memory of John Austin was unclouded by a need to gloss over the past. Harriet Grote, having witnessed Sarah's suffering in her marriage, recalled John as a brilliant misfit—as one obsessed with 'indecisive, morbid, fastidious contemplations,' and when Sarah made some reference to his career, she wondered whether 'such a drifting, floating, existence can be so called.' Though scornful about him, for Sarah, Mrs. Grote felt genuine sympathy, alloyed with considerable insight. 'Poor Sarah [she told Richard Monckton Milnes] is once more free. "The Philosopher" having succumbed, on Saty. last, to the inevitable fate—you will see that she will miss her *fardel* [burden] as much as tho' it were a *pleasure* lost to her—we women have the talent of turning sacrifices into enjoyments. Lucky it is so, for we do not get much of any positive sort.'

It was a prophetic statement. Far from seizing her independence, Sarah clung to her burden by continuing the quest for the recognition she had always wanted for her husband. In her eyes he had been destined to leave a legacy of work that would illuminate a path for others, and she was as convinced as ever that his University of London lectures on jurisprudence would do just that. From the start she had aimed to be the partner of a man who accomplished significant work and had made sacrifices and suffered deprivations to enable him to do this. But his refusal to publish his lectures—like his lack of success as author, barrister, university lecturer, and government official—undermined the assumptions of her life and threatened to render it meaningless. To avoid this consequence, she now set to work.

Where John Austin had declined to publish, Sarah did not hesitate. Publication—and a successful reception—of his lectures on jurisprudence became her intense preoccupation. Years earlier John Neal recognized that she was 'both adventurous and ambitious,' and now, a year after her husband's death, she displayed these qualities as she renewed her longstanding '*wifely* ambitions.' 'Yet you see,' she explained, 'now when he is in his grave, *that* survives or rather *re*vives, and my young ambition was not more fervent than that which is now the sole unextinguished passion of my old age.' First she negotiated the reprinting of Austin's first book which as a result of her initiative had been published in 1832; then she turned to editing her husband's papers to create a more comprehensive work that would be 'an inestimable gift to posterity.' Her determination to rescue John from oblivion was never greater. 'What labours, what hopes, and schemes of usefulness! All frustrated and void! I hope however to be able to shew more clearly than has yet been done what an inappreciable treasure the country had which could not find an asylum or a pittance to enable him to work for its good.' Apart from preserving the treasure, she would exonerate her husband from the suspicion that indolence had kept him from writing the book that had been his life's work. This project, she explained, 'gives an interest to life I could find nowhere else . . . I am never weary of it, for I see in a future (so remote that I *can* see it only with the eye of faith) my husband's fame and usefulness increasing with every page I finish.' Her faith—it was really a mission—kept her going: it was 'the sole gleam of light in my darkness. It is this which enables me to bear solitude and keeps me from utter despondency.'

Her success was greater than she dreamed possible. The book had an uninviting title—*Lectures on Jurisprudence*—but it enjoyed surprising sales and influence soon after publication: 'The reception given to my book, the honour done to my revered husband's memory, exceed all my hopes.' It went into a second edition before she died (and five others before another twenty years passed). She had helped create 'a really great work,' which in fact became a landmark in legal literature and a statement of what is still known as the Austinian theory of law. Her sense of satisfaction was boundless: 'My dear husband's fame and authority are constantly rising.' She claimed that 'his most earnest and constant desire—to be of use to his country—had been accomplished.' Of course that desire was hers far more than her husband's, as she acknowledged in saying that fame and even usefulness had been 'so long and ardently coveted *for* him.' By gaining recognition for him she established his importance and confirmed that her difficult life had not been lived in vain.

As Sarah grew older, the dread that her letters to Hermann might surface gradually diminished. Perhaps she was reassured by Goethe's observation about Pückler: 'His experience of the world enables him to terminate any little *affaires du coeur* without violence or indecorum.' The letters remained locked in his desk drawer, and in this instance he acted with that underlying good nature she had always attributed to him. She heard about him from his friend Varnhagen in 1857 (the letter has not survived), and in a reply that gives no hint of special interest she asked to be remembered to him 'with all the cordiality of an old friend—if he will allow me to say so.' After this it was not clear if she even knew that he was still alive: in fact, he survived her by four years, dying at age eighty-six in 1871.

In the last decade of her life Sarah seems to have laid to rest the specter of the letters, but it was a challenge to reconcile them with her conscience and her image of herself as the devoted wife. She now judged her former self as having been imprudent rather than immoral. 'We all do foolish and wrong things,' she told a friend, 'at least I *do*, but I hope I am not a bad woman in the main.' Wrongdoing, she now claimed, was a matter of conduct, and she had, after all, stopped short of action; she had broken the spirit, not the letter, of her marriage vow. 'A woman's heart is best revealed in her life,' she declared, and by this standard she was not culpable. She was 'not a bad woman in the main.'

Sarah's friend François Guizot helped her reach some reconciliation with the past. She first met Guizot, then ambassador in London, in 1840; later, she and John lived in Paris while Guizot was the beleaguered prime minister of France, and they became friends. After his downfall in the revolution of 1848, a correspondence developed between them, Sarah once again exchanging letters with a foreigner who provided the affection, intimacy, and emotional sustenance that were meager in her marriage. They corresponded about politics and family affairs for another seventeen years, until Sarah's death. Guizot's sensitivity to women, his own melancholy history, his stoic example in face of political defeat and personal tragedy made him an ideal comforter, and she turned to him for 'solace of the soul,' especially with regard to her role as wife. After Austin's death he asserted, 'one must absolutely possess, entirely to oneself, a human creature, and belong exclusively to her (or him). This is the power of marriage, even for those who meet with many imperfections.' In the same spirit, he also assured her that 'Austin must have been proud to have inspired in a soul such as yours a tenderness so profound, so respectful, so enduring.' His reconciling approach led Sarah to say, 'you are one of the persons to whom morally and intellectually I owe the most.' Guizot, after all, offered her assurance that her marriage had been worthwhile and that she had been an exemplary wife.

In old age she became determined more than ever to affirm her image as the conventional model wife. She ascended the pedestal of Victorian wifehood and played and overplayed the loyal and submissive part so emphatically that, to one who knew her well, it seemed her life was 'enfolded in his.' This was reflected in the epitaph she composed for herself in preparation for her own death. She had it inscribed on her half of the tombstone she and John would share. It read (in Latin): 'Sarah, who in her bereavement had placed this monument to her much lamented husband John Austin, after painfully surviving him for 8 years, at last gladly rests beneath the same stone.'

Her enchantment with the German romantics, who had sought to loosen conventional bonds, especially those of marriage, had to be revised to fit her role as the dutiful wife. She now admired domestic virtues in women and wrote about their most sacred duties as wives and mothers. Even Goethe, her 'Abgott' [near God] in the 1830s, was censured (and by implication his disciple Pückler) for having cast doubt on so many societal arrangements. The 'dear Original' who had assaulted bourgeois assumptions was utterly demoted. The general rules of society had to be enforced or everyone might claim the right to deviate from them.

A thousand pretenders to originality ... would arise; and what a *débordement* [an overflowing] of folly, conceit and nonsense would take place, were there no inconvenience attached to singularity, and to the breach of general rules!—What arrogant claims to indulgence! What sacrifice of the general good to the vanity or the caprice, self-indulgence of individuals! I have therefore not much sympathy with the distresses of this sort of *Non-conformists*, and find more grandeur in the submission of extraordinary persons to ordinary rules.

Having begun in rebellion against Victorian morality, she eventually became its ardent defender.

In spite of establishing herself as a model wife and winning fame for her husband, Sarah's last years were shadowed by grief. Lucie, her 'main prop,' was so severely afflicted with tuberculosis that she had to leave husband and children in England while she sought gentler climates, first in South Africa in 1861, and a year later in Egypt, at Luxor, where she spent the last seven years of her life. A supremely intelligent and adventurous traveler, she even encountered a sign of the ubiquitous Pückler. He had left a mark on

Egypt thirty years earlier while on those travels that left
Sarah to her nervous collapse at Boulogne. Lucie discovered
his graffiti while visiting ancient monuments. 'The scribbling of names is quite infamous—beautiful painting is
defaced by Tomkins and Hobson—but worst of all Pückler
Muskau has engraved his, and his *Ordenskreuz*! [an insignia
of his rank] in huge letters and size on the naked breast of
that august and pathetic giant who sits at Abu. Simbel. I
wish some one wd kick him for his profanity.'

Tragic as Lucie's illness was, there was nothing gloomy
about her letters, which provided excellent material for a
book. She had an anthropologist's eye and shared her
mother's unusual capacity for sympathy with and understanding of non-Europeans. She sent home descriptions of
a 'remote and almost fabulous' way of life that had survived
for centuries on the edge of the Nile but which, she realized,
would soon disappear. Lucie's *Letters from Egypt*—really
extracts from her letters—was edited by Sarah and published in 1865. Three editions were printed that year and
many more after. It was the nineteenth book that Sarah was
associated with either as author, translator, or editor.

As Lucie's condition worsened, Sarah was racked by
'constant anxiety for my dearest daughter, and my longing
for the darling children [Lucie's] fill my mind and render
it incapable of other thoughts. I try to read, and in the midst
my heart's treasure stands before me, and one question
follows another in my restless mind.' While awaiting news
during the long intervals between letters she helplessly visu-
alized Lucie's suffering. Lucie tried to spare her mother but
did not entirely conceal the inevitable symptoms—the
coughing, fever, palpitations, gasping for breath, noises in
the chest which disturbed sleep, and the inevitable blood-

spitting. Mother and daughter arranged what each knew would be their last meeting. In mid-1865, though both were extremely ill, they met in the Alpine village of Soden, as Lucie was forbidden to visit her native country, with its damp climate. After returning to Luxor, Lucie wrote to Sarah about the possibility that 'I die first, which I hope for your sake, dearest Mütter, I shall not. That sounds a strange sort of wish, but *you* know why I say so well enough.' The minor irritations between them dissolved as these two independent and remarkable women courageously faced death.

The corroding anxiety about Lucie did not help Sarah's own health—an amalgam of heart and kidney troubles, gout and obesity. She had suffered recurrent heart pains since 1845 and grew worse in the 1850s, but she did not let them keep her from life's work. 'When my heart seems as if it would stop altogether,' she explained, '*I* stop, and by dint of ether, ammonia, etc. give it a spur.' On top of her chronic illnesses, she injured her arm and hand in a serious fall, making it difficult and painful for her to write. She who had the light, energetic step now could no longer get around, but resourceful as ever, she had herself pulled about in a pony chaise. The end, she knew, would come suddenly and soon, but she displayed her old contempt for death. In 1864 she made a last journey to Paris, where she was overtaken by illness, and a year later, returning from that sorrowful meeting with Lucie at Soden, she could say, 'I am so entirely stupefied by sickness and sorrow . . . that I have no spirit to do anything.' Yet in spite of her complaints about illness and 'settled gloom,' she continued to assert opinions. In November 1866, less than a year before she died, she felt such keen excitement about English approval for the expanding German state—Prussomania, she called it—that she sent articles to newspapers protesting the swallowing up of Bohemia and Saxony by Prussia. Toward the end, with her own family out of reach, she took a maternal interest in her servant's children. She took in her cook's nine-year-old daughter, and when her young gardener, also living under her roof, had a third child, she looked forward to more. 'As there are no limits to English productiveness, I expect if I live, to have a swarm. But all this gives a feeling of *belongingness*.'

She did not live to see the swarm, for her daughter's wish was granted: Lucie survived her mother, but only by two years. Sarah died on August 8, 1867, at age seventy-four. There was the inevitable sorting and distribution of property, and Lucie asked for Sarah's old watch—probably the one that a rejected suitor had thrown into her carriage following the wedding ceremony—and for the 'locket she always wore with Da's hair in it.' Presumably Lucie had no idea that the hair in the locket just might have been Hermann's.

Lucie evidently entertained no suspicions*—but what about John Austin? Apparently he died unaware that there had been more to Sarah's correspondence with Pückler than those innocent passages that Sarah read aloud to him. And

---

*According to Gordon Waterfield, Lucie's great-grandson, 'she had no idea at that time [in the early 1830s] that [Sarah] was in love with [Pückler].' *Lucie Duff Gordon in England, South Africa and Egypt* (New York, 1937), 59. The phrase 'at that time' seems to imply that at a later date Lucie did know, but no evidence in support of this was presented. Of course, one can speculate about the possibility that before her death Sarah, recognizing that her letters to Pückler could surface after she was gone, confided to Lucie about them. While this is conceivable, there is no evidence to suggest that it happened.

yet one cannot be certain. We know that early in their correspondence he objected to Pückler's portrait in the sitting room, and he certainly knew about gifts from Hermann and about Sarah's extensive purchases for the prince, since some of them were packed in their house. When writing from Malta imploring Pückler to write prudently or not at all, Sarah said, 'It is true that he knows that I have never known you [i.e., have had a meeting with you],' but she added that her husband had some ideas that would make a meeting between them especially difficult. She also mentioned to Hermann that she and John had a frank discussion which placed their marriage on a new footing. One can only speculate whether Pückler's name had come up during that discussion.

Yet much argues against carrying such speculation very far. If John objected to the portrait because he suspected that his wife was exchanging love letters with Hermann, she would not have merely moved the portrait to her dressing room; there would have been a blow-up that Sarah would have described to Pückler; and then the flow of letters would have stopped. We may also conclude that the orgy of shopping is not likely to have aroused John's suspicion, for Sarah was constantly rendering a whole range of services to foreign friends. Whatever discussion John and Sarah had, there is no evidence that John knew about the real character of Sarah's relationship with Hermann. From Malta Sarah pleaded with Pückler to be cautious, pointing to the risks she faced, but this was language that would not have been used if the feared consequences had already fallen. Finally, if she thought her husband was suspicious, she would not have met Hermann and exchanged polite letters with him in Berlin during the winter of 1842–43.

Sarah escaped the shame and scandal that would have come with exposure, but the episode with Hermann left her with somber reflections about the demands of sexual passion and the constraints of marriage. As much as she ostentatiously played the part of the dutiful wife, she did not depreciate the powerful passions that led to her love for Hermann. Some women, she said, had 'omitted in their calculations *one female* item, *sex* and all that it brings with it,' and failed to understand 'the unconquerable force of the physical relations of women.' Having been swept up by such a force, she acknowledged its reality, but she also accepted that society would insist on its control. Here was a conflict between passion and the restraints imposed by society. In a happy marriage the conflict could be resolved. But Sarah's observation and, above all, her own experience of marriage made her aware that this was not always the case, and thus she thought that, 'Of all the problems which society seeks in vain to solve, the most difficult by far are those which regard the relations between the sexes.' This, for her, was an insoluble problem. 'There was (and when and where has there *not* been?) so much to condemn and to deplore, so much of injustice and falsehood, of corrupting license and corrupting restraint.' Each alternative had a sad cost. She had been tempted by, but had narrowly avoided, 'corrupting license' and was left with 'corrupting restraint,' which, she acknowledged, left a gap that she longed to fill. Neither alternative was satisfactory, she concluded, and for her this became one of the 'unfathomed sources of the most poignant sorrows of human life!'

APPENDIX

The appendix includes seven of the eighty-two letters and fragments from Sarah Austin to Hermann Pückler-Muskau in the Varnhagen Collection at Cracow. Sarah Austin's first surviving letter is dated November 9, 1831, but there were a few earlier ones. Most of the correspondence dates from 1832 and 1833; it becomes sporadic from 1834 to 1837; and from then onward there are only four more letters, written in the early 1840s.

Before this you have my letter. I shall have your sitting room engraved too. Send me more. Baron Bülow[1] is as fischblutig [cold-blooded] as any English lord and very stupid. It was base in him to insinuate that the English *public* was hostile to you. You know it is wholly untrue, and that the hostility was nearly confined to the tools of the aristocracy. As to any steps to be now taken, all I wait for is opportunity. Nothing is so bad as an inopportune appeal to the public. I want therefore to *get up* an occasion of speaking of you again in print. The little account of Muskau will afford one, but that must not be published yet because nobody will listen to anything but Reform,[2] and because as soon as the *dead* time is past, and the General Election over, *we* shall come out again and then I will take care that all these proceedings and their causes shall be set in their true light. Meantime I intend from time to time to send any little notices I can to the Examiner and the Spectator so as to keep your name before the public, as living and active. I shall send the passage descriptive of Göthe's death[3] as *from you to me*. Also perhaps, if I may, your report of Leopold Schefer's[4] opinions which delight me. Your charming account of the terms you are upon with your labourers, which does you much honour, and is such a severe rebuke to our haughty nobles I should like to give. May I? Send me any little bits that cost you no trouble, characteristic of the manners and condition of your people. Put into them your own acuteness of

---

[1]Heinrich von Bülow (1792–1846), Prussian statesman, ambassador in London at this time.

[2]The Reform Act had recently passed.

[3]On March 22, 1832.

[4]Leopold Schefer (1784–1862), author, composer, traveler, administrator of Pückler's estates since 1813.

observation, and your own noble generous heart. Be your own interpreter and defender. All the best hearts and heads of England will understand and appreciate you. Or if you could write something longer? An essay on any subject for a Magazine. What think you of a paper on Göthe, or on any one of his works? Or an account of any new book, actor, opera? But do nothing unless you feel a *Beruf* [calling] to do it. I showed John Romilly[5] the print of your castle. He said, *that* to English minds contained evidence of all the talents and all the virtues. I expect him to dinner today to meet a very agreeable American, Dr. Macauley of Baltimore.[6] I wish you could see a book which has lately been published and hailed with enthusiasm by the same people who detest yours—called *The Domestic Manners of the Americans*.[7] It is by a woman and full of the vilest mis-representations. On Friday I went to the German opera in company with this same *Yankee*, who is nearly as enthusiastic an admirer of the Germans as I. He is just returned from the continent. He says 'We and the French talk about democracy and republicanism but the true republican feeling pervading intercourses of society exists nowhere but in Germany.' Tell me what is said at Berlin of our three days?[8] Were they not sublime? A people excited to the highest possible degree, *absolutely without a government*—congregating by hundreds of thousands and not a window broken—not a creature injured, not a law violated. The meeting of the 3 great parishes of Marylebone, St. Pancras and Paddington took place near my house, and it was a grand sight,—for hours one unceas-

---

[5]John Romilly (1802–1874), member of parliament for Bridport at this time, later solicitor general, attorney general, and master of the rolls.

[6]Dr. Patrick Macauley.

[7]Published in 1832; by Frances Trollope (1780–1863).

[8]An allusion to the July [1830] revolution in Paris; some regarded the impasse in London over the Reform Bill in May 1832 as comparable to the event in France.

ing tide of men, cheerful, quiet and resolute. Your friend the Queen has played a disastrous game. She can never recover it. I pity her for I have no doubt her English advisers are the causes of it. Lord Munster[9] and his sister Lady Sophia Sidney are also done for. What idiots, not to see that their only means of gratifying their rapacity and ambition was through the popularity of their father whom the people would have indulged in his schemes for his bastards to almost any amount had he continued true to them. It was their interest to be ultra reformers instead of affecting the claims of high birth. So much the better for our pockets! They will get no more. The Duke of Wellington[10] is not only *crotté* [filthy] but *dans la boue* [stuck in the mud], and the Tories, as a party, destroyed. Out of all this what will come? I know not. I am not so sanguine as my Radical friends. The commercial plague-spot is, in my mind, the greatest of our evils, and one which no form of government will change.

By the bye, pray do not mention to anyone the idea I spoke of in my last letter—of our coming to seek employment at Berlin. My husband and I had a long conversation about it last night. He wishes it *more and more*, but as he says, it would never do to announce any such project. We have, as I think I told you, £200 a year, which his father gives him and £100 a year which my father left me—an equal share with his six other children. On this we could live at Berlin I know, better than on our present £500 here. What I want him to do is to give up the thankless task of instructing a people who have no desire for profound instruction, who regard knowledge merely as *stock in trade*, and to go to live among men by whom I am confident he would be

---

[9]George Augustus Frederick Fitzclarence, first earl of Munster (1794–1842), major general, orientalist, author of works on Asiatic subjects and military history.

[10]Arthur Wellesley, duke of Wellington (1769–1852), field marshall, hero of Waterloo, prime minister 1828–1830.

appreciated. His fear is, however, and I cannot say it is groundless, that his father would not consent to his going to live in what he would call *idleness*, i.e., absence of lucrative employment; and that it would be necessary to hold out to him the prospect of some sort of advantage beyond that of tranquillity and a congenial people. You cannot imagine the depth and force of his mind, the *sincerity* of his acquirements, his lofty indifference to present fame and gain, and his equally lofty confidence that he could, if favourably placed, labour efficiently at the great work of constructing a complete System of Law. He says the Prussian government is the only one capable of appreciating such a work or such a man,—that he wishes to live under it, that he has no political opinions which wd make it disagreeable to him to do so—since he has no confidence in popular government in the actual state of the popular mind. Now my friend, be quite candid with me.

Lay aside all your Mephistopheles nature and do not think I am labouring to gratify my own desires under the mask of consulting my husband's interests. I advised him to remain in Germany when we were there 4 years ago. I have never ceased to tell him it was the country for him, and I should [have] equally persuaded him to go to Berlin if you did not exist. That some selfish feelings creep in I do not deny, but never, never could I be base enough to counsel him to his disadvantage.

You would like to have me near you—that I cannot doubt—but yet be sincere and if such ideas are quite wild, tell me so at once.

I have had a letter from Fr. von Kottwitz[11]— She is no friend or admirer of you, dearest; but take care how you betray me. I will tell you honestly that I asked her some questions about you, which she has answered. She says 'je compte sur votre discretion' [I count on your discretion], and I feel that she has reason to complain of my abuse of her confidence; but I wish you to *know*

---

[11]See pages 141–44 and 148–53.

her as she is going to Muskau and you will talk to her of me. Be very polite and very cautious. I know not how she will speak of me. I think she is angry that you did, as you say, 'overlook her dans la foule [in the crowd].' She wants to send me a packet and begs me to ask you to offer to convey it. Do as you like. She writes to me with the *fondest* expressions of attachment. I do not feel certain how much of it is real. At all events, she is not a person to whom I should choose to entrust myself. She presses me very warmly to visit her. Oh that I could. I have told you nothing of my health. It is better but still very feeble. I am going on Tuesday to a cottage one of my Brothers has at Cheshunt in Hertfordshire and shall stay a week. Lucy goes with me of course. I hope to return better—[?]¹²

A thousand thanks for the lock of hair and for having it enclosed in such a manner that my lips can touch it. I am however afraid to wear the medallion. My child and I have had no separate existence.— She has been always with me and sees all I do and all I wear. I would neither conceal it from her nor lie to her (*you* don't like the word—*I* hate glosses and palterings with what one means). I must have the hair put into some concealed place where I may wear it invisible to all eyes but mine. I can wear the medallion as your gift or at least keep it—may I not? The ring I wear constantly, and ever shall. 'Tis very pretty. I only wish it were plainer.

Have you recd my old shoe? What a gift! Dear love, du schwärmest [you gush] like a boy of 18— How I love you for it. Happy, happy you who can indulge such fantastic visions. I sit down wearied in body and in spirit and can hardly find energy to write to you. He is ill in bed in a high fever—such as, poor pitou [dear] often attacks him— This almost invariably happens if I have any little scheme of recreation in prospect. I have just written to my Brother to bid him not expect me.

---

¹²Three words here are illegible.

This is a specimen of my whole life. And it comes after a day of indefatigable labour on the proof sheets of a little book I am publishing.[13] It is the work of my early days—a selection of all the noble poetry, religion and morality which is to be found in the Old Testament mixed with such terrible and disgusting alloy. It is arranged under heads. I did it in the house of my dearest Father, who *was* a Christian such as *you*, dear, would have acknowledged. I have been prevailed on to publish it and you shall have it of course. It is very tedious in the detail of the press, but I must get through it now.

At the same time I have in hand for my friend Romilly *a history of Prussian Law Reform* from the commencement, including all the details of the formation of the Allgemeines Landrecht [public law] and a wonderful, glorious letter of your immortal Frederic [sic] to his Chancellor von Carmer.[14] I shall take occasion to expose the ignorance and folly of Lord Dover[15] (Honble. Agar Ellis when you were here) who has presumed to lay his dilettante hands on the life of that august man. Now, caro, take the field under my orders—see if you can help me. I am to make two papers for the Jurist, a periodical work. That done I go to Göthe and Schiller, which is already announced in the newspapers and all the world is *ravi* [delighted] that pretty Mrs. Austin is going to employ her '*exquisite talent*,' as one Magazine of this month says, on those great men. Pretty Mrs. Austin had rather be playing the fool[?][16] at Muskau with a certain other great child. But I must make a virtue of necessity wear my laurels as if I thought them worth caring. This bête [fool] public won't understand one word in ten of Göthe and Schiller when I have

---

[13]*Selections from the Old Testament* (London, 1833).

[14]Johann Heinrich Casimir von Carmer (1720–1801).

[15]George James Ellis (1797–1833), created Lord Dover, 1831, member of parliament, 1818–1831, patron of the arts, author, editor.

[16]One word here is illegible.

done it. Je me donnerai au moins la jouissance [I will at least give myself the pleasure] of telling them so—sordid, manufacturing creatures. Mes hommages to M. Schefer. Tell him our souls are in cotton and steam. Oh Cielo, I was near forgetting a [?].[17] My friend Victor Cousin[18] writes me from Paris, 'J'ai vu votre Original le P.P.M. [Prince Pückler Muskau] l'autre été à Berlin, et en effet c'est un original très amiable.' Juges si celà me plait. [I have seen your original P.P.M. in the summer at Berlin; indeed he is original and very pleasant. You can imagine whether this pleases me.] You are quite mistaken beloved, if you think I don't like you to write in English. I repeat I doat on your English and it is only *fear* that makes me prefer the German character. I *can* write to more. I shall fall off my chair. 'Oh Jupiter how weary are my spirits!' One moments rest for my head on that dear shoulder—one kind look from the blue eye, one long soft kiss, and I should forget it all. Goodnight I sleep alone tonight and will wear your hair and kiss that. Tuesday morng. This is courier day. I must leave you. I work in my little garden and fancy myself employed like my own distant one. Strange, strange how I love you. How sure I am that we should pass blessed hours together. Farewell coeur de mon coeur. Be happy and love me as much as you can without injury to your happiness. Above all be most kind and gentle to that woman or I cannot love you. It seems to me that her attachment to you binds me to her. Here is a long kiss for you.[19]

Your S——

---

[17]One word here is illegible.

[18]Victor Cousin (1792–1867), author of histories of philosophy and of the Report on Prussian education which Sarah Austin translated into English.

[19]She drew a circle here to represent a kiss.

Yesterday Geliebter [beloved] brought me your dear letter and I have this instant after thousand interruptions accomplished the reading of it all. Don't regret this for me, love. I tell you again it is delicious to hang for hours over your letters, and to catch the 'thoughts that breathe and words that burn,'[1] one by one. But before I proceed to answer all that is sweet and dear in your letter or to tell you any thing of myself, I must vider mon coeur [empty my heart] about one part, which has deeply wounded me. Were I an ordinary woman, pleased with the customary flatteries of men, or subject to the ungenerous vanity of women, you could not have laid a more acceptable tribute at my feet than the quotations from the letters of your poor friend. But you ought to know me better. You saw, or I tried to make you understand, that even in translating, my scruples and omissions arose not from servile fear, but from a constant recurrence to the thought of others' pain; let me say so from a kind and loyal heart. You know that I told you that if any other woman had claims upon you, I could not accept what was stolen from her. This unhappy one's claims on you are not exactly of the kind I meant, but what then? they are better than mine. Her grief rends my heart. I see and feel her desolation. I hate myself and almost you, as the causes. Remember that disloyalty to women—above all to a loving woman—is a crime in my eyes of atrocious cruelty and of despicable baseness, and that had you sent me her letter or told me her name, I should never have answered your letter at all. And for what, Hermann, would you expose the wounds of a bleeding heart ? That I may see how a pretty woman loves you? Do you think I am a person to love from imitation, or that the taste of other women, were they queens of beauty and fashion,

---

[1]Thomas Gray, *Elegy Written in a Country Churchyard* (1750).

would influence mine? Do you think me capable of the meanness of weak women, of triumphing in a conquest, torn from another? God is my witness, my only impulse on reading her expressions was grief, remorse and the deepest sympathies. I shed tears for her and wished only to console her. My life—since my marriage—has been one of labour, anxiety and constant self denial and self control—*you* cannot ever conceive of this.—You will call me cold and reasonable. I am not so, but I have been disciplined to forget myself, and not even passion can make me unmindful of the sufferings of others. You, my Prince, have had a different training, and are more wilful. I do not blame you, nor extol myself, but I should ill deserve to be your friend, your petite femme, your Ambassador,—to lay my head on your shoulder, and to have *your* head in my bosom, if I did not tell you when I think you wrong. Your apology, of a sort of Necessity, dearest, is an apology for every thing. However your confidence in me is not misplaced. The frailties of any woman would be safe with me, and her sorrows sacred. I have no English rigour on that subject. Not that I do not think all violation of promises and vows, wrong—nay criminal—but those given in our marriages are so impracticable of observance, that what *man* does observe them? Like all overstrained attempts at compelling virtue it defeats itself. This institution (of which au reste I am an ardent admirer) wants entire remodelling. Is not neglect, unkindness, indifference as much a violation of the vow as infidelity? Can a man be said to 'love and to cherish' a woman for whose comfort, advantage, happiness, he shews not the least solicitude, and whose devoted efforts to please him he receives with sullen apathy, or worse? Yet this, or corresponding conduct on the part of a woman, is *censé* [accounted] no infraction of the treaty!

Depend upon it, Liebling, I want no corroboratives to make me love you. It is yourself and no other person who will persuade me that you are loveable.

For a long while after I read your letter I sat in a kind of melancholy dream, comparing the life you describe with that which is actually mine. And yet what should I be were I with you? The two things that have strengthened me to bear a weary life—self esteem and the esteem of others—gone. Self esteem, not because I chose to live with you and devote myself to your happiness without asking the world's leave, but because I could prefer *any thing* to my child's welfare. As to the esteem of others, as I have told you, I owe *all* the consideration I enjoy (and it is not little) to *myself*, and perhaps that makes me feel the value of it. Nobody would feel more keenly contempt *which I could not retort*. But I need not preach and speculate. Oceans divide us, my heart, and I can but dream about you.

Now for the proposition you make to me as to the *manner* of our meeting;—if ever we meet; you know not half I could dare, or half I could imagine, for the man I love. I *have thought and felt it all. It should be as you wish*. I want not to act any reserves or scruples. If I love you at all I love you entirely. Besides you are right. I could not look on a face I never saw and say, *that is mine*, though it seems to me I could wake in your arms and feel that I was at home. All these preliminaries are however needless. We cannot meet—at least not of years—and years will change us sadly, in one way or another. This summer it is decreed that we all go to Polvellan in Cornwall—the place whence I wrote you my first mad letters—so gaily! We shall go and return together. So no hope of Bonn for this year. Another *perhaps*, and only perhaps, and even then I may be so surrounded as to make our meeting impossible; for I take for granted you would not choose to see me always in the presence of others. *I* could not bear that.

I am almost sorry to hear of your *Sehnsucht* [longing] and begin to wish you did not love me so much. I would not cost you one uneasy thought, love. Ne te montes pas la tête [Don't let it go to your head]. You would very likely be disappointed in me,—you who have had so much beauty and talent and *agrément* [pleasure]. Your fancy is herrlich [wonderful] and I love you for it and did from the first. I would *fantasiren* with you to the limits of possibility, and beyond. I would humour you in your wildest vagaries and desires,—but do not let it trouble your repose. Tu te possèdes—c'est bien mon ami—tiens toi bien en ta possession—je ne desire pas usurper. Mon amour est beaucoup plus tendre qu'exigeant. [You are in command of yourself—that's good my friend—keep in command—I do not wish to usurp. My love is far more tender than demanding.] All I ask is that yours may be the same but you will tell me that is not in man's nature. Alas, do I not know it? I must go. Good night. I kiss your hair and your portrait.

I received your packet last night through the hands of le petit Chancellier[1] who drank tea with me. We quarrelled a little about Prussian politics but parted good friends. I find he sent my last letter and parcel by Count Poten to Hamburg, which I didn't like, indeed, on the well known dishonesty of Diplomates about letters I am in a constant fright about ours, dearest, more especially in these troubled times.

Thank you most tenderly for the books, the bracelets, the extremely elegant collier de l'ordre de quoi? de St. Hermann? de l'amour? de tout ce que vous voulez—ce que vous voulez? traitre c'est que je porte tes fers. Eh bien, je les porterai, mais gare—car si tu me rends esclave je crois en conscience que j'en [*sic*] serai des plus [soutiens?], quelquefois, quelquefois aussi oh des plus soumises, des plus empresseés devouées. Mais ———— [elegant chain of the order of what?—of St. Hermann? of love?—of anything you wish—what do you wish? villain, that I should carry your chains. Oh well, I will carry them, but take care, for if you enslave me, I think I shall be the most [supportive?], sometimes, and sometimes also the most submissive, the most fervent [and] devoted. But————]

Sunday July 29. I had begun this letter, dear, as you see with the hope of sending it off last Tuesday. *That* I found to be impossible and as I had heard from Wagner[2] that they now send only one courier in a week (on Tuesdays) I was obliged to defer writing. I am glad I was, for I can now answer your beloved letter which arrived today.

My dearest friend, whom unknown I have so admired, loved

---

[1]Pückler's way of describing his agent in London.

[2]Johann Emil von Wagner, born 1805, diplomat, and Pückler's agent in London at this time.

and trusted, for whom I feel that few would do so much as I who shall probably never behold your face—if I have given you pain, forgive me. I read your letter with commissione di [more?] [sense of condemnation] and a sort of penitent tender self-reproach. And yet I ought not to reproach myself for it was natural and indeed just that I should feel as I did. In the first place—but you know me not—you cannot know me—I who have borne up bravely against a world of misery that would have crushed and extinguished half a dozen ordinary women, who am regarded by the wisest and the best that England contains as the stay and support of my husband and as a person really worthy of all reverence—pardon if I am too proud to bear to be considered as the mere mistress of any man. I would not be that to Alexander the Great or Caesar if *they* regarded me as no more. I would exchange equal love and equal respect but I would be the mere minister of no man's pleasures. And yet if you knew what rapture it would be to me to minister *in any way* to the pleasures of a man who loved me as I desire and deserve. All that you can imagine and more I would do—but then—I must see *distinctly* that I was not valued for that alone, and I must feel that spite of it all I was treated as if I were a vestal and a queen, when I chose.

But apart my pride, think sweetest and dearest of my position, ground to death worn down with care and sorrow, all the animal part of me mortified more than with weeks of fasting and [?][3] *Could* I summon up images of joy and volupté, even *with you*? No dearest, I thought of you, as ever, but it was of the comfort of seeing your face, of hearing a kind voice;—of a walk in the evening to refresh myself in the calm and beneficient air;—of tears poured out in your bosom;—and, at most, of sleep on your shoulder or in your arms. Hermann, dearest, you have never loved one like me in character or in circumstances. Measure no one against me—nor me against any one. Mine was no marriage

---

[3]One word here is illegible.

of *convenience* but of passionate love and religious devotion. The first has been dead for years—*he would have it so*, or it would have been eternal—*the latter remains*. To die for him were as light to me as to go to sleep. This feeling can never change, nor while he lives, could any thing on earth induce or force me to live away from him—*not even his own unkindness*—for I know that he could not live without me. I am certain of it. Therefore your poor Victoire[4] was very differently circumstanced. Perhaps she could love you more. I know not, but this I know, that what might, in me, all turn to the fervour of passion had I such a husband as hers, is now perhaps half consumed in deep, solemn compassion and enthusiastic devotion to a man I revere and have sworn to God and myself—never to forsake—never—for he is unhappy and unloving, uncomforting; nobody but I can know him, though all revere his probity and his intellect.

Make yourself no more chimeras of Chancelliers. I am sorry I used the word since it has led you so astray. John Romilly![5] —oh dearest, you need fear no lovers in my *entourage* of young men. They are Mr. A's friends. Would to Heaven you could see and hear them speak with me or of me. John Romilly has a true and deep regard for me—for us—but he would as soon think of making love to the planet Venus. So of many others. Indeed I think no woman was ever so happy in *friends*. There are at *least* half a dozen men to whom I *would* trust myself, my child, every thing—*certain* that not by look or word would they ever ask for any return for all their kindness but what a sister might grant. Am I not rich? The two Romillys (Edwd[6] is married) are among these and are as much Mr. A's friends as mine. *John is delicacy and honour in person*. I called him your true Chancellier because he

4See pages 159–160.

5See page 239, note 5.

6Edward Romilly (1804–1870), member of parliament 1832–1835, 1837–1866.

takes such a lively interest in your affairs—more than little Wagner. I am free (I mean *franche* [natural] not *libre* [loose]) in my manners—cordial nay affectionate—to a fault, but I am not coquettish and they understand me, as I am. Mets ton coeur en paix [have no fear] as for that. I plead guilty—if guilt it be, to the half Italian nature which you say the little moustaches betray—but, dearest, there is no such cure for this as constant occupation of body and mind, and those small carking cares which, more than all things, destroy romance and voluptuousness. Were I a nun, God help me. I can imagine that it would go hard with me in the hours of leisure and contemplation: for religion such as I feel it softens rather than hardens the heart, and tranquillity, opportunity of thinking on oneself—one's own being, state, and affections,—as I can imagine that I should die of it, or go mad. But you who know human nature well under some aspects, you perhaps know it not on this side, how the active business, the reiterated small cares and occupations of a mistress of a family in narrow circumstances effectively divert the mind from all such thoughts and weary the body too much to leave that very importunate. I talk to you as you bid me, without reserve, for I think I may. I love you. I wish to have you for a friend. I wish to be yours. But now I am going to be still more *franche* [forthright] and on that very subject. A friend of mine who has heard me repeatedly say that I wrote to you spoke to me very seriously and earnestly the other day on the matter, imploring me as I valued my peace and reputation not in any way to commit myself to you. Not that he guessed how far I was likely to commit myself, *indeed have actually done*, nor in what way. *That* he would never suspect me of. *But* he said 'take great care what you write. Tell him nothing that you would not *print*. Tell him nothing of any body, that he can injure or hurt them or you by repeating.' He added 'I do not know him, I never saw him, but I hear of him continually in society from persons who knew him well; and I must say the universal impression he left is that though an agreeable, clever man, he is decidedly not a man to be trusted. That he is indiscreet and has no *delicatesse* about betraying to the world all he sees and hears, you yourself see and admit from his book; but more than this, I am convinced he is universally regarded as a slippery person. Again I say take care what you write.'

Now for my own preservation (supposing it to be true) all this comes too late. If I broke off all communication with you tomorrow you have more than enough, (did you think it worth your while to destroy me), to place me in a situation in which I would not live 24 hours. Don't think this is from mere solicitude about my own good *name*, though *of that* I, who have so little else in the world perhaps alone know the value—were I a Duchess I might afford to brave or disregard it. But I can imagine that there are circumstances which would induce me utterly to [contenu?] [put aside?] even that to live with a man I loved, and chose, and trusted above all the world, careless of all the world might think or say.—But never, never will I live to see my dishonour stamped upon my husband, or reflected back upon my child. Therefore, Hermann, know fully and distinctly that my life is as much in your hands as that of an eastern slave in his sovereign's; and that an indiscretion on your part—the vanity of shewing a letter, of quoting a fond sentence, might as effectually kill me, as if you poured down my throat the poison I should swallow. Cruel and treacherous, I cannot, will not, think you for an instant. On the contrary—would to God I had you here by me that with tears and fond embrace I might tell you how fully I trust to the generosity and tenderness of your heart. But tell me dearest, what does this mean? So many people have said the same thing to me—so many cautions I have received. I have, God knows, regarded them little, as you know, but they disquiet me, for as my friend said, so general and fixed an impression has always *some* ground or other. Is it *légèreté*? [frivolousness] What is it? Be candid with your *petite femme*. Examine *yourself* and trace the causes of this. N.B. that it is not only here that these things are said of you but all over Germany. A German of rank, whose name I forget, complained to the friend of a friend of mine that you had made some improper use of things he had communicated to you. This is no 'demi confidence,' for I forget the names and all the circumstances having been told of it months ago. Do not be angry with me dear for being uneasy. How can I help it? I know you only from report—your own, and that of others— facts observed by myself I have none, to set against any thing that may be said. I must be mad or stupid not to see the risks I run, nor could you, a man of sense, be flattered by such blindfold, insane [assumption of] security. Nevertheless I love you so dearly, and my nature is so frank and confiding, that I shall invent no pretexts to back out of my dangerous position. I tell you all—and I leave it to you—who love me—to reassure and comfort me. If you can trust yourself with the sacred deposit of the life and happiness of three persons each of no common value—then I will trust you. But in the name of God, Hermann—as you are a man and a gentleman—if you doubt your discretion, your self com- mand, your earnest sense of the solemnity of what I say to you—in the name of God—be frank and candid and save me save us all from peril.—Imagine me on my knees before you and with streaming eyes. Do not think all this exaggerated. Be my friend—I shall ever be yours.

As to Madame de Kottwitz[7]—since you desire it I send you her letter though I dislike doing it because it exposes her folly and want of principle. You will see what she says about her own affairs. I need not add how deeply it disgusted me—or how indignant I was at her wanting me to write to that brave honest old Rittmeister v. Laroche to suppress what he knew and I knew of her affair with Faldern. I have never answered her letter et voilà pourquoi [and that is why]. But I must, as I brought it upon myself by my foolish eagerness to hear about

---

[8]See pages 141–44 and 148–53.

you. You will see or guess what I asked her, namely, what sort of man you were? and whether it was true as I had heard that you had been married, divorced and remarried. So far as I remember this was all—I begged her to tell me all she knew or had heard. The mention of the Ladies of your family I send with great repugnance. I need not add that it made no impression on me—any more than the personal description of yourself—which I had heard enough of you from English men and women to know to be false. To caution you about secrecy and care were absurd. You extort this from me and if you abuse it . . . what can I think? What but that your enemies are kinder to you than yourself. I am ashamed to have felt the interest I did in this weak and selfish woman but she was young and unhappy. Judge me not by her, I conjure you.

I find from Wagner that a certain Mr. Meroni is a wellknown person in Berlin. If you see him he may remember me. He and his wife travelled with us from Köln to Rotterdam. He was very polite and gave me his card at parting, urging us extremely to go to Berlin and offering us all sorts of civilities. That is four years ago. But I am very little altered, if at all. I shall write to Henry[8] to hasten to Muskau—the people at Munich who are very kind to him have persuaded him not to pass the winter at Berlin but there. I have not time to discuss the matter but do, you my dear kind friend advise the poor boy. It is difficult for a widowed mother to judge.

Thank you most herzlich [heartily], liebster [dearest], for Falk.[9]— At this moment I ought to be translating it—mais tu me detournes de tout [but you distract me from everything].

---

[8]Henry Reeve (1813–1895), Sarah Austin's nephew, author, journalist, editor of the *Edinburgh Review*, 1855–1895.

[9]Johannes Daniel Falk (1768–1826), author of satires, plays, and a volume of recollections of Goethe (1832), which Sarah Austin included in her *Characteristics of Goethe* (1833).

Wilson[10] authorized me immediately to do it—'on my own terms' and I want to finish it before I go into Cornwall. I have done 20 pages. How interesting it is!

As to Landscape Gardening, all that must of course stand over till my return. We go in a week i.e., on the 7th or 8th and return the middle or end of Sept. I think it safest and best for you not to write to me thro' the Embassy while I am away—calculate so as to let a parcel arrive the 1st week in Oct. You can write by post [but] not more than *once* as it will attract notice and mind not a word of English or French except what I may read aloud. The letters arrive at Polvellan[11] at breakfast time and are laid on the table before a score of people all eager for 'news.' I know my treacherous face and the rush of blood from my heart to it, that will follow the sight of your hand. Perhaps, indeed you had better not write, unless you have some *manifestly* pressing reason. *I will write to you*, and bear the privation as I may. If you have any packet to send now, it would come to me safely enough if it came hither as usual. Our young friend John Mill[12] joins us at Polvellan early in Sept. and will bring any thing. On the whole this is safer than the post, as I may receive and read it *alone*—but for once be cautious what you write—mettez y de l'amitié tout [confine yourself to pure friendship]. Be quite easy about my proceedings at Polvellan. I shall never be away from Mr. A—a day or a night—perhaps never above an hour at a time and there is no creature who has the project of making love to one. I take at random a handful of notes from the young fellows who frequent my house. I know well enough that they prove nothing as to the nonexistence of a Chancellier but they prove that I live,

---

[10]Effingham Wilson, London publisher of Sarah Austin's translation of Pückler's *Tour of a German Prince* (1832).

[11]The place in Cornwall where Charles Buller lived.

[12]John Stuart Mill (1806–1873), economist, philosopher, political reformer.

as I said, on very cordial *affectionate* terms with them, without an idea of love making. The one from Normanby[13] I send because it relates to you. As to your commission. Mr. Otway Cave[14] called just as I was reading your letter. He laughed heartily at your setting me to provide for the continuation of the equine species at Muskau. He says Tattersall[15] is perfectly honest and honourable—that from the immense number of horses that pass through his hands he can buy better and cheaper for you than any private gentleman and charges only his regular commission, that he is perfectly in the habit of executing such commissions for the Continent—but that if you like, he, Mr. O.C., will look at the horses—if you give Tattersall a commission, though he says no man in England is so good a judge. He says if you write to Tattersall he will send you something like an estimate—though of course it cannot be precise—Mr. Hanbury a great sporting man told me he lately sent up his whole stud, 20 horses of first rate quality, to Tattersall to sell and left the whole thing entirely to him.

As to the curtains beloved Étourdi [scatterbrain]. You tell me neither the number of windows nor the height of the rooms—Oh I beg your pardon, Liebling, you ask for Proben [samples]— You shall have them by next Tuesday's Courier. They must be of chintz (Indienne English) lined with a plain colour harmonizing with the room. 'Tis pity you did not send me patterns of the colours—blass rot [pale red] may be so very various according to the proportion of blue or yellow in the red. But I will do my best, and when I return you will have decided and I can buy them for you. They are not very costly. They are highly glazed when

---

[13]Constantine Henry Phipps, 1st Marquis of Normanby (1797–1863).

[14]Robert Otway Cave (c. 1796–1844) member of parliament, 1826–1844.

[15]Tattersall's was an auction room for horses, founded by Richard Tattersall (1724–1795).

new and when washed, should be what it is here called calendered i.e., glazed again, that is done by dyers, not washerwomen. The glazed surface prevents the dust from adhering so that they keep clean for a long time with careful brushing.— If you can't get them properly cleaned, send them to me when they are dirty.— They have as you know generally a fringe on the drapery at the top and are bound with some sort of galon [braid]. Should I get these things to match. I don't like much drapery or fringe but donnes mois tes idées et je m'orienterais la dessus [give me your ideas and I will inform myself on the subject].

If the rooms are South and you inhabit them only in Summer I should recommend muslin—either all white woven in elegant patterns—on white raye or flowered with some colour harmonizing with the room. These cost very much less and are extremely light and elegant for summer, but give no air of *snugness* in a cold evening with fire and candles. I have just bought some flowered with purple and green for Polvellan— These are washed and *starched* (comprends tu) [do you understand] like a muslin handkerchief.

Je suis toute enchantée d'entre dans les details de ton ménage. Laisse moi l'arranger quelque chose de plus. En attendant puisque tu seras occupé à mesurer beaucoup de choses voilà une chose qui sort de mon work basket et que tu porterais dans ton waistcoat pocket. J'ai mis un baiser sur chaque pouce [I am delighted to involve myself in the details of your household. Let me arrange some more things for you. Meanwhile, since you will be so busy measuring many things, here is something from my work basket which you could carry in your waistcoat pocket. I have kissed every inch].—I had appropriated poor Lucy's parure [ornament] but I shall keep it for her. I had already bracelets of the kind, and earrings neither of us shall ever wear car nous n'avons pas ce goût des sauvages [for we do not share this barbaric taste]. My ears are intactes. I shall change them for something which will be equally *yours* and which she shall wear.

I can't say a word on politics. We are all furious against you Prussians. I thought your King less stupid. What a Beruf [task] he had if he could have seen and felt it! Leader of civilized enlightened Germany Ye Gods and to reject that to be the tool of Russia and ally of Austria.

I am as aristocratic as you dear and in the same *sens*. We should agree perfectly. I *am no democrate*—I only wish to see men happy and enlightened.

God bless you my friend and love. Your last letter is very sweet, I send you a shower of kisses for it and remain most tenderly yours

S———

[Point de?] Sara's Weg [Sara's Path]— Tu me ruines [You are my downfall]—I have spent my whole morning in scrawling to you. Can you read it?—

P.S. Tuesday

If Mme de K. is at Muskau give her the enclosed. If not send it by post. Burn her letter of course immediately. I *think* she had as strong an affection for me as such a being is capable of, but we shall see. Notez that I am not a woman's beauty: I know that. They look for regularity of features and as Walter Scott[16] somewhere says '*don't understand the points of* a fine woman.' You do ou je me trompe fort [or I deceive myself]. Don't encourage her to send me a quantity of Commissions which may be troublesome to me both as to time and money. You can say that it will not do to load M. de Bülow's bag too heavily. I must leave you instantly. My husband was yesterday again attacked by fever and is in bed. I was not *in* bed all night. I lay down on the outside comme je pouvais [as best as I could] in my dressing gown. God

---

[16]Walter Scott (1771–1832), novelist.

bless and keep *thee* dearest. I have just got the Morgenblatt with your letter of 16 June and shall translate it and send it to the Examiner.

Your own S.

Dearest Friend

Your letter (recd yesterday the 20th) makes you far dearer than ever to me and what is more raises my opinion of you. There is a calm gentle generous tone—an absence of all vanity, all egotism, all the tyranny of a 'spoiled child.' It is the letter of a man who wishes to love and be loved worthily not only to be excited nor enjoy, nor to rule. Dearest Hermann if you were here and oh, how I wish you were—I should say, there—there's my hand—I am your friend for life—your ally—your confidant—your comforter—for you may want even that. My heart opens as I read that letter and I see in it all your own generous nature—your real sensitivity—your candour and noble honesty. Alas! I love you so for it, que peu s'en faudrait [how little it takes] but I should throw my arms round your neck at once and kiss you heartily—taking the risk of your turning your cheek to me—I would take some odds however that it would not be so bad as that. But it is useless to speculate. Here we are—the sea is between us, and we have nothing for it but poor fancy. As for my tastes, I will just tell you. Boys I never liked—beauty in men is of very subordinate and doubtful effect—a good person and the air of a gentleman, with a look of feeling and sense is all I ever cared about. As for the other point—I do assure you, and you will believe me—that at no time of your life would any very astonishing achievements *sur ce champ de bataille* [on the battle field of love] have been any recommendation to me. I suppose it is an *idiosyncracy* of mine. Vehement, intense, mad as I have sometimes felt this enjoyment, I never could stand a repetition of it. I am inclined to think that women who *laissent faire* [let it happen], are perhaps sooner *disposes* [available] again; or there may be insatiable natures—Kurz [in short], mine is not one—very far from it—and it requires fondness, endearment—*love* in short, to make me care for it. Aussi très souvent cela m'a eté une supplice [Also very often it was a torture to me], not from any personal disgust, but for want of the preliminary commotion de coeur [stirring of the heart]. Ainsi des prouesses [Thus physical prowess] would be worse than thrown away on me. I am not one of those ladies who as Lady Aldborough said '*look only at shoulders and* [?]'[1]

Tuesday Morng. I was obliged to leave off last night because my eyes were so painful. They are no better today so dearest friend you will give me credit for far more than I write, of love, kindness, and traulich [intimate] gossip. Imagine it all and with it the highest respect for your talents, your qualities and above all your charming sincerity, wh breathes in every line of your letter. There is all your better nature in it, my own dear friend, and it wins and touches my heart far more than my voluptuous raptures, or vehement professions. Yes—*now* I feel confident that we should meet with the kindest and most confiding sentiments—meet as if we had loved and parted in another world and were reunited; and if no grain of passion mingled with this—yet, dearest Hermann we must think ourselves lucky to find each other. Would to God I could take your hand and look in your eyes for the confirmation of this feeling. I know I should find it there.

What you say of my husband is just. You could never have so dangerous a rival and he grows more and more so. Ten years ago, how gladly would I have separated from him! I *was* very near going to my Father twice. Now, not for worlds would I leave him. I have conquered him by love, patience, gentleness and courage, and who would not prize such a conquest? And indeed he is a noble being. He is now ill in bed and I have much to do. I have just had to write to all his class to announce that he cannot lecture tonight.

Now as to *our* business. *You belong to me*, dearest Hermann, and

---

[1]One word here is illegible.

your affairs are mine—therefore no more of scruples or thanks. Only this—if I *seem* dilatory or slow, you will *never* doubt my zeal. You will give me time and I will do all with true hearty pleasure. The chimney piece commission I accept with great delight. I flatter myself I shall shine in its execution, for I am famous for picking up odd and pretty things. This however above all requires time, for les jolies choses ne se presentent pas toujours [pretty things are not always at hand], and rather come upon one au hazard [by chance]. The perfumery I did hope to send today. You shall be *certain* to have it next week—and some prettinesses—I hope you will have recd the book and papers I sent last week. As it is decided that the Cousins cannot take the furniture I think the best thing will be, as soon as you decide on the chintz (of which I sent patterns), to have that, the squat and cushions, the blue striped chintz for the study, the damask stuff, kurz [in short] *all*, properly packed and shipped by Waithman[2] for Hamburg. Heller[3] suggests directing them to the Preuss. Gen. Port Director at Hamburg but you know best. Heller has given me £10 more—in all £30 of which I have spent £21-0-3. He has £20 more in hand. This will pay all the smaller things but of course not Waithman for the rest, which I should think will be about £50 more. I think it best to pay at once because I get a large discount and the best things by that means. All that I have bought has been considerably under the credit price.

I am glad to relieve Heller who is really a good and tatenvoller [active] Junge vif [lively fellow] and precipitate, but with genuine upright and good feelings. Nobody here understands him, as you may believe, for he is very Deutsch. And he is rather vain and wants to jouer un *rôle* [play a part] in society and is angry with people who won't attend to him. I see that this country will

---

[2]The shipping agent that packed and shipped goods purchased for Pückler by Sarah Austin.

[3]Pückler's agent in London at this time.

do him good—though tis a disagreeable medicine—and as he has really head and heart, I hope he will turn out something. You will not now, dear Hermann, reply to this by those jokes which are a little *fades* [tasteless]—but believe that I *can* take interest in a promising human being without wanting to go to bed with him. Besides, I do believe Heller has a great respect and regard for me and for my husband and would not wish to turn that matter into an intrigue. Such a man as Wagner would have been far more likely to try, simply because he could less understand me and less attach himself to what is best in me, and would see only what all men do—a very fine woman, very lively and good natured. All this you must know.

Au reste—the looking glass may deceive but one thing cannot—the eyes and the voices and the manners of men, and I can tell you I should have no want of soupirants [lovers] if I chose.

I must have done. I long to see your books. Continue to write. Authorship will always be a *hors d'oeuvre* in your existence as well as in mine, for I am no bluestocking and am much more in my element riding, dancing etc. But for different reasons it is good for me.

Adieu, my beloved friend for a week.

Your
Sara—

Lord Grey² is old—Lord Althorp³ is stupid. Lord Brougham⁴ is at variance with all his colleagues and trying to trip up their heels—(he will not much care *how*) the people are suspicious and angry and nothing is done to conciliate, humanize or enlighten them except what is done in a bad *sens* and with bad views. With all that, their good sense and energy comes to light and may, probably *will*, work to good results. But the process is odious and I, for my part, had rather *not* be in the scramble. So says my good friend and partner here and we think we shall be very quiet and happy at Berlin. In Septr. we quit this house and mean to take another, and unless something is done (wh I don't expect nor wish) to keep him here we shall be at Berlin next winter. A gentleman was employed last week to say to me that if I would point out to Ld Brougham *what* he could do for Mr. A—what sort of emploi [work] I thought wd suit him, he would give it him. I replied I would have nothing to do with it. That Ld B—as a lawyer knew better than I what such a man was fit for—that he had, as I knew, read his book and that I should never solicit any thing from him nor from anybody. That the country that could neglect such a man was unworthy of him and that I for my part desired nothing so much as to live in Prussia.

I trust this was conveyed word for word to Lord B—qui est un franc Charlatan et hait le merite [who is a plain charlatan and

---

¹The beginning of this letter is lost.

²Charles, second Earl Grey (1764–1845), prime minister 1830–34.

³John Charles Spencer, Viscount Althorp, later third Earl Spencer (1782–1845), politician.

⁴Henry Brougham (1778–1868), author, member of parliament, 1810–12, 1815–30; lord chancellor, 1830–34; one of the founders and major contributors to the *Edinburgh Review*.

hates merit]. I am just sending off a copy of Mr. A's book to the Duc de Broglie[5] who knows and admires his writings. I should like to send one to you but I don't imagine you wd. read it.

My Bible[6] [is] un grand succès. I care for this, insofar as it brings me money. I must now say one thing to you, to my dearest Hermann. For the first time in my life it seems to me possible we may meet. And now I beg you to regard all that has been written by you as no wise binding on you to receive me (if I come) otherwise than as a person entitled to your esteem, and capable of appreciating your mind and conversation and disposed to take no common interest in all that concerns you. I have thought of this maturely and I will not have you meet me with the feeling of an obligation to make love to me. If we meet, we meet, *mind*, as acquaintances, nay friends, for I cannot be *less* than a friend to you, but free as air. We may not be smitten with each other and imagine any thing so fade [tasteless] and ridiculous as to have to affect it. *You* have had too much of enjoyment and experience not to be very fastidious and *difficile*, and *I* may have the caprice of not liking that de près [close at hand] which I have been dreaming about de loin [from a distance]. If we met *as you proposed* and I agreed and I saw in a few days that you were *satisfied*, *que tu en avois assez* [that you had enough], that I did not fulfill all your expectations and desires, *you* would have nothing to regret—but I—I should die of mortification and humiliation. I still *think* you would like me, but with a man so *blasé* who can be sure. Therefore I repeat you are free, and till you have [assurance][7] that you like nothing else so much you shall not have me, and not then unless I am of the same mind.

---

[5]Achille Leon Victor, Duke of Broglie (1785–1870), politician, diplomat, author.

[6]See note on p. 243.

[7]Two words here are illegible. The second word appears to be 'assurance.'

And if you do not make love to me at all, don't think I shall be angry—point du tout [not at all]. I shall be amused and amuse you, and we shall discuss and agree and disagree and romance and philosophize and I, dearest friend, shall feel an unutterable interest in all you say and do and shall never by word or look remind you of the projects you imagined in the dark. Can you trust me for this? You may and may therefore put me perfectly at ease and as a stranger or rather as an old friend.

Can it be that I shall see you? We talk of Berlin daily—yet I cannot think that he will be let to go. Enfin nous verrons [Well, we will see].—And now good night. I am still not recovered and am soon fatigued. God bless you. Don't talk of war and of volunteering. Je viendrai être ton bon écuyer [I will come and be your equerry]. Thank M. Varnhagen v. Ense[8] for me. I only wait to find some book to send him. As for you, Mon Prince, I send you a pocket handf. wh. I made and I have worn in cravate to ride in, and so now you may attach what value to it you will. Goodnight—mille bais[ers?] [a thousand kisses]. [?][9]

---

[8]Karl August Varnhagen von Ense (1785–1858), politician and author.

[9]Four words here are illegible.

Friday July 19 [1833]
26 Park Road

Amatissimo Principe [Most Beloved Prince]

I have nothing for you this week but news—and even that I must condense as much as possible. We do not leave England. Whether to rejoice or not, I in my secret heart know not, but *to all appearance* this is matter of great congratulation. So all our friends say and think. The Chancellor[1] has just appointed a commission of five, for the revision of our Criminal law, whereof my husband is one. This will be £500 a year for two years and will also afford Mr. A an opportunity of shewing what he can do. All he fears is, that an[y] collaborations will obstruct his views by their prejudices as mere English practical lawyers. However I hope it will give him occupation useful to himself and the public and will thus keep his mind in a cheerful and tranquil state. This will be an immense gain to me—far more than the money were the hundreds, thousands. On the other hand, the Rhine, Germany, and the cherished hope of seeing the beloved Unknown are for the present gone. All I can look forward to now is the possibility of a *visit* to Germany which our more ample means may permit us to make hereafter. But then years pass and we cannot remain as we are. And yet, dearest Hermann, my heart tells me that at no period of our lives can we meet without finding in each other something that we have sought in vain elsewhere, and that the Wahlverwandschaft [affinity] will retain its power as long as we live. Mais hélas—ce n'est pas tout—et je voudrais bien ———————— Remplissez cette lacune de [?][2] mieux vous ne pouvez pas l' exagérer. [But alas—this is not all—and I would like ———————— You fill this empty

---

[1]Lord Broughman. See note 4, page 265.
[2]One word here is illegible.

268

space as best you can; whatever you put in it will not prove to be an exaggeration.]

Well—besides this commission there is a chance of a Lectureship at the Inner Temple, the richest of our wealthy Law Associations called Inns of Court, which you must have heard of. This is our dear friend Bickersteth's[3] doing. He came on Saturday to tell me of it, for my husband has been so ill and nervous that nobody thinks of speaking to him about any thing that can agitate him. This is yet undecided— If he gets it, it will give him about £200 to 300 a year more—but at present only one year is certain. You know our English proverb 'It can't rain but it pours.'—So, on Saty this happened; on Sunday Mr. Austin *père* arrived and had a tête à tête with me at night [and] made known his intentions of giving us whatever was necessary to our living here, and of instantly making his will with such provisions for my husband, self and child as will place us beyond the reach of anxiety, and secure to the dear girl a very good fortune at our death. On Monday came the announcement from the Chancellor. My husband had a thousand difficulties and scruples about accepting it and I was obliged to write to Bickersteth and on the Monday morning (unknown to him) to drive all over the town to Mr. Mill,[4] John Romilly[5] etc. to collect their advice which I knew wd. determine him. They were unanimous for him to serve. These three days were a perfect drama. I wish I could write it all as it occurred.— Well, on Sunday Mr. Austin leaves us and goes to his other sons. On Monday I begin my *démé[nagement]*. On Saty—tomorrow week (July 27) we quit this house— One of my brothers takes in my furniture—another lends us his house which he and his family have quitted for their house in Wales.

---

[3]Henry Bickersteth (1783–1851), barrister; master of the rolls, 1836; created Baron Langdale, 1836.

[4]See page 256, note 12 above.

[5]See page 239, note 5 above.

There we shall remain till about the 6th of August when we shall go I suppose to Sandgate near Dover there to remain till the end of October. Then I must return to London, find a house and once more establish ourselves in this huge city. So you will not lose your Commissionaire dearest and she will be as much as ever at your service—as much as ever happy, delighted to do any thing for you—as much occupied about you and attached to your image.

If you think I am very violently happy you are mistaken. I *acquiesce* in the beneficial effects of all these arrangements on those to whom I am more nearly and tenderly and dutifully bound. I thank God for them—I see a more tranquil existence for myself, less toil—less care and privation—but I am not at all blind to the fact that the necessity for labour—the endless petty cares and distractions of my life have stifled the craving of my heart which in ease and leisure would have sometimes been intolerable. A character so strong and energetic as mine—feelings so warm and acute must be employed somehow. The whole force of my nature has found employment in fighting with adversity—in shielding those I am bound to from evil—in being, to repeat Jeffrey's[6] words 'the heroine of domestic life.' I have felt a sort of triumph in the midst of circumstances other women wd have found overwhelming and humiliating. It has been my pride and glory to make to myself a position in this haughty and slavish English society by dint of inward pride and courage—to spurn at their trumpery distinctions—to assert and proclaim my poverty and to force those who were affecting to be 'genteel' to give way to my real individual predominance and to the simplicity, good nature, liveliness and yet intrinsic superiority of my manners *wh are* superior simply because I affect nothing and do not

---

[6]Francis Jeffrey (1773–1850), author, politician, judge; member of parliament, 1831–34; one of the founders, editor, and major contributor to the *Edinburgh Review*. Lord Advocate for Scotland.

condescend to borrow consideration from any *body* or any *thing*.

If once I am at ease, rich, and the wife of a prosperous and popularly distinguished man all this is over. I share in the vulgar claims. I can no longer go in an omnibus for sixpence to a party and *say* that I came so and in five minutes see myself the object of more respect and attention than all the carriage ladies. I shall have no more waves to struggle with. However this is a curious taste, and shews you the vehemence that lies at the bottom of a very gentle, complying affectionate, gay nature. *You* will understand what passion there is in it. I must leave off. The casts next week. Adieu—adieu dearest. Write pray write.

London July 13, 1834.

Though I am still in the greatest uncertainty about you and your plans, and that ever to be and never actually existing Reise [journey]. I cannot longer delay writing to give you some information about our plans. We like every body else are plunged into some uncertainty by this change of ministry or rather this suspension—for whether after all it will be a change or not seems doubtful. The reappointment of the Criminal Law Commission depends upon the stability of Lord Brougham,[1] at least so we imagine. But for this we should start in about a week for the sea side. Our project is to go to Jersey—if we like it, to remain there, if not, to cross over to Granville and take up our abode on the Norman coast. We shall probably remain there till the end of October and then return to Lectures, Commissions and the horrors of London. The Marchioness of Lansdowne with whom I dined about a week ago was the first suggestor of Jersey and on enquiry we find much to tempt us—beauty of scenery—quiet, cheapness etc. I was asking her about the coast of Kerry which I have longed amazingly to visit ever since I translated your description of Bantry and Glengariff. But Lady L—— rather put me off by saying we should find few accommodations and above all not those for bathing—the most essential of all to my husband. Besides the journey is longer and more complicated and expensive. My thoughts, hopes and fears and actions centre more and more in that one point, his health, and I really cease to think of any enjoyment or happiness beyond the one of seeing him restored to that measure of health and mental efficiency without which there is neither 'health, peace nor competence' (the three things without which life is little more than a burthen) for me. I have not been able to prevail on myself this spring to leave him even for the shortest period and after having engaged to accom-

---

[1]See page 265, note 4 above.

pany my sister to the house of a dear old friend at Oxford and made all my arrangements I gave it up from an Ahnung [premonition] of evil. And lucky I did. He had a severe attack that very week.

And now my dear, dear and generous friend, does not this sufficiently reply to your letter? If more and more I withdraw from the least thing, a country excursion, an opera or a ball which may give him any disturbance or annoyance, what can I say to what would rob him of all his remaining consolations. No dear Hermann if you would come and see us—if you knew him—if you saw his sufferings and if you saw how entirely and absolutely he rests on his wife for support and assistance, never I am certain (would you consent) to add one care or grief to one already so overcharged. Your good and noble heart would strengthen me in all my best resolves and you would say, persevere to the end, fulfil your appointed task. All your ideas of my imaginations of you are quite déplacées [misplaced]. If you reflect on *my own* age you will feel how little it is that of great pretensions, or of wild illusions. I think it most likely that I should prefer you *now* to what you were in the triumph and wilfulness of your earliest and gayest days. But let us not lose our time in vain discussions. *Friends* dear and valuable, each to the other we can be, and this can and will last when the rest shall have all vanished. For me, my friend, the path of duty becomes every day narrower and sterner. Who knows [how] long I may have it to tread? No one not a heartless brute *could* deviate from it under my circumstances. The hardest heart must be troubled. Would to God I could die to restore him to health. This I cannot. But I *can* watch over him and nurse him in sickness. And that I *must* do. And now, my dear and kind Hermann, there is a thing you could do to contribute to my peace and comfort. These letters—ah if you knew how the thousand casualties of life sometimes rise like demons before my eyes to torment me. While I was quite obscure I dreaded them less, but now I cannot conceal from myself that what I write would excite curiosity—and a curiosity sharpened by malignity—by all the proud triumph of the *mediocre* the cold and the worldly over one who has gained for herself respect and love—a name and a place in society whom many envy. If you see in this a changed mind, or a selfish suspicious spirit you wrong me much. You would not, if you knew me. But Hermann, the shadows of life fall around me and I have but one bright light— the hope that I diminish *his* sufferings and next to that the respect I enjoy. When I think that these letters would convert all to darkest night, can you wonder if I appeal to your generous solicitude for me and, let me add, for one much more worthy of it, if I ask you to relinquish any personal gratification you say, and which I am but too pleased to think, you find in their possession, in favour of my tranquility. I think I once told you I would never ask this again.

My confidence in *you* is not the least altered or impaired. But several circumstances lately have occurred within my knowledge to prove how vain are all precautions save the one—destruction. To this I am at last reluctantly and with a heavy heart about to resort in respect to your's. Till now—I have kept them—but I must do so no longer. In a few days I shall go to this melancholy work reading and burning—reserving all I dare and may.— Before I leave England again I shall do this with what regret I need not, cannot say.

Tell me if mine have always reached you properly sealed. A friend of mine said to me some days ago 'I advise you not to send any letter you care about having seen by the Ambassador's bag.' I could not make him explain but he said he had good reason for giving me this caution. Is it possible they can be so base?

At all events I shall send this by post. Mr. [Meyer?] and his wife have been here twice. They are gone back to Berlin. Dr. Julius[2] is now in London. I have seen him often and like him

---

[2]Nikolaus Heinrich Julius (1783–1862), physician, and prison reformer.

much. Have you heard of the work of Frau von Arnim?³ Tell me something of her. She is the *Lady of the Ring* I perceive. She must be an extraordinary woman. You will perhaps see my friend Mrs. Jameson⁴ at Berlin, if you are there. If you do, be kind to her for my sake and her own. Elle est remplie de talens [she is most talented], and very amiable. She will tell you of me and my Lebensart [way of life]. Write to me if you think it can arrive within a fortnight. If not stay till I can tell you where to direct.—Ever and ever your most true and

affectionate
S.A.

My darling girl is well. I am not quite well but very passably. P.S. Capt. Spencer⁵ sent me the Tutti Frutti with a complimentary note. Have you yet seen it? I have not read it—a friend borrowed it of me, but it seemed to me very well done. I have had a very kind letter from Hr. v. Altenstein.⁶

---

³Bettina von Arnim (1785–1859), author, close friend of Goethe, supporter of reform movements.

⁴Anna Brownell Jameson (1794–1860), prolific author, especially of works on the history of art; lived in Germany for long periods; heroine to many mid-century British feminists.

⁵Edmund Spencer translated Pückler's *Tutti Frutti* into English in 1834.

⁶Karl Sigmund Altenstein (1770–1840), Prussian statesman.

NOTES

The following notes provide the sources of quoted passages and other significant information. The quoted passages are identified in the notes by the last words of the quotation. When two or three consecutive quotations in one paragraph are from the same source, only the last quotation has been cited in the notes. In the interest of brevity we have used abbreviations.

Since most of the manuscripts referred to in the notes are in the Varnhagen Collection in the Jagiellonian University Library at Cracow, Poland, only those notes identifying manuscripts in *other* collections and libraries include the name of the collection or library. All others—including all of those referring to letters from Sarah Austin to Pückler and from Pückler to Sarah Austin—are located in the Jagiellonian University Library.

For information about Pückler we have especially relied on Ludmilla Assing, ed., *Briefwechsel und Tagebücher des Fürsten Hermann von Pückler-Muskau*, 9 vols. (Berlin, 1873–76); Ludmilla Assing, *Fürst Pückler-Muskau. Eine Biographie* (Hamburg, 1873); Eliza M. Butler, *The Tempestuous Prince* (London, 1929); Irma Gaab, *Fürst Hermann Ludwig Pückler-Muskau (1785–1871)* (Munich, 1922); and Jost Hermand, Introduction to *Briefe eines Verstorbenen* by Hermann, Fürst von Pückler-Muskau, ed. Wolfgang F. Taraba (New York, 1968). Flora Brennan's spirited translations in *Pückler's Progress* (London, Collins, 1987) also have been helpful. These works are cited in the notes only if passages from them have been quoted.

ABBREVIATIONS

Beevor	Papers of Mrs. Carinthia Beevor
BL	British Library, London
Blakiston	Papers of Mrs. Georgiana Blakiston, London
Bowood	Bowood House: Papers of the Marquess of Lansdowne
CLC	*The Collected Letters of Thomas and Jane Welsh Carlyle*, Duke-Edinburgh edition, eds. Charles Richard Sanders and Kenneth J. Fielding. Durham, N.C.: 1976–81
CW	*Collected Works of John Stuart Mill*, ed. John M. Robson. Toronto, 1963–
Durham	Durham University Library
Fragments	*Fragments from German Prose Writers*, translated by Sarah Austin, illustrated with notes. London, 1841
Germany	Sarah Austin, *Germany, from 1760 to 1814; or, Sketches of German Life, from the Decay of the Empire to the Expulsion of the French*. London, 1854
Guizot	Guizot Papers, Archives Privées, Archives Nationales, Paris
Houghton	Houghton Papers, Trinity College Library, Cambridge
JA	John Austin
LDG	Gordon Waterfield, *Lucie Duff Gordon in England, South Africa and Egypt*. New York, 1937
MA	Archives of John Murray, publisher, London
NLS	National Library of Scotland

Osborn — James M. and Marie-Louise Osborn Collection, Yale University Library

P — Hermann von Pückler-Muskau

SA — Sarah Austin

SA, Preface — Sarah Austin, Preface to *The Province of Jurisprudence Determined*, second ed. London, 1861

St. Bride — St. Bride Printing Library, London

TG — Janet Ross, *Three Generations of English Women, Memoirs and Correspondence of Susannah Taylor, Sarah Austin, and Lady Duff Gordon*, revised ed. London, 1893

Tour — Hermann von Pückler-Muskau, *Tour in England, Ireland, and France, in the years 1828 and 1829*, translated by Sarah Austin. Philadelphia, 1833

Tr F — Translation from French

Tr G — Translation from German

UCL — University College, London

UCLA — University of California, Los Angeles

Verstorbenen — *Briefe eines Verstorbenen. Ein fragmentarisches Tagebuch aus England, Wales, Ireland, und Frankreich, geschrieben in den Jahren 1828 und 1829* (Stuttgart, 1836), volumes 1 and 2; *Ein fragmentarisches Tagebuch aus Deutschland, Holland und England, geschrieben in den Jahren 1826, 1827 und 1828* (Stuttgart, 1836, 1837), volumes 3 and 4. (New York, 1968)

Waterfield — Papers of the late Mr. Gordon Waterfield

Weimar — Nationale Forschungs- und Gedenkstätten der Klassischen Deutschen Literatur in Weimar

Yale — Yale University Library

Introduction

is in Krakow,' *The American Archivist*, *44*, no. 3, summer 1981, 223–28.

10   STYLUS . . . TISSUE PAPER: See W. B. Proudfoot, *The Origin of Stencil Duplicating* (London, 1972), 25.

11   'WILD WAY OF WRITING': SA to P, March [23]–29 [1832].

11   'QUICKLY AS I THINK': SA to P, March 23 [1834].

13   'WHAT A MIRACLE': SA to Fanny Wright, May 3, 1827, University of South Carolina Library.

13   'WITH FICTIONS': SA to Ottilie von Goethe, August 9, 1840, Weimar.

13   'REGARDS OUR SEX': TG, 71.

13   'SEX—POVERTY—EVERY THING': SA to P [*c*. late May 1832].

13   'CANNOT STAND INFAMY': SA to P, October 15 [1832].

13   'ITS OPINIONS': SA to Varnhagen, February 19, 1835.

13   'ALL I THINK': SA to Ottilie von Goethe, August 9, 1840, Weimar.

13   'WILD, MAD CORRESPONDENCE': SA to P, April 13 [1832].

14   'FOLLIES BE PRINTED?': TG, 356.

Chapter One

15   'LOVE SHE ACCEPTS': George Eliot, *Felix Holt* (Harmondsworth, 1979), 524–25.

15   'OF BEING A WIFE': TG, 364.

15   'LEFT BEHIND': Susanna Taylor to Richard Taylor, July 11, 1819, St. Bride.

16   AUGUST 24, 1819: *Norwich Mercury*, August 28, 1819. There are a few letters from John Austin addressing Sarah as his wife, which are erroneously dated 1818.

17   'ACQUISITION OF KNOWLEDGE': LDG, 13.

18   'HIDDEN IN HIM': John Knox Laughton, *Memoirs of the Life and Correspondence of Henry Reeve* (London, 1898), *2*, 323.

18   'ICY RESPONSE': Margaret C. W. Wicks, *The Italian Exiles in London 1816–1848* (Manchester, 1937), 236 (Tr. Italian).

18   'DON'T KNOW WHY': Louise von Kottwitz to SA, May 13, 1832.

18   'WELL-FILLED': Edward L. Pierce, *Memoir and Letters of Charles Sumner* (Boston, 1877), 46.

18   'DEEP GRAND': TG, 117.

18   'LUSTROUS': John Neal, 'Mrs. Sarah Austin,' *American Phrenological Journal*, 47 (April 1868), 128.

19   'HAVE NO RELATION': *The Letters of Sydney Smith*, ed. Nowell Smith (Oxford, 1953), *2*, 624.

19   'HECTICALLY INTENSE': CLC, *5*, 386–87.

19   'SCRAPES': TG, 40.

19   'DISPLAY AND FLIRTATIOUSNESS': Franklin Fox, ed., *Memoirs of Mrs. Eliza Fox* (London, 1869), 75.

20   'ATTRACTIVE, AND IMPOSING': *Ibid.*

20   'LITTLE MISSES': *I Too Am Here, Selections from the Letters of Jane Welsh Carlyle*, eds. Alan and Mary McQueen Simpson (Cambridge, 1977), 33.

20   DYNASTY OF TALENT: W. R. Brock and A. J. Meadows, *The Lamp of Learning: Taylor and Francis and the Development of Science Publishing* (London, 1984), 1–16.

22   'THEIR USEFULNESS': *Family Poems, Songs, Addresses*. Address by Rev. Philip Taylor, August 3, 1814, pp. 97, 104, 119–20.

22   'SCIENTIFIC CULTURE': TG, 302.

22   'THEY HAVE DONE': TG, 321.

23   'SUBDUING CHAIN': *Monthly Repository*, 21 (August 1826), 486.

23   'UNITARIAN BREEDING': Harriet Martineau, *Autobiography*, ed. Maria Weston Chapman (Boston, 1877), *1*, 88.

24   'FOR *HIS* CHILDREN': Susan Reeve to Richard Taylor, October 13, 1814, St. Bride.

24   'INTO A PLAY': Sarah Taylor to Richard Taylor, [*c.* 1811], St. Bride.

24   'HISTORICAL COMMERCE': TG, 54.

24   'ALL AROUND HER': Joseph Hunter, 'Notice of Taylor Family of Norwich,' April 19, 1830, BL, Add. 36527, f. 71.

25   'MENDING STOCKINGS': Philip Hemery Le Breton, ed., *Memoirs Miscellaneous and Letters of the late Lucy Aikin* (London, 1864), 125–26.

25   'FOR ANOTHER': TG 39–40.

26   'JUST KINDLED': TG, 25.

26 'LINEN, LACE ETC.: *Anna Jameson, Letters and Friendship, 1794–1860*, ed. Beatrice [Mrs. Steuart] Erskine (London, 1915), 166.

26 'FROM THEIR ALTITUDE': Le Breton, *Memoirs*, 133.

26 'COULD NOT SEW': Harriet Martineau, *Autobiography*, ed. Maria Weston Chapman (Boston, 1877), *1*, 20.

27 'WORD, OR DEED': TG, 31.

27 'VIEWS AND FEELINGS': TG, 43.

27 'VANITY AND SELFISHNESS': TG, 36.

27 'LITTLE FOLLIES': *Ibid.*

28 'IF POSSIBLE, CONSIDER': TG, 40.

28 'LOVED, AND LOVING': SA to P, August 27, 1832.

28 '*MAY* HAVE ERRED': LDG, 29.

28 'HUMAN HEART': TG, 42.

28 'LOVING CHARACTER': SA to P, March 18, 1833.

29 'STORES OF REPENTENCE': SA to P, March [23]–29 [1832].

29 'OF OUR YOUTH': Harriet Martineau, *Autobiography*, *1*, 20.

29 'OUR NEIGHBOURS': *Ibid.*, *1*, 62.

31 'CONDITIONAL PROPOSALS': LDG, 25–29.

32 'TO BE DREADED THE LEAST': *Ibid*, 26–27.

32 ARMY DIARY: *Ibid*, 13–15.

33 'STRONGEST OF ALL MOTIVES': *Ibid*, 29.

34 'PURITY AND SAFETY': *Ibid*, 26–29.

34 'PROFERRED LOVE': *Ibid*, 28–29.

34 'AND YOUR STAY': *Ibid*, 28.

35 'PUT BEFORE HER': SA, Preface, vi.

35 'THIS TEMPTED ME': TG, 373.

35 'DESTROYERS OF MANKIND': *Ibid*, 44.

36 'WILL FOLLOW AFTER': John Taylor to SA, June 16, 1824, Osborn Collection, Yale.

36 'MUCH IN UNISON': Betsy Rodgers, *Georgian Chronicle, Mrs. Barbauld and Her Family* (London, 1958), 235.

37 'OF DEEP INTEREST': Susan Reeve to Richard Taylor, November 22 [1814], St. Bride.

37 'TREMBLING ANXIETY': Susanna Taylor to Richard Taylor, December 4, 1814, St. Bride.

38 'FUTURE DESTINATION': *Ibid.*

38 'LAMENTED, FOR EVER': Susan Reeve to ?, November 22 [1814], St. Bride.

38   'EXCELLENT ONE': John Taylor to Richard Taylor, November 17, 1814, St. Bride.

38   'ON OUR PART': Susanna Taylor to Richard Taylor, December 4, 1814, St. Bride.

39   'HAPPILY SEALED': LDG, 30.

39   'GIRL IN THE WORLD': *Ibid.*

39   'TO SEE HIM': *Ibid.*, 31.

39   'CALL OUR BROTHER': John Taylor to Richard Taylor, November 17, 1814, St. Bride.

39   'UNBOSOM ITSELF': John Taylor to SA, June 16, 1824, Osborn.

40   OF HOURLY CONDUCT: Harriet Martineau, *Autobiography, 1,* 87.

40   'INCLINATION TO CONSULT': SA to Richard Taylor, December 30, 1814, St. Bride.

40   'OF HIS CHARACTER': LDG, 31.

40   'WORLD COULD': *Ibid.*

41   'IN MY LIFE': *Ibid.*

41   'THE MAN FOR SALLY': Susan Reeve to Richard Taylor, November 22 [1814], St. Bride.

41   'COMPREHENSIVE VIEWS': LDG, 28.

42   'DETERMINE HER CHOICE': Susanna Taylor to Richard Taylor, December 4, 1814, St. Bride.

43   'AT LENGTH MY FRIEND': Lucy Aikin, *Epistles on Women* (Boston, 1810), 91, 93.

43   'HUSBAND AND FRIEND': JA to SA, December 15 [1819, misdated 1818], Trinity College, Cambridge; JA to SA, n.d., William L. Clements Library, University of Michigan.

43   'ENGAGE MY ATTENTION': TG, 364.

43   'HIGH-MINDED ADVICE': *Ibid.*

43   'STEEP OF LEARNING': *The Lewin Letters. A Selection from the Correspondence and Diaries of an English Family 1756–1884* (London, 1909), *1,* 180.

43   EROTIC AND THE TUTORIAL: Patricia Beer, *Reader, I Married Him* (New York, 1979), 99–103.

44   'MANNERS AND HABITS': Franklin Fox, ed., *Memoir of Mrs. Eliza Fox* (London, 1869), 75.

44   'WHAT IT SHOULD BE': John Taylor to Richard Taylor, September 14, 1819, St. Bride.

44   'VENTURING A LITTLE': Betsy Rodgers, *Georgian Chronicle, Mrs. Barbauld and Her Family* (London, 1958), 235.

45   'COMPANION AND FRIEND': Le Breton, *Memoirs of Lucy Aikin*, 147.

45   'IN THE EVENINGS': John Taylor to Richard Taylor, September 14, 1819, St. Bride.

45   'FOR THE BETTER': *Ibid*. This letter was written three weeks after the wedding, presumably when Sarah and John finally departed from Norwich after having returned to retrieve their belongings.

45   GOLD WATCH: Lina Waterfield, *Castles in Italy: An Autobiography* (New York, 1961), 229.

Chapter Two

46   'DEATH PART THEM': *I Too Am Here. Selections from the Letters of Jane Welsh Carlyle*, eds. Alan and Mary McQueen Simpson (Cambridge, 1977), 80.

46   'HUMAN ANGUISH': George Eliot, *Adam Bede* (New York, n.d.), 243–44.

46   'RELIGIOUS DEVOTION': SA to P, July 24–31, 1832.

47   'BEST OF MEN': Lucy Aikin, *Epistles on Women* (London, 1810), vi.

47   'WHO IS ALSO A WIFE': SA to P, March 11–[14] [1832].

47   'NOBLE ACTIONS IN MEN': SA, *Fragments*, 269.

48   'PRINCIPLES OF LAW': 'Sir John Patteson,' *Law Magazine and Review*, *12* (1862), 205–6.

49   'ARE ENGAGED IN': JA to Jeremy Bentham, July 20, 1819, UCL.

49   'MUCH AS MYSELF': *Ibid*.

50   'ON THE BARS': Henry Reeve, 'Autobiography of John Stuart Mill,' *Edinburgh Review*, 139 (January 1874), 99.

51   'PERNICIOUS PREJUDICES': SA to P, June 19 [1832].

51   THIS DISTINCTION: *Ibid*.

51   'BELLE PASSION': TG, 70.

52   'NO HELP FOR HIM': Henry Crabb Robinson, *Reminiscences*,

vol. 2, ff 100–1, Dr. Williams's Library, London; *Suffolk Chronicle*, December 26, 1874, p. 5.

53   'SUCCESS IN BUSINESS': SA, Preface, vii.

53   'EARNEST TIMID EYES': James A. Froude, *Thomas Carlyle: The First Forty Years of His Life, 1795–1835* (New York, 1882), 123.

53   'FREQUENT ILLNESSES': CW, *12*, 170.

53   'HYPOCHONDRIACAL MAN': TG, 78.

54   EXCESSIVELY SHY: TG, 89.

54   'BAFFLED YOUTH': Byron, 'Lara,' section XVIII, in *Poetical Works*, eds. Frederick Page and John Jump (Oxford, 1970), 307.

54   'HE COMPLAINS': SA to Richard Taylor, December 30, 1814, St. Bride.

54   'MY OLD DISEASE': TG, 67.

54   'HIS NORMAL STATE': TG, 469.

55   'EGYPTIAN PYRAMID': SA to P [1832].

55   'A HARD CASE': CLC, *6*, 404.

55   'MOST RIGID ECONOMY': John Taylor to SA, June 16, 1824, Osborn.

55   'SINGLE HANDED': SA to Gladstone, January 22, 1853, BL, Add. 44373, f. 323.

55   'A SERIOUS CALAMITY': John Neal, *Wandering Recollections of a Somewhat Busy Life: An Autobiography* (Boston 1869), 299–300.

55   THESE YEARS AS CRUEL: TG, 80.

55   'EVIL TO ME': TG, 82.

55   'MIND AND SPIRITS': SA to P [*c.* November 1832].

56   'MIGHT NOT BE ANXIOUS': SA to P, March 11–[14] [1832].

56   'HIS OR HERS': TG, 80–81.

56   'WOMAN IN THE WORLD': TG, 99.

56   'IN *OUR FIRM*': SA to Besser, October 18 [*c.* 1841], Staats- und Universitätsbibliothek, Hamburg.

56   LEISURE AND REST: Margaret C. W. Wicks, *The Italian Exiles in London 1816–1848* (Manchester, 1937), 235.

57   'INDULGE ME THUS': SA to Varnhagen, February 19, 1835.

57   'DOMESTIC LIFE': SA to P, July 12, 1833.

57   'ARE UPON YOU': CLC, *9*, 394.

58 'SUPPORT AND COMFORT': SA to P, April 13, 1835.

58 'WHICH ILLNESS PRODUCES': SA to Varnhagen, January 17, 1835.

58 'YOUR STAY': LDG, 28.

58 'MY HUSBAND': SA to P, July 24–[31] [1832].

58 'NEGLECTED, OVERLOOKED': SA to P [1832].

59 'REDOUBLES ITSELF ON ME': SA to P, January 19, 1836 (Tr F).

59 'NEVER PASSED FOR MUCH': George Grote, *Posthumous Papers*, ed. Harriet Grote (London, 1874), 75.

59 'RECEIVING THEM': SA to Harriet Grote, August 25, 1865, UCL.

59 'ABYSS OF MISERY': *Fragments*, 320.

59 'FORGOTTEN THE WIFE': *Ibid.*

59 'SYMPATHIZING FRIENDS': *Ibid.*

59 HER PARENTS'S HOUSE: SA to P, January 19, 1836 (Tr F).

59 'I MARRIED HIM': SA to P, August 9 [1833]

59 PRIZED HER FREEDOM: SA to P, August 9 [1833].

59 'SEPARATED FROM HIM': SA to P, January 21 [1833].

60 'WHAT A MIRACLE': SA to Fanny Wright, May 3, 1827, University of South Carolina Library.

60 'NEGLECT AND UNKINDNESS': SA to P, August 27, 1832.

60 'UNLOVING, UNCOMFORTING': SA to P, July 24–31 [1832].

60 'AFFECTIONS AND DUTIES': Wicks, *Italian Exiles in London*, 99–100, 231–3.

60 '*THAT* IS HOPELESS': SA to Anna Jameson, September 26–28, 1835, Osborn.

61 'MARRIED LIFE': SA, *Fragments*, 303.

61 'WEARY HOURS': SA, *Germany*, 231.

61 'INCURABLE RECLUSE': SA to Gladstone, April 1 [n.y.], BL, Add. 44356, f. 231.

61 '*AGREEABLE* TO VERY FEW': SA to P, June 23–25 [1833].

61 'GREAT EFFORT TO LOVE': CLC, *9*, 39.

61 'NOTHING BUT ACID': CLC, *9*, 52.

62 'WELL IN LONDON': CW, *12*, 293.

62 'DAMNED BORE': J. B. Priestley, *Thomas Love Peacock* (London, 1927), 77.

62 '*CHOICE* OF WORK': CW, *12*, 347.

62   'HARBOUR OF REFUGE': TG, 174.

63   'IN THE WORLD': SA, Preface, xviii.

63   'A GERMAN PROFESSOR': 'Mr. Charles Austin,' *Pall Mall Budget*,
       January 2, 1875, p. 21.

63   'TRADITIONAL *CULTE*': SA to P, March [23]–27 [1832].

63   'MONSTROUS GREAT GIRL': TG, 81.

63   'MUTTERSPRACHE': SA to P, March [23]–29 [1832].

64   'GERMAN CHILD': *Ibid.*

64   'HALF-EDUCATED': TG, 83

64   'UNDISCIPLINED, AND INDEPENDENT': TG, 81.

64   'VIGOUR AND ANIMATION': TG, 83.

64   'I FEAR NOTHING': TG, 72.

64   *VERDEUTSCHT*: CLC, 5, 386.

64   'IN DEAR GERMANY': SA to Francis Lieber, March 15, 1834,
       Huntington Library.

64   CONTENTMENT: SA to P, October 15 [1832].

64   'SINCE MY MARRIAGE': SA to P, February 11, 1833.

65   'OF WHAT AWAITED': *Ibid.*

65   'FOR THE LECTURER': Henry Crabb Robinson, 'Reminis-
       cences,' vol. 2, f. 101, Dr. Williams's Library, London.

65   'CLANGING METALLIC': CLC, 5, 397.

65   'HAD EVER READ': LDG, 44.

66   'AS WELL AS DISCOURAGED': JA to Leonard Horner, November
       5, 1830, UCL.

66   'TILL THE END': Henry Cole, Diary, March 21, 1831, Victoria
       and Albert Museum, London

66   'AGITATE HIM': SA to P [July 1833].

66   '*OUR* COURAGE': SA to P, November 13 [1832].

66   'UNDER OUR FEET': SA to P [*c.* November 1832].

66   'LONDON UNIVERSITY': SA to Francis Lieber, March 15, 1834,
       Huntington Library.

66   'IS TO BE DONE': SA to P, July 6 [1832].

67   'ETHEREAL VITALITY': SA to P, December 2–3, 1834.

67   'COMMANDING STATION': John Neal, 'Mrs. Sarah Austin,'
       American Phrenological Journal, 47 (April 1868), 128–9.

67   'AND DID IT': SA to P, October 21, 1833.

68   'ALIVE AND WELL': *Ibid.*

69 'OF MAN TO YOU': *Ibid.*

69 'HAD SHE CONTINUED': John Neal, 'Mrs. Sarah Austin,' *American Phrenological Journal*, 47 (April 1868), 128–9.

69 'RIVER OF TALK': CLC, *5*, 387; *8*, 82.

69 'TALK OF ENERGY': John Knox Laughton, *Memoirs of the Life and Correspondence of Henry Reeve* (London, 1898), *1*, 100.

70 'TO *MYSELF*': SA to P, June 3 [1832].

70 'OR ANY *THING*': SA to P [July 1833].

70 'ADMIRED AND CARESSED': SA to P, June 29 [1832].

70 'PROTECTING SAINT': TG, 63.

70 'CAVALIER SERVIENTI': SA to P, July 18, 1832.

71 'JOBBING COUNTRY': SA to P, March 11–[14] [1832].

71 'PERSONS OF DISTINCTION': SA to P, May 14, 1833.

71 'THAT ENGLAND CONTAINS': SA to P, July 24–[31] [1832].

71 'IMAGINATIVE SYMPATHY': John Sterling to SA, [1832], Lacaita-Shelburne Collection, University of Michigan Library.

71 'PERSON IN COMPANY': SA to P, July 6 [1832].

72 'SOMETHING FEVERISH': CLC, *5*, 387.

72 'AS I AM': SA to P, July 24–[31] [1832].

72 'LOVERS IF I CHOSE': SA to P, January 21 [1833].

72 'LOOKING LOVE TO ME': SA to P, January 13 [1832].

73 'NEEDED TRANSLATION': John Neal, 'Mrs. Sarah Austin,' *American Phrenological Journal*, 47 (April 1868), 128–9.

73 SANTA ROSA: Wicks, *Italian Exiles in London*, 234.

73 'IN LOVE WITH [HER]': SA to P, March [23]–27 [1832].

73 MAN OF GALLANTRY: SA to P [1832].

73 '*VERY ADORING*': SA to Guizot, November 27, 1861, Guizot.

73 BICKERSTETH: SA to P, October 15 [1832].

74 'VALUES HIS PEACE': SA to P [*c.* October 1832].

74 'GET INTO SPIRITS': SA to P [1832].

74 'ABOUT ALL THINGS': SA to P [1832].

74 'ARE VERY FLOURISHING': SA to P [*c.* November 1832].

74 'CELEBRATED MRS. AUSTIN': CLC, *8*, 43.

74 'LONDON DISTINGUISHED FEMALE': CLC, *8*, 92.

74 'UPON ME LATELY': SA to P, April 13, 1835.

74 'WOULD SUBMERGE MANY': SA to P, February 11, 1833.

74 'CONTRADICTION IN MY LIFE': SA to P [1832].

75 'OVERWHELMING AND HUMILIATING': SA to P [July 1833].

75 'HALF A DOZEN ORDINARY WOMEN': SA to P, July 24–[31] [1832].

75 'TO LIVE AND ACT': SA to P [1832].

75 'ANY MANY MIGHT ENVY': SA, *Germany*, 335.

75 'SPARKLING CUP': SA to P, April 13, 1835.

75 'ANNOYANCE AND CARES': SA to P, July 6 [1832], (Tr F).

75 'BITTER SUFFERING': SA to P, March 11–[14] [1832].

75 'HOPE OR FEAR': TG, 78.

76 'DO ALL AND BEAR ALL': SA to P, June 23–25 [1833].

76 'COURAGE TO MEET IT': SA to P, June 29 [1832].

76 'HIMSELF AGAIN': SA to P [*c*. November 1832]; Sarah paraphrased a passage from *King Richard III*, Act V, scene 3, adapted from Shakespeare by Colley Cibber.

76 'PERHAPS HAVE ATTAINED': SA to Henry Taylor, March 12 [1848], Bodleian Library, Oxford.

76 JOHN STUART MILL: CW, *12*, 170.

76 JOHN STERLING: Sterling to SA [1832], Lacaita-Shelburne Collection, University of Michigan Library.

76 SOUTHEY, ROGERS: SA to P, February 14, 1834.

76 CLEAR-FLOWING ENGLISH: CLC, *9*, 396.

76 'A HIGHER TASK ONE DAY': CLC, *9*, 397.

77 'BEST LIVING TRANSLATOR': Dionysius Lardner to J.C.L. Sismondi, November 23, 1833, private communication from the late H. O. Pappe.

77 'HIS SOLE EMPLOYMENTS': SA to P, March [23]–27 [1832].

77 'FORGET ALL THAT': SA to P, January 13 [1832].

77 'TO FORGET MYSELF': SA to P, June 3 [1832].

78 'BEEN MY LIFE': SA to P, August 9 [1833].

Chapter Three

79 'THE DESERT I HAD LEFT': Charlotte Brontë, *Villette* (Harmondsworth, 1986), 121–2 (chapter 7).

79 'INSIDE OUT TO YOU': SA to P, August 9 [1833]

80 'PLAN WE HAVE NONE': TG, 83.

81   'HOPE YOU WILL NOT': SA to John Murray, December 25
        [1830], MA.

81   'MANUSCRIPT ELSEWHERE': SA to John Murray, March 22
        [1831], MA.

82   'DESCRIBING IT': SA to John Murray, December 25 [1830],
        MA.

82   'AS MY OWN': SA to P, November 9, 1831.

83   'MY INNER SUN': *Tour*, 513.

83   'THE HIGHEST PLACES': *Tour*, 143.

83   'COMFORTABLE CARRIAGE': *Tour*, 315.

83   'LIFE IS TO ME': *Tour*, 386.

83   'ESPECIALLY IN ENGLAND': *Tour*, 315.

84   'NEW AND INTERESTING': *Tour*, 206.

84   'NOR ANGEL': *Tour*, 315 (Tr F).

84   'HERE BELOW': *Pückler's Progress, The Adventures of Prince
        Pückler-Muskau in England, Wales and Ireland as told in letters
        to his former wife, 1826–9.* Translated by Flora Brennan, Lon-
        don, 1987, 171.

85   'TRUEST FRIEND': *Tour*, 180.

85   'BEST COMFORT': *Tour*, 75.

85   'WELL BEING': *Tour*, 139.

85   'MUTUAL UNDERSTANDING': *Tour*, 360.

85   'YEARS OF TENDERNESS': *Tour*, 49.

85   'KINDNESS AND INDULGENCE': *Tour*, 75.

85   'SQUEEZED INDISCRIMINATELY': *Pückler's Progress*, 95.

85   AT HIS LODGINGS: *Tour*, 249.

85   'IS ATTRACTED': Sophie Grafin von Arnim, *Goethe und Fürst-
        Pückler* (Dresden, 1932), 30.

85   'CHARIOTS OF LOVE': *Pückler's Progress*, 171.

86   'FINGERS OF HER HAND': *Verstorbenen*, 3, 269 (Tr G).

86   'PEARLY FACE': *Pückler's Progress*, 103.

86   'MY SENSES LEFT ME': *Verstorbenen*, 3, 412 (Tr G).

86   'ACQUAINTED WITH LUST': *Verstorbenen*, 3, 270 (Tr G).

87   'LIVELY AS QUICKSILVER': *Pückler's Progress*, 97.

87   'GREATEST CHARM': *Pückler's Progress*, 187.

87   'FIRE OF THE SOUTH': *Verstorbenen*, 2, 215 (Tr G).

87   'BEAUTIFUL AFRICAN': *Ibid.*, 1, 253.

87   'WILD GENRE': *Tour*, 495.

87   'UN-ENGLISH': *Ibid.*

88   'CANNOT HELP IT': SA to P, November 18 [1831].

88   'CONTROVERT WITH YOU': SA to P, November 9, 1831.

88   'TALKED TO YOU': SA to P, April [8?]–9 [1832].

88   'SO GAILY!': SA to P, June 3, 1832.

89   'THE DEAD': P to SA [August 1831], draft.

89   'DEAR ORIGINAL': SA to P, November 9, 1831.

89   'DEAD MAN': *Ibid.*

89   'TRANSLATOR OF THE DEAD': P to SA [August 1831], draft.

89   'DISGUISES AT ONCE': SA to P, November 9, 1831.

90   'THINK YOU A TRAITOR': SA to P, November 9, 1831.

90   'OR SHOULD BE': SA to P, November 27–30 [1831].

90   'BUT MYSELF': SA to P, November 9, 1831.

90   'CANNOT BE': *Ibid.*

90   'WON'T YOU?': SA to P, November 27–30 [1831].

90   'UN PEU FOLLE': SA to P, November 9, 1831.

91   'PICKLING MUSTARD': E. M. Butler, *A Regency Visitor* (New York, 1958), 17.

91   'HOLD INTERCOURSE?': SA to P, November 9, 1831.

91   'LES ROSES *DEINETWEGEN*': SA to P, March 11–14 [1832].

92   'BELIEVE ALL THIS?': SA to P, November 9, 1831.

92   'IT WAS TRUE': SA to P, March 11–14 [1832].

92   'CHOSE TO LOOK': *Ibid.*

92   'WILL AMUSE ANYBODY': *Ibid.*

92   'MONEY TRANSACTIONS': *Ibid.*

92   'DOSE OF THE SAME': P to SA [*c.* February–March 1832], draft.

93   'OF COURSE': *Ibid.*

93   SEXUALLY ABUSED: E. M. Butler, *The Tempestuous Prince*, 136, 265.

94   'THE INDIFFERENT': *Briefwechsel*, 7, 211 (Tr F).

94   'BECOME A PRUSSIAN': A. I. Ehrhard, *Fürst Pückler* (Berlin, 1935), 45 (Tr G).

95   'GUIDING ANGEL': *Briefwechsel*, 7, 219 (Tr F).

95   'OTHER I': Assing, 2, 39.

95   'SCHNUCKE [LAMBKIN]': *Pückler's Progress*, 99.

95   'MERELY VEGETATED': *Briefwechsel*, 7, 240 (Tr G).

96   'COST AND TIME': P to SA, May 24, 1833.

97   'ON A HOT STOVE': Assing, *1*, 193.

98   'A BITTER MEDICINE': *Briefwechsel*, 6, 370 (Tr G, Tr F).

98   'UNFORTUNATE SUM': *Briefwechsel*, 7, 63.

98   '200,000 POUNDS': *Pückler's Progress*, 155.

98   VENUS HERSELF: *Briefwechsel*, 6, 386.

99   'THAN YOU THINK': *Pückler's Progress*, 188.

99   'HINDRANCE TO ME': *Ibid.*, 98.

99   'TWO CHILDREN': *Ibid.*, 182.

99   'TERRIBLY NAUSEOUS': H. Ch. Mettin, *Fürst Pückler Rerst Nach England* (Stuttgart, [1965?]), 169 (Tr F, Tr G).

99   'DEVIL OF A MARRIAGE': *Pückler's Progress*, 188.

100   'CHURCH STEEPLES': P to SA, May 24, 1833, copy (Tr G).

100   'GRACEFULLY TOUCH': SA to P, November 9, 1831.

101   'YOU WILL BELIE': SA to P, November 27–30 [1831].

101   'I TRANSLATED': SA to P, November 9, 1831.

101   'NOT TOO BAD': *Ibid.*

101   'INTIMATE FRIEND': SA, Preface to volumes 3 and 4 of *Tour*.

101   'INTEREST IN YOU': SA to P, March 11–14 [1832].

102   'RESMELT THEM ENTIRELY': *Briefwechsel*, *3*, 24 (Tr G).

102   'TO MY HEAD': *Verstorbenen*, *2*, 132 (Tr G).

102   'LESS CRUEL': *Verstorbenen*, *4*, 142; *Tour*, 208.

102   HENRIETTA SONTAG: *Verstorbenen*, *4*, 360–62.

103   HARRIET L——: *Verstorbenen*, *1*, 253–64.

103   THIS DELETION: P to SA [*c.* August 1831], draft.

104   'HIGH PRIEST': P to SA [*c.* February–March 1832], draft.

104   'DIRT OF YOUR BOOK': SA to P, March 11–14 [1832].

104   'DISGUSTING': *Ibid.*

105   'SUCH A TRANSLATOR': SA to P, January 13 [1832].

105   'MY HANDS OF YOU': SA to P, March 11–14 [1832].

106   'TO ENGLISH READERS': P to SA [*c.* February–March 1832], draft.

106   'SOMETHING WICKED': SA to P, March 11–14 [1832].

106   'YOUR COWARDICE': P to SA [*c.* February–March 1832], draft

106   'AWAY ALL THAT': SA to P, March 11–14 [1832].

107   'NOT A GERMAN PEN': P to SA [*c.* February–March 1832], draft.

107 'SECOND EDITION': SA to P, November 27–30 [1831].

107 HIS TRANSLATOR: Varnhagen to P, January 5, 1832, *Briefwechsel, 3,* 83.

107 HUGE BALE: SA to P, November 27–30 [1831].

107 BUT THE TRANSLATION: SA to P, November 18 [1831].

107 'DISTINGUISHED PERSON': *Briefwechsel, 8,* 215.

107 'ENGLISH TRANSLATORS': SA to Varnhagen, February 19, 1835.

107 'HEAR THAT': SA to P, March [23]–27 [1832].

108 'OF THE ENGLISH': SA to P, June 23–25 [1833].

108 'I HAVE WRITTEN': P to SA [*c.* February–March 1832], draft.

109 'NEVER PUNISHED': *Ibid.* (Tr F).

109 'INTEREST IN YOU': SA to P, January 13 [1832].

109 'TO LOOK AT': SA to P, February 16 [1832].

109 'AS MISTRESSES': SA to P, January 13 [1832].

110 'EVER KNOW YOU': SA to P, January 13 [1832].

110 'PERHAPS, YOU ME': *Ibid.*

110 'ONE AND THE OTHER': P to SA [*c.* February–March 1832], draft.

111 'WRITE AT ALL': *Ibid.*

111 'MY BEST GENRE': Ludwig Stern, *Die Varnhagen von Ensesche Sammlung,* 620.

112 'ON MY TONGUE': Charlotte Brontë, *Villette* (Harmondsworth, 1986), 591 (chapter 41).

112 '*HOW DEEPLY*': SA to P, May 20–[21] [1832].

112 'SHOULD NEVER MEET': SA to P, March [23]–29 [1832].

112 'JE ME RUINES': SA to P, July 6 [1832] (Tr F).

112 'TELL IT YOU': SA to P, March [23]–29 [1832].

112 'CHATTING WITH YOU': *Ibid.*

113 'PLAUDERN': SA to P, January 13 [1832].

113 'FRIGHTENS ME': SA to P, February 16 [1832].

113 'LEAVE IT ALONE': SA to P, November 13 [1832].

113 'DEVOUR IT': SA to P [*c.* late May 1832].

113 'AS I OUGHT': SA to P, January 13 [1832].

114 'INTO OTHER HANDS': SA to P, March [23]–29 [1832].

114 'SOON IMPROVE': *Ibid.*

114 'GERMAN CHARACTERS': SA to P [*c.* late May 1832].

114 'SCHADE': SA to P [*c.* late May 1832].

114   'YOUR HAND': SA to P, June 5–6 [1832].

115   'HEAR FROM YOU?': SA to P, June 29 [1832].

115   'PRIVATION AS I MAY': SA to P, July 24–[31] [1832].

116   'PURE FRIENDSHIP': *Ibid.*

116   'WOUNDED MIND': SA to P, June 29 [1832].

116   'DEAR FRIEND': SA to P [1832].

116   'TRANQUILITY BY DAY': SA to P, July 6 [1832].

116   'SELF CONSTRAINT': SA to P [1832].

117   'A HUNDRED TIMES': SA to P, March 11–14 [1832].

117   'IN VAIN': SA to P, June 29 [1832].

117   'MUST BE BORNE': SA to Julia Smith, January 6, 1834, Cambridge University Library, Add. 7621.

117   'INCAPABLE OF ENJOYMENT': SA to P, April 13, 1835.

117   'LOAD OF LEAD': SA to P [*c.* November 1832].

117   'RESIST NO LONGER': *Ibid.*

117   'DISTASTEFUL TO HIM': TG, 360.

117   'BURTHENSOME TO HIM': Margaret Wicks, *The Italian Exiles in London, 1816–1848* (Manchester, 1937) 233.

118   'HAVE BEEN DISAPPOINTED': SA to P, July 18, 1832.

118   'WEEKS OF FASTING': SA to P, July 24–[31] [1832].

118   'CARE FOR IT': SA to P, January 21, 1833.

119   'HEAV'N KNOWS': SA to P, July 18, 1832.

119   'LOVE SUSTAIN ME': SA to P, July 6 [1832].

119   'SMILE UPON ME': SA to P, May 20, 1833.

120   'ANNOYS YOU': SA to P, August 27, 1832.

120   'PASSION ARE OVER': SA to P [*c.* late May 1832].

120   'WORLD I LIKE': SA to P, March [23]–29 [1832].

120   'GENEROUS SMILE': *Ibid.*

120   'A FULL HEART': SA to P, June 3 [1832].

120   'FORGET IT ALL': *Ibid.*

120   'TO MY HEART': SA to P, August 9 [1832].

120   'LONGING FOR YOU': SA to P, June 5–6 [1832] (Tr G).

120   'UNKNOWN DIVINITY': SA to P, June 5–6 [1832].

121   'UNKNOWN IDOL': SA to P, May 20–21 [1832].

121   'BELOVED SHADOW': SA to P, March [23]–29 [1832].

121   'DEAR VISION': SA to P, February 16 [1832].

121   'HONOURED ONE': SA to P, April [8?]–9 [1832].

121 'SWEETEST AND DEAREST': SA to P, July 24–[31] [1832].

121 'MY HEART': SA to P, May 20–[21] [1832].

121 'MY LIFE': SA to P [*c.* October 1832].

121 'MON PRINCE': SA to P, May 20–[21] [1832].

121 BESTER: *Ibid.*

121 LIEBLING: SA to P, June 3 [1832].

121 GELIEBTER: SA to P, June 5–6 [1832].

121 CARO: SA to P, June 3 [1832].

121 CARISSIMO: SA to P, June 19 [1832].

121 IDOL MIO: SA to P, April [8?]–9 [1832].

121 BIEN AIMÉ: SA to P [*c.* April 1832].

121 COEUR DE MON COEUR: SA to P [*c.* late May 1832].

121 MON ÂME: SA to P, March [23]–27 [1832].

121 LOVING KISS: SA to P, May 20–21 [1832].

121 SHOWER OF KISSES: SA to P, July 24–[31] [1832].

121 AN ITALIAN KISS: SA to P [*c.* April 1832].

121 A LONG KISS: SA to P [*c.* late May 1832].

121 HOT KISSES: SA to P, June 5–6 [1832].

121 '*mille baisers*': SA to P, June 19 [1832]

121 'YOUR EYELIDS': SA to P [*c.* November 1832].

121 'RAVING': SA to P, April 13 [1832].

121 'FORGET YOU': SA to P, April 13 [1832].

121 'LOVE YOU': SA to P, June 3 [1832].

Chapter Four

122 'WRECKING PRUDENCE': Charlotte Brontë, *Shirley* (Harmondsworth, 1987), 569 (chapter 36).

122 'CHILDISH FOLLY': George Grote, *Posthumous Papers*, ed. Harriet Grote (London, 1874), 148.

122 'UNKNOWN IDOL': SA to P, May 20–[21] [1832].

123 'YOUR FRIEND': SA to P, February 16 [1832].

123 'I AM MYSELF': P to SA [*c.* February–March 1832], draft.

123 IN THE WORLD: SA to P, March [23]–29 [1832].

123 'JOBBING COUNTRY': SA to P, March 11–[14] [1832].

123 'THEIR CORE': SA to P, May 20–[21] [1832].

123   'COTTON AND STEAM': SA to P [*c.* late May 1832].

123   SUBLIME LITERATURE: SA to P, November 18 [1831].

124   'SCREAMIKIN': CLC, 5, 397.

124   'AND INTELLECTUAL': SA to P, July 18, 1832.

124   'HOURS TOGETHER': SA to P [*c.* late May 1832].

124   'FOUND TWICE': SA to P, July 18, 1832.

124   'TO BE YOURS': SA to P, July 24–[31] [1832].

124   'AN ENGLISHWOMAN': SA to P, March [23]–29 [1832].

125   'ASK ANYBODY': SA to P, January 14 [1833].

125   'MILITAIR HORSES': SA to P, March [23]–29 [1832].

125   'SENSUOUS WAY': Patricia Beer, *Reader, I Married Him* (New York, 1979), 181.

125   'WHITE WAVES': SA to P, November 9, 1831.

125   'PROFESSORIN': SA to P, June 19 [1832].

125   'NEVER SAW EQUALLED': SA to P [1832].

125   'LIKE DEER': P to SA, April 16, 1832, copy.

126   'ANIMAL ORGANIZATION': SA to P [1832].

126   'TAME ANIMALS': SA to P, March [23]–29 [1832].

126   'OF MY LIFE': SA to P, January 14 [1833].

126   'OF AN AUTHOR': SA to P, November 27–30 [1831].

126   'GOOD FOR ME': SA to P, January 21 [1833].

126   'CAPACITY FOR LOVE': SA to P, March [23]–29 [1832].

126   'EMPLOYED SOMEHOW': SA to P [July 1833].

127   'VERY IMPORTUNATE': SA to P, July 24–[31] [1832].

127   'TO CONCLUDE IT': SA to P [*c.* late May 1832].

128   'SAY YOU ARE': SA to P, March [23]–29 [1832].

128   'MANIE SYLPHE': *Ibid.*

128   'FOND LONGING': SA to P, August 27, 1832.

129   'SOUND MORALITY': SA to P, October 15 [1832].

129   'ANTIPATHIES OF BIGOTRY': SA to P, August 27, 1832.

129   'INTELLIGENT CREATURE': *Ibid.*

130   'SINGLE TWINGE': SA to P, October 15 [1832].

130   'NOT TRUST HIM': *Ibid.*

130   'TASTE ALONE': *Ibid.*

130   'FOR AN HOUR': SA to P [*c.* November 1832].

130   'WE AGREE': SA to P, October 15 [1832].

131   'ENTIRE REMODELLING': SA to P, June 3 [1832].

131   'CALL VIRTUE HERE': SA to P, March 11–[14] [1832].

131   'OF THE TREATY!': SA to P, June 3 [1832].

131   'A GREAT VICE': SA to P, October 15 [1832].

132   'OUR PRESENT RELATIONSHIP': P to SA [*c.* April 1832], draft (Tr G).

132   'BODY AND SOUL': P to SA, April 16, 1832, copy (Tr G).

132   'OVER UNRESERVEDLY': P to SA [*c.* April 1832], draft (Tr G).

132   'POSSESS ME ENTIRELY': P to SA, April 16, 1832, copy (Tr G).

133   'ENOUGH *HERE*': SA to P, April 13 [1832].

133   'ODD PEOPLE': P to SA, April 16, 1832, copy.

134   'ENOUGH OF THAT': SA to P [*c.* late May 1832].

134   'I PERISH': P to SA, April 16, 1832, copy (Tr G).

134   'WILD VOLUPTUOUSNESS': P to SA [*c.* April 1832], draft (Tr G).

134   'TO FRIENDSHIP': P to SA, April 16, 1832, copy (Tr G).

135   'JOYFUL THINGS': P to SA, April 16, 1832, copy (Tr Latin).

135   'ONE BY ONE': SA to P, June 3 [1832].

135   NOURISHED BY THEM: SA to P, June 19 [1832] (Tr F).

135   'YOU DARLING': SA to P, June 5–6 [1832] (Tr G).

135   SECRET PAPERS: Butler, *Tempestuous Prince*, 177. For mention of Pückler's erotic writing, also see Jost Hermand, Introduction to *Briefe eines Verstorbenen* by Hermann, Fürst Pückler-Muskau, ed. Wolfgang F. Taraba (New York, 1968) and Irma Gaab, *Fürst Hermann Ludwig Pückler-Muskau (1785–1871)* (Munich, 1922).

135   '*TOO MUCH*': SA to P [*c.* October 1832].

135   'JOY AND VOLUPTÉ': SA to P, July 24–[31] [1832].

135   'HOW DEEPLY': SA to P, May 20–[21] [1832].

135   'POSSIBILITY, AND BEYOND': SA to P, June 3 [1832].

136   'YOUR RAPTURES': SA to P [*c.* October 1832].

136   'STICKY AND GREEDY': SA to P [*c.* late May 1832] (Tr F).

136   'MONSIEUR LE PRINCE': SA to P, June 5–6 [1832] (Tr F).

136   'LITTLE MOUSTACHES': SA to P, July 24–[31] [1832].

136   'BARBATA BELLISSIMA': Francis Jeffrey to Thomas Carlyle, February 14, 1833, NLS.

137   'DO NOT UNDERSTAND': SA to P, June 5–6 [1832].

137   'TO MY MIND': *Ibid.* (Tr G, Tr F).

137   'DESPISE ME': *Ibid.* (Tr F).

137   'WANDERING SPIRITS': SA to P, June 5–6 [1832]. The translation is from 'The Satyricon of Petronius Arbiter' in *Petronius*, trans. by Michael Heseltine, revised by E. H. Warmington (Cambridge, 1975), 185.

137   'LOVE ME': SA to P, June 5–6 [1832] (Tr F).

137   'FIND THEM GOOD': SA to P, August 27, 1832 (Tr G, Tr F).

138   'SUCH THINGS': *Ibid.*, (Tr F).

138   'VAGARIES AND DESIRES': SA to P, June 3 [1832].

138   'DESIRE AND DESERVE': SA to P, July 24–[31] [1832].

138   HIS HAIR: SA to P, March [23]–29 [1832].

138   TOUCH IT: SA to P [*c.* late May 1832].

138   'NEVER QUIT ME': SA to P, May 20–[21] [1832].

139   '*TOUT SIMPLE*': SA to P, July 6 [1832].

139   'WHAT ONE MEANS': SA to P [*c.* late May 1832].

139   'WERE PLAINER': *Ibid.*

139   'SHALL WEAR': SA to P, July 24–[31] [1832].

139   'DEVOTED. BUT': *Ibid.*

140   'WHAT A GIFT': SA to P [*c.* late May 1832].

140   'FANTASTIC VISIONS': *Ibid.*

140   'DEAR FACE': SA to P, July 6 [1832].

140   'A THOUSAND TIMES': SA to P, June 5–6 [1832] (Tr G).

140   'IMAGINATION CAN DO': P to SA, April 16, 1832, copy (Tr G).

140   'TINGE OF SILVER': SA to P, March [23]–29 [1832].

140   TO BED: SA to P, June 3 [1832].

141   'SPRING OF ALL': SA to P, June 5–6 [1832].

141   'MY OWN HEART': *Ibid.*

141   'AND COARSE': SA to P, August 27, 1832.

141   'SIX MONTHS AFTER': SA to P, March [23]–29 [1832].

142   'WHAT AWAITS YOU': SA to Louise von Kottwitz, March 28, 1832 (Tr F).

142   'RIDICULE AND MOCK': Louise von Kottwitz to SA, May 13, 1832 (Tr F).

142   'TOLD ABOUT HIM': *Ibid.* (Tr F).

143   'EXCITE HIS CURIOSITY': Louise von Kottwitz to SA, May 13, 1832 (Tr F).

143   'WHISPERED WORDS': Louise von Kottwitz to P, September 14, 1832; [*c.* October–November 1832] (Tr G).

143*n.*   'LOVE TO YOU, HÉLAS': SA to P [*c.* March 31]–April, 1 [1833].

144   'THEY ARE WRAPPED': SA to P, May 20–[21] [1832] (Tr F).

145   'MÄNNLICHE FRAU': SA to P, March [23]–29 [1832].

145   'NOT PRETTY': SA to P, October 15 [1832].

145   MERELY PRETTY: SA to P, March 11–[14] [1832].

145   'TO ADMIRE ME': SA to P, October 15 [1832].

146   'ORDINARY MEN': *Ibid.*

147   'BEAUTIFUL WOMAN NEVER': *Ibid.*

147   'ACCURATELY FORMED': *Ibid.*

147   'YOUR BEAUTIFUL LIMBS': P to SA, November 24, 1832, copy
         (Tr G).

148   'YOU WISH, I'LL DO': SA to P, October 15 [1832] (Tr Italian).

148   'WHAT A FOOL I AM': SA to P [*c.* November 1832].

148   'WOULD I': *Ibid.*

148   'STUPID LETTERS': P to SA, November 4, 1832, copy (Tr G).

148   'IMPROVE MYSELF': P to SA, October 28, 1832, copy (Tr G).

149   'AS I DO': *Ibid.*

149   'DESPISE ANY BODY': SA to P, January 11, 1833.

149   'I CONJURE YOU': SA to P, July 24–[31] [1832].

149   'DIFFERENT ELEMENT': SA to P, October 15 [1832].

150   'DISGRACE AND YOURS': SA to P, October [16]–21 [1832].

150   'WEAKNESS AND SHAME': *Ibid.*

150   'YOU, DEAREST': SA to P [*c.* late May 1832].

150   'EXTORTED': SA to P, July 24–[31] [1832].

150   'BLONDE SHEEP': P to Louise von Kottwitz, November 8, 1832
         (Tr F).

151   'OVER A YEAR': Louise von Kottwitz to P, October 7, 1832 (Tr
         F).

151   'FOX LIKE MYSELF': P to Louise von Kottwitz, November 8,
         1832 (Tr F).

151   'SUCH A DISLOYALTY': SA to P, January 11, 1833.

152   'MY IDEAL WOMAN': SA to P, October [16]–21 [1832].

152   'COMPLEXION AND FACE': SA to P, October 15 [1832].

152   'THINK ME JEALOUS': SA to P, October [16]–21 [1832].

153   '*YOURSELF* AND TO THEM': SA to P, March 23 [1834].

153   'TILL I DIE': SA to P, March [23]–29 [1832].

153   'MY DANGEROUS POSITION': SA to P, July 24–[31] [1832].

154   'A SLIPPERY PERSON': *Ibid.*

154   'TO DESTROY ME': *Ibid.*

154   'COURAGEOUS AND RESOLUTE': SA to P [*c.* late May 1832].

154   'I SHOULD SWALLOW': SA to P, July 24–[31] [1832].

155   'DEAD—ASSASSINATED': SA to P, June 5–6 [1832] (Tr F).

155   'FROM PERIL': SA to P, July 24–[31] [1832].

155   'FOR AN INSTANT': SA to P, July 24–[31] [1832].

155   'AN ITALIAN CUSTOM': Leslie Marchand, *Byron; a Biography* (New York, 1957), 316.

155   CAROLINE LAMB: *Ibid.*, 130.

156   'HARD SENSUALITY': SA to P, June 29 [1832].

156   'MEPHISTOPHELES NATURE': SA to P, July 18, 1832.

157   'THEM TO SHAME': P to SA, November 4, 1832, copy (Tr G).

158   'BEDLAM TASTES': SA to P, January 11, 1833.

158   'ENGLISH PRUDERY': SA to P [*c.* November 1832].

158   'SMALL TRIUMPHS': *Ibid.*

159   'HORRIBLE RAGE': *Ibid.*

159   'GIVE YOU UP': P to SA, December 17, 1832, copy (Tr F).

159   'PERHAPS VERBALLY': P to SA, February 3, 1833, copy (Tr G).

159   'FRIGHTENS ME': SA to P, August 27, 1832.

159   'I FEEL SICK': SA to P, August 27, 1832 (Tr G, Tr F).

159   'WANING PASSIONS': Gaius Suetonius Tranquillus, *The Twelve Caesars*, trans. by Robert Graves, rev. by Michael Grant (Harmondsworth, 1983), 135.

160   'SO UNLIKE': SA to P, August 27, 1832.

160   'INCOMPREHENSIBLE TO ME': *Ibid.*

160   'VESTAL BLUSH': SA to P, August 27, 1832.

161   'DISCOVER THE LONGITUDE': *Ibid.*

161   'TO BED WITH HIM': SA to P, January 21, 1833.

162   'THE LATTER': SA to P, March [23]–29 [1832].

162   'IN YOUR ARMS': SA to P, July 24–[31] [1832].

162   'WOULD BE MISUNDERSTOOD': SA to P, November 18 [1831].

162   'IN ANOTHER': SA to P, March [23]–29 [1832].

163   'NO MAN'S PLEASURES': SA to P, July 24–[31] [1832].

163   'OF ALL ENGLAND': SA to P, August 27, 1832.

163   'GENUINE FEELING': SA to P, July 18, 1832.

163   'GLORIOUS CREATURE': SA to P, March 23 [1834].

164   'MY HEART': SA to P, March 11–[14] [1832].

Chapter Five

165   'EYES OPEN': SA to Kate Whittle, February 4, 1849, Waterfield.

165   'PASSION IS INSISTENT': Stendhal, *The Charterhouse of Parma*, trans. Margaret R. B. Shaw (Harmondsworth, 1978), 345 (chap. 20).

165   LITTLE *WEIBCHEN*: SA to P, October 3, 1834.

165   SHADOW WIFE: SA to P, June 29 [1832] and October 3, 1834.

165   *PETITE FEMME*: SA to P, July 18, 1832 and [December 24, 1834].

165   'ÉPOUX CHERI': SA to P, July 18, 1832.

165   'LITTLE WIFE': P to SA, November 24, 1832, copy, May 20, 1834, copy, and March 30, 1833, copy (Tr G).

165   'SHADOW HUSBAND': P to SA, June 13, 1833, draft (Tr G).

166   'HUSBAND IN GERMANY': P to SA, November 24, 1832, copy and n.d., draft (Tr G).

166   'POOR WEIBLEIN': SA to P [*c.* late May 1832].

166   'CHATTING': SA to P, March [23]–29 [1832].

166   'I CANNOT GO ON': SA to P, June 5–6 [1832].

166   'TROUBLES BETWEEN US': P to SA, June 13, 1833, draft (Tr G).

166   'POSSIBLE TO ME': SA to P, April [8?]–9 [1832].

167   'YOU AND ME': SA to P, August 27, 1832.

167   'SPOUSE IN GERMANY': P to SA, June 13, 1833, draft (Tr G).

167   'EVERYTHING FOR ME': P to SA, November 24, 1832, copy (Tr G).

167   'FOR THE BELOVED': SA to P [*c.* November 1932].

167   'LITTLE HELLER': SA to P [*c.* November 1832].

168   'BETTER COMMISSIONER': SA to P, January 14 [1833].

168   'BEFORE YOUR EYES': SA to P [*c.* October 1832].

168   'MORE THINGS': SA to P, July 24–[31] [1832] (Tr F).

168   'PAY TOO MUCH': SA to P [*c.* March 1833].

168   'HOUSE AND HAND': SA to P, October [16]–21 [1832].

168   'EXQUISITE': SA to P, February 11, 1833.

168   'EASTERN PATTERN': SA to P, October [16]–21 [1832].

168   'EMERALD GREEN': SA to P [*c.* April 1833].

169   'ABSOLUTE POWER': SA to P [*c.* October 1832].

169   'PRETTY THINGS': SA to P, January 21 [1833].

169 'AFFAIRS ARE MINE': *Ibid.*

169 'BUSINESS DETAILS': SA to P, October [16]–21 [1832] (Tr F).

169 'THAT BOUDOIR!': SA to P [*c.* November 1832].

169 'SUPER-CARGO': SA to P, January 14 [1833].

170 'PAPER AND INK': P to SA, July 24, 1833, copy (Tr G).

170 'YOU KNOW WHAT': P to SA, December 17, 1832, copy (Tr G).

170 'KISSED THEM ALL': SA to P, May 20–25, 1833.

170 'MAKE ME VOLUPTUOUS': P to SA, June 13, 1833, draft.

170 'HAVE FURNISHED': SA to P, August 10 [1833].

170 AUSTIN COLLECTION: P to SA, January 5, 1833, copy (Tr G).

170 'SEE WHAT YOU SEE': SA to P [*c.* November 1832].

170 'WHAT A DELIGHT': SA to P, August 9 [1833].

171 'STAND IN MINE': SA to P, April [8?]–9 [1832].

171 BE SELF-RELIANT: SA to P [*c.* October 1832].

171 GAIN A RICH WIFE: SA to P, [*c.* October 1832] and [*c.* March 1833].

171 HONORABLY WITH WOMEN: SA to P, June 3 [1832].

171 'THOUSAND TIMES MORE': SA to P, May 20–[21] [1832].

171 'A LOVING HEART': *Ibid.*

171 'SEA BETWEEN US': SA to P, April 9 [1832].

172 'WHO LOVE[D] HIM': *Ibid.*

172 'DREAM ABOUT YOU': SA to P, June 3 [1832].

172 'ELYSIAN FIELDS': SA to P, April [8?]–9 [1832].

172 'BUT NO OTHERWISE': *Ibid.*

172 'THAT I CLASP': SA to P, June 19 [1832].

172 'ÜBERIRDISCH LOVE': *Ibid.*

173 'NOBODY BUT YOURSELF': *Ibid.*

173 'REALITY NEAR YOU': *Ibid.*

173 'ALL A DREAM': SA to P, August 9 [1832].

173 'INTO YOUR BOSOM': SA to P, August 27, 1832.

173 'RESTORED TO YOU': SA to P, October 15 [1832].

173 'GAITY IS GONE': SA to P, April 13 [1832].

174 '*ALL* IS MADNESS': SA to P, August 9 [1832].

174 UNLIKELY TO HAPPEN: SA to P, June 3 [1832]; [*c.* late May 1832].

174 HEART WAS IN MUSKAU: SA to P, May 17, 1832

174 'YOUR BLUE EYES': SA to P, March 11–[14] [1832].

174 'BLOWING VOYAGE': SA to P, March [23]–29 [1832].

174   'ON THE SALT WAVES': SA to P [c. late May 1832].

174   'OUR MEETING': SA to P, June 3 [1832].

175   'BEFORE I KNEW YOU': SA to P [c. late May 1832] (Tr F).

175   'HIS DISADVANTAGE': SA to P [c. late May 1832].

175   'WOMAN, PASSIONATELY': SA to P, February 11, 1833.

175   'AFFLICT OTHERS': SA to P, June 5–6 [1832].

175   'THE OTHER HELPLESS': SA to P, August 9 [1832].

176   'A BRUTE TO DO SO': SA to P, March 11–[14] [1832].

176   'ALMOST WORSHIP': SA to P, June 29 [1832].

176   'I AM CERTAIN OF IT': SA to P, July 24–[31] [1832].

176   'BY MISFORTUNE': SA to P, November 13 [1832].

176   'NEVER TO FORSAKE': SA to P, July 24–[31] [1832].

177   'NEARLY EXTINCT': SA to P, March [23]–29 [1832].

177   'PICTURE OF YOURSELF': P to SA, [c. February–March 1832], draft.

177   'SCHWÄRMEN WITH YOU': SA to P, March [23]–29 [1832].

177   'HAVE TOGETHER': SA to P, August 27, 1832.

177   'PLAY WITH YOU': Lucie Austin to P, n.d. [1832].

177   MOTHER'S SECRET: P to SA, n.d., draft; February 28, 1834, copy (Tr G).

178   REGULAR OCCUPATION: SA to P [c. late May 1832]

178   'AT ONCE': Ibid.

178   'COMBINE ALL THIS': SA to P, April 13 [1832].

178   'SEEN AND KNOWN': SA to P, April 9 [1832].

178   'COULD NOT BEAR THAT': SA to P, June 3 [1832].

178   'WITHOUT GLITTER': P to SA [c. April 1832], draft (Tr G).

179   'IN THE SUMMER': P to SA, April 16, 1832, copy (Tr G).

179   'GO TO POLVELLAN': SA to P, June 3 [1832].

179   'THAT IS OVER': SA to P, June 5–6 [1832].

179   'I WOULD': Ibid.

179   'LIVE AT BERLIN': SA to P [c. April 1833].

180   'PLEASURE IN ME': SA to P [1832].

180   'LOVE YOU ENTIRELY': SA to P, June 3 [1832].

180   'LIKELY TO MEET': SA to P, October 15, 1832.

180   'MAKES THE THIEF': SA to P, August 27, 1832.

181   'COME HERE': P to SA, December 20, 1832, copy; also, December 17, 1832 (Tr G).

181   'NOT IN YOUR NATURE': P to SA, January 5, 1833, draft (Tr G).

182   'your husband': *Ibid.*

182   'while i . . .': SA to P, April 13 [1832].

182   'no longer for me': SA to P, July 18, 1832.

183   'feeling the effects': P to SA, April 16, 1832, copy (Tr G).

183   'my new chancellier': P to SA, November 4, 1832, copy (Tr G).

183   'flight of those dreams': SA to P, February 11, 1833

183   'dreams that it had': *Ibid.*

183   'perhaps more': *Ibid* (Tr F).

184   'far from it': SA to P, January 21 [1833].

184   'so bad as that': *Ibid.*

184   'living decently': SA to P [1832].

184   'talk of berlin daily': SA to P [*c.* May 1833].

184   'you and i to meet': SA to P, April 1 [1833].

184   he would visit: SA to P, June 23–25 [1833], July 19 [1833], August 9 [1833].

185   'we may meet': SA to P [*c.* May 1833].

185   'for always': P to SA, March 30, 1833, copy (Tr G).

185   'my sweet sara': P to SA, May 24, 1833, copy (Tr G).

185   'that exclamation': SA to P, June 23–25 [1833].

185   'true german heart': P to SA, June 13, 1833, draft (Tr G).

186   'dreaming about de loin': SA to P [*c.* May 1833].

186   'mortification and humiliation': *Ibid.*

186   'trust me for this?': SA to P [*c.* May 1833]

186   'not leave england': SA to P, July 19 [1833].

187   'you are mistaken': *Ibid.*

187   'i would like': *Ibid.*

187   'remain as we are': SA to P, July 19 [1833]

188   'severed than ever': SA to P, November 6 [1833].

188   'let me hear something': SA to P, December 9, 1833.

189   'with ever less hope': SA to P, February 14, 1834.

189   'your plans': SA to P, September 8, 1834 (Tr F).

189   'quitting me': SA to P, February 14, 1834.

189   'in this castle': P to SA, February 28, 1834, copy (Tr G).

189   'gone—for ever': SA to P, October 3, 1834

189   'fall around me': SA to P, July 13, 1834.

189   'triste i am': SA to Julia Smith, January 6, 1834, Cambridge University Library, Add. 7621.

189 'BREAKING DOWN': SA to Henry Brougham, February 22 [c. 1834], UCL.

189 STRONG ATTACHMENT: E. M. Butler, *The Tempestuous Prince*, 141.

190 'WITHIN YOUR REACH': SA to P, March 23 [1834].

190 'INNER SELF': *Briefwechsel 1*, 330–1.

190 'JUST AS RAPIDLY': Irina Gaab, *Fürst Hermann Ludwig Pückler-Muskau* (Munich, 1922) 12 (Tr G).

190 MUSKAU PROPERTIES: *Briefwechsel, 2*, 24.

190 EVEN ASKED SARAH: P to SA, April 16, 1832, copy (Tr G).

191 'LETTERS TO ME FOR': SA to P, January 14 [1833].

191 VOGHT: *Briefwechsel, 8*, 173, 327–9.

191 ZWEIBRÜCKEN: Ludwig Stern, *Die Varnhagen von Ensesche Sammlung in der Königlichen Bibliothek zu Berlin* (Berlin, 1911), 620–21; E. M. Butler, *The Tempestuous Prince*, 175, 264.

191 '*FOOLISH* SARA': P to SA, June 13, 1833, draft (Tr G).

192 'DEAR FANTASY PICTURE': P to SA, February 28, 1834, copy (Tr G).

192 QUESTION FOR HER: P to SA, December 15, 1833, copy; February 28, 1834, copy (Tr G).

192 'THAT IS SO SAD': P to SA, December 15, 1833, copy (Tr G).

192 'FEARS THIS MIGHTILY': P to SA, February 28, 1834, copy (Tr G).

192 'TOLERATES NONE': P to SA, May 20, 1834, copy (Tr G).

192 'TO GROW WEAK': P to SA, July 24, 1833, copy (Tr G).

192 THINGS SHE HAD SENT: SA to P, June 23–25 [1833].

193 REMAIN AT HAMBURG: SA to P, October 21, 1833.

193 NOT EVEN BE UNPACKED: P to SA, February 28, 1834, copy (Tr G).

193 'STRANGER TO MY HOUSE': SA to P, May 20–[21] [1832].

193 'NEED NOT, CANNOT SAY': SA to P, July 13, 1834.

194 'THOSE CRAZY LETTERS': SA to P, March [23]–29 [1832].

194 'SO NEEDLESSLY ANXIOUS': P to SA, July 24, 1833, copy (Tr G).

194 'DARKEST NIGHT': SA to P, July 13, 1834.

194 'VANITY BE GRATIFIED': SA to P, March 23 [1834].

194 'DOING SOMETHING SECRET': SA to P, January 19, 1836 (Tr F).

194 'TORMENT ME': SA to P, July 13, 1834.

194 'QUIET DESPERATION': SA to Julia Smith, January 6, 1834, Cambridge University Library, Add. 7621.

194   'HOPING OF [HER] FAMILY': CLC, *6*, 323.

194   'INQUIETUDES AND FATIGUES': SA to P, October 3, 1834.

195   'VANITY OF VANITIES': SA to P, December 2, 1834.

195   'SEAS OF TROUBLES': SA to P, May 14, 1833.

195   'LET ME DEPART': SA to P, December 2–3, 1834.

196   'MY FATE': SA to P, December 2–3, 1834.

196   'APATHY OF AGE': SA to P, August 9 [1833].

196   'WILD ILLUSIONS': SA to P, July 13, 1834.

196   A GALLEY SLAVE: SA to P, April 1 [1833].

196   'WOULD DIE LAUGHING': SA to P, November 13 [1832].

196   'HOPELESS CARES': SA to P [*c.* November 1832].

197   'HIS NEW OFFICE': SA to P, August 9 [1833].

197   'AFFECTIONATE GAY NATURE': SA to P, July 19 [1833].

198   'I SHOULD THEN SINK': SA to P, December 2–3, 1834.

198   DISAGREED WITH COLLEAGUES: SA, Preface, xvi.

198   'PROFITABLE OCCUPATION': SA to P, April 13, 1835

198   'PITIABLE MAN': CLC, *7*, 175.

198   'ALIVE NOR DEAD': P to SA, November 10, 1835, draft (Tr G).

198   'SO ENTIRELY DISCOURAGED': SA to P, October 3, 1834.

198   'SURFACE OF THE WATER': SA to Thomas Carlyle, July 1 [no year], NLS.

199   'RETURN TO TOWN': SA to P, April 13, 1835.

199   'EFFORT AND DIFFICULTY': SA to Varnhagen, June 1, 1835.

199   'THAT SHE EVER EXISTED': CLC, *8*, 111.

200   'ON TO OTHER SHORES': SA to P, September 8, 1834 (Tr F).

200   'HOUSE NOR HOME': SA to John Murray, May 5, 1835, MA.

200   'BANISHMENT': SA to P, April 13, 1835

200   'WHICH ATTEND IT': SA to P, April 13, 1835.

200   'CHASTISEMENTS OR PROBATIONS': SA to Anna Jameson, September 26–28 [1835], Osborn.

201   'TO PURIFY ALL': SA to Heine, January 19, 1836 (Tr F), Heinrich Heine, *Briete au Heine 1823–1836* (Berlin–Paris, 1974), *24*, 373–4.

201   'WITH DUE SUBMISSION': SA to P, February 23, 1836.

202   'YOUR APPOINTED TASK': SA to P, July 13, 1834.

202   'TASTES AND PLEASURES': SA to P, December 2–3, 1834.

202   'NARROWER AND STERNER': SA to P, July 13, 1834.

202   'NOW COME TOO LATE': SA to P, August 9 [1833].

202   '*IMAGINE* LEAVING HIM': SA to P, October 3, 1834.

203   'FAG DAY AND NIGHT': SA to Francis Lieber, November 21, 1835, University of South Carolina Library.

203   'NEARLY HALF DEAD': SA to John Murray, May 14, 1836, MA.

203   'YOUR SLAVE': SA to John Murray [1836], MA.

203   'THEMSELVES TO ME': SA to P, January 19, 1836 (Tr F).

203   'TEPID GLASS OF WATER': SA to Anna Jameson, September 26–28 [1835], Osborn, Yale (Tr F).

203   'THAT I MAY': SA to Jane Welsh Carlyle, June 1 [1835], Historical Society of Pennsylvania.

203   'I HAVE GROWN OLD': SA to P, January 19, 1836 (Tr F).

Chapter Six

204   'NOT MADE FOR ME': SA to P, December 16, 1836.

204   'WERE NOT SUFFERING': George Eliot, *Adam Bede* (New York, n.d.), 460 (chapter 50).

205   'QUITE OVERPOWERING': TG, 127.

206   'MEMBER OF THE COMMISSION': Sarah S. Bunbury, *Life and Letters of Robert Clement Sconce* (London, 1861), 2, 13.

206   'PROPERTY OF THE PUBLIC': SA to John Stuart Mill, March 3, 1837, British Library of Political and Economic Science, London.

206   'DESPICABLE TO ME': TG, 133.

206   'ON THEIR CONDUCT': TG, 129.

207   'AMONG THE MALTESE': *The Harlequin*, no. 31, October 27, 1838, 121.

207   'THE ENGLISH LADIES': SA to John Stuart Mill, March 3, 1837.

207   'THEIR TALENTS MERIT': SA to P, April 16–18 [1837].

207   'MOTHER TO US ALL': [Philip] Meadows Taylor, *The Story of My Life*, ed. A. M. Taylor (London, 1877), *1*, 156–7.

207   'LA SIGNORA COMMISSIONARIA': *Malta Government Gazette*, June 20, 1838, 253.

208   'MY SAD CIRCUMSTANCES': SA to P, January 19, 1836 (Tr F).

208   'SO MUCH FRIENDSHIP': SA to P, December 16, 1836 (Tr F).

209 'THE LATTER DIFFICULT': *Ibid.*

209 'AFTER MY MISFORTUNES': *Ibid.*

209 'COMPROMISE HIS LADY': SA to P, March 23 [1834].

209 'ITS PUBLIC VISIBILITY': SA to P, December 16, 1836 (Tr F).

209 'STINGING THISTLE FOR OTHERS': P to SA, April 16, 1832, copy (Tr G).

210 'EXCELLENCIES *FAIR PLAY*': SA to P, April 16–18 [1837].

210 'FAIL TO LOVE YOU': SA to P, February 14, 1834.

211 'THAT PRECIOUS PEACE': SA to P, December 26 [1836], (Tr F).

211 'NOW EXPRESS ONCE MORE': *Ibid.*

211 'MISFORTUNE PURSUES US': SA to P, December 16, 1836 (Tr F).

211 'SOME SERENE DAYS': SA to P, December 16, 1836 (Tr F).

212 NINE HOURS A DAY: SA to Lucy Taylor, n.d., Blakiston.

212 'ANYTHING BUT GAY': Lucie Austin to Signor Prandi [1839], copy, Beevor.

213 CONSENT TO MARRY: Lucie Austin to JA [1839], Beevor; LDG, 93–95.

213 AUSTIN SENIOR: SA to P July 19 [1833]; August 9 [1833].

213 'SPOT WHERE I AM': TG, 165–66.

214 'THE REST OF MY LIFE': SA to P, August 29, [1841].

214 'REMEMBRANCE OF OUR MEETING': SA to P [*c.* late 1842–early 1843].

214 'YOUR *OLD, NEW* FRIEND': SA to P [c. late 1842–early 1843].

214 'EXPRESSED FOR A STRANGER': SA to P, August 29 [1841].

214 'NOT FORGET ME': P to SA, July 24, 1833, copy (Tr G).

215 'LOVE ADVENTURE': *Südöstlicher Bildersaal* (Stuttgart, 1840), *2*, 383 (Tr G).

215 'LOVE IS A NECESSITY': *Ibid.*, *2*, 447 (Tr G).

215 'TO ITS DEPTH': *Ibid., 3*, 92–95 (Tr G).

215 'MIGHT HAVE ADMIRED': *Ibid., 2*, 385 (Tr G).

215 'TRANSPORTS OF RAPTURE': *Ibid., 3*, 190–91 (Tr G).

215 'NO ORDINARY WOMAN': *Ibid., 2*, 448 (Tr G).

215 'ALOUD WITH YOU': *Ibid., 2*, 438, 443; *3*, 44 (Tr G).

216 'HER GREATEST NEED': *Ibid., 3*, 91, 95 (Tr G).

216 'STRENGTH OF MY SOUL': *Ibid., 2*, 440–41 (Tr G).

216 'ALL MY SENSES': *Ibid., 2*, 440–42 (Tr G).

217 ST. HILAIRE EXPLAINED: Jules Barthelémy-Saint-Hilaire, *M. Victor Cousin, La vie et sa Correspondance* (Paris, 1895), *3*, 127.

217   'DEALT WITH ADMIRABLY': H. H. Houben, *Gespräche mit Heine* (Frankfurt am Main, 1926), 566–67 (Tr G).

217   SYDNEY SMITH: TG, 202.

217   'WAS INTERESTING': Harriet Grote to Richard Monckton Milnes, March 25, 1844, Houghton.

218   SEEMED TO AGE: Lucie Duff Gordon to C. J. Bayley, July 20, 1851, copy, Beevor.

218   HEART ATTACK: Mrs. Stair Douglas, *The Life and Selections from the Correspondence of William Whewell, D.D.* (London, 1881), 416.

218   ENORMOUSLY FAT: Alexander Duff Gordon to Georgiana Duff Gordon, January 19, 1852, Beevor.

218   'CANNOT MANAGE HER': Alexander Duff Gordon to Caroline Duff Gordon, March 17, 1852, Beevor.

218   'THIS ACQUAINTANCE': SA to Henry Brougham, July 17 [1852], UCL.

219   'BE BRIGHT IF POSSIBLE': Alexander Duff Gordon to Caroline Duff Gordon, March 17, 1852, Beevor.

219   'VERY DREARY': Alexander Duff Gordon to Caroline Duff Gordon, April 3, 1852, Beevor.

219   EXERTION: SA, editor's preface, 2, v, *A Memoir of the Reverend Sydney Smith. By his daughter, Lady Holland. With a Selection from his letters* (London, 1855).

219   '*DONOTHINGNESS*': SA to Julia Smith, May 14 [1858], Cambridge University Library, Add. 7621.

219   *CONTINENT, AND ENGLAND*: 'Mr. Murray's General List of Works' (February 1851), 3.

219   'STRENGTH OR EASE': Alexander Duff Gordon to Caroline Duff Gordon, April 13, 1852, Beevor.

219   'TO SIT UNDER ALWAYS': Alexander Duff Gordon to Caroline Duff-Gordon, April 28, 1852, copy, Beevor.

220   'RAVEN SARA': Lucie Duff Gordon to C. J. Bayley, May 18, 1851, copy, Beevor.

220   'HIS GREAT POWER': SA to Macvey Napier, July 27 [1846], BL, Add. 34626, f. 299.

221   'WORK IMMEDIATELY': SA to John Murray, January 22, 1849, MA.

221   'DESIRE FOR SOCIETY': SA, Preface, xxvi–xxvii.

221   'WEARY AND WORN': SA to Julia Smith, May 14 [*c.* 1858], Cambridge University Library, Add. 7621.

222   'INJUSTICE OF MEN': TG, 325.

222   'FACULTIES IN ANY WAY': SA to Julia Smith, May 14 [*c.* 1858].

223   'HE DOES NOTHING': *Ibid.*

223   'WONDERFULLY ELASTIC': Harriet Grote to John Murray, January 18, 1853, MA.

223   'NOT GIVE UP': TG, 311.

223   'REMAIN UNSHAKEN': SA to Susan Reeve, October 13, 1853, Beevor.

223   'FOR THE WINTER': SA to Susan Reeve, October 13, 1853, Beevor.

223   SYDNEY SMITH: *A Memoir of the Reverend Sydney Smith. By his daughter, Lady Holland. With a selection from his letters, edited by Mrs. Austin.* (London, 1855), 2 volumes.

223   'EVENLY, AND JUSTLY': TG, 326.

223   'SUFFERING BODY': SA to Karl Varnhagen von Ense [March 5, 1843].

224   'CHECKS THEM': TG, 326.

224   'WHAT HE IS': SA to Murray, October 22 [1855], MA.

224   '*TEN* TALENTS WERE GIVEN': TG, 324-25.

224   'RECONCILED TO IT': SA to Lansdowne, October 18 [1858], Bowood.

224   'BRIGHT AND SERENE': TG, 378.

225   'LONG HONEYMOON': M.C.M. Simpson, *Many Memories of Many People* (London, 1898), 117.

225   'CAN PRODUCE': TG, 360.

225   'WAKE INTO FRESH LIFE': SA to Guizot, February 9, 1850, Guizot.

225   'CHOOSE THE SAME LOT': SA to Lansdowne [1847], Bowood.

225   'CONVULSIONS OF SORROW': SA to Hepworth Dixon, July 17 [1860], UCLA.

225   'HALF HERSELF': Alfred T. Story, *The Life of John Linnell* (London, 1892), *1*, 128.

226   ARTEMESIA: Harriet Grote to Lady William Russell, July 13 [1861], Blakiston.

226   'SETTLED THAN MINE': SA to Hepworth Dixon, July 17 [1860], UCLA.

226   '*ENTIRE* AND INCURABLE': *Ibid.*

226   'FASTIDIOUS CONTEMPLATIONS': George Grote, *Posthumous Papers*, ed. Harriet Grote (London, 1874), 151.

226   'CAN BE SO CALLED': Harriet Grote to John Murray, January 31, 1869, MA.

226   'ANY POSITIVE SORT': Harriet Grote to Richard Monckton Milnes, December 22, 1859, Houghton.

227   'ADVENTUROUS AND AMBITIOUS': John Neal, 'Mrs. Sarah Austin,' *American Phrenological Journal*, 47 (April 1868), 128–29.

227   'PASSION OF MY OLD AGE': SA to Laura [Peyronnet] Russell, January 1, 1866, Blakiston.

227   'GIFT TO POSTERITY': SA to Anna Jameson, September 26–28 [1835], Osborn, Yale.

228   'WORK FOR ITS GOOD': SA to Harriet Grote, April 16, 1860, Beevor.

228   'EVERY PAGE I FINISH': SA to Lansdowne, January 22, 1862, Bowood.

228   'UTTER DESPONDENCY': SA to Laura [Peyronnet] Russell, January 1, 1866, Blakiston.

228   'EXCEED ALL MY HOPES': SA to Guizot [1863], Guizot.

228   'REALLY GREAT WORK': SA to Lady William Russell, November 1866, Blakiston.

228   'CONSTANTLY RISING': SA to Guizot, November 29, 1865, Guizot.

228   'HAD BEEN ACCOMPLISHED': SA to 3rd Earl Grey, November 6, 1863, Durham.

228   'COVETED *FOR* HIM': SA, Preface, xxviii (italics added).

229   'VIOLENCE OR INDECORUM': P, *Tour in England, Ireland, and France* (London, 1832), advertisement in vol. 1.

229   'ALLOW ME TO SAY SO': SA to Varnhagen, January 15, 1857.

229   'IN THE MAIN': TG, 355–56.

229   'REVEALED IN HER LIFE': *Fragments*, 344.

230   'SOLACE OF THE SOUL': SA to Guizot, August 10, 1861, Guizot.

230   'MANY IMPERFECTIONS': TG, 359.

230   'SO ENDURING': Guizot to SA, May 1, 1861, Guizot (Tr F).

230   'I OWE THE MOST': SA to Guizot, August 21, 1861, Guizot.

230   'ENFOLDED IN HIS': SA, Preface, xxvii.

230   'THE SAME STONE': Weybridge parish church records.

231   'ORDINARY RULES': SA to Varnhagen, August 3, 1857.

231   'MAIN PROP': SA to Francis Lieber, March 15, 1834, Huntington Library.

232   'HIS PROFANITY': Lucie Duff Gordon to Alexander Duff Gordon, February 11, 1863, Beevor.

232   'ALMOST FABULOUS': Lucie Duff Gordon, *Letters from Egypt* (London, 1983), 209.

232   'RESTLESS MIND': SA to Laura Russell, August 4 [1865], Blakiston.

233   'WELL ENOUGH': Lucie Duff Gordon to SA, November 23, 1866, Beevor.

233   'GIVE IT A SPUR': SA to Julia Smith, May 14 [1858], Cambridge University Library, Add. 7621.

233   'TO DO ANYTHING': SA to John Murray, October 23 [1865], MA.

233   'SETTLED GLOOM': TG, 421.

233   PRUSSOMANIA: TG, 422.

234   '*BELONGINGNESS*': SA to Lady William Russell, December 23, 1865, Blakiston.

234   'HAIR IN IT': Lucie Duff Gordon to SA, August 8, 1867, Beevor.

235   PÜCKLER'S PORTRAIT: SA to P, March [23]–29 [1832].

235   'NEVER KNOWN YOU': SA to P, December 16, 1836 (Tr F).

236   'RELATIONS OF WOMEN': SA to Ottilie von Goethe, August 9, 1840, Weimar.

236   'BETWEEN THE SEXES': SA, Preface, *Letters from Egypt, 1863–65* (London, 1865), ix.

236   AN INSOLUBLE PROBLEM: SA to Hepworth Dixon, May 4 [n.y.], UCLA.

236   'SORROWS OF HUMAN LIFE': SA, 'Goethe's Character and Moral Influence,' *Edinburgh Review*, 106 (July 1857), 225.

About the Authors

LOTTE HAMBURGER graduated from the London School of Economics. She has worked as a writer and researcher for various institutions in England and the United States and with Joseph Hamburger is coauthor of *Troubled Lives*.

JOSEPH HAMBURGER received his Ph.D. from the University of Chicago. He teaches political science and history at Yale University and is the author of books and articles on philosophy, politics, and the history of the Victorian era in Britain.